THE BOY IN THE CELLAR

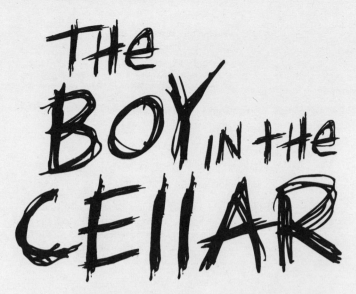

THE BOY IN THE CELLAR

Trapped for thirteen years then abused by my carers.
A shocking **true story** of survival.

STEPHEN SMITH

With Veronica Clark

JOHN BLAKE

Published by John Blake Publishing,
The Plaza,
535 Kings Road,
Chelsea Harbour,
London SW10 0SZ

www.facebook.com/johnblakebooks ❶
twitter.com/jblakebooks ❷

First published in paperback in 2019

Paperback ISBN: 978 1 78946 175 6
eBook ISBN: 978 1 78946 176 3

British Library Cataloguing-in-Publication Data:

A catalogue record for this book is available from the British Library.

Design by www.envydesign.co.uk

Printed and bound in Great Britain by Clays Ltd, Elcograf S.p.A.

1 3 5 7 9 10 8 6 4 2

MIX
Paper from
responsible sources

Dedicated to Gail and all my children.
Without their support, I would never have found
the courage to tell my story.

CONTENTS

Today had been a good day because, today, I'd got to leave my room. I'd travelled in a car and had seen things I'd never seen before. I'd even been inside a hospital. Today, I also found out two things for the very first time.

My name is Stephen Smith. And I am seven years old.

PROLOGUE

D amp glistened against the bricks and mortar. It sparkled like diamonds caught in the half-light peeking through the small opening to the world outside. The thick red bricks seemed to soak up and retain the unbearable coldness, the room felt like a long-forgotten tomb buried deep beneath the earth.

The little boy shifted over in the corner as Peter moved quickly across the floor, refusing to stop even for a moment, dust, dirt and cobwebs the only decorations hanging in the gloom. The room was full of shadows and sparsely furnished; just a makeshift bed, a small table and space for a dark wooden chair. The floor was made of stone and as ice-cold to the touch as it looked. Peter ran across it and over towards the concrete plinth. Lifting himself, he climbed up onto it and scurried along, his long legs moving quickly and nimbly until he'd reached the boy's arm draped away from his body to one side. Peter felt safe; in certain areas, the room was plunged into darkness, so there were several places he could hide. But right now, he wanted to be with the boy. The tickling sensations against the child's skin made him stir momentarily, causing him to stop dead in his tracks like an impromptu game of musical statues. He waited to see if the boy would wake and, for a moment, was certain he would. But the child fell back into a deep slumber, leaving Peter to continue on his way.

Once the boy's breath had regulated to a steady pattern, Peter continued, inching a few more steps. Soon, he'd quickened his pace. Journeying along the child's arm, he climbed down onto his soiled blue shirt. The fabric was stained with food and it rose up and down in waves of creases. Peter should have found the complexities of such fabric challenging, but he'd done this so many times before. Shadows beneath the fabric seemed both dark and welcoming, so he tucked down and made his way underneath. He felt the warmth of the boy's body as he dashed over his young skin. Tracing along the thin torso, he scurried quickly over red welts and temporarily healed scars – a landscape of pain. The same scars would soon be broken again, but for now, they had time to recover.

The sensation of Peter prickling against his back caused the child to wake. Without warning, he sat bolt upright. His sudden movement caught Peter unawares and he tumbled down, landing against the soft but cold mattress. Crawling out of the shadows, he moved away from the boy, who turned and brushed long strands of unkempt hair from his face. Lifting a dirty hand, he wiped crusted sleep from the corners of his eyes and stared down at Peter.

'I wondered where you'd been,' he said, straightening up. 'I've not seen you for a couple of days, I was worried.'

The boy stretched both hands above his head and yawned

loudly. He placed an open palm against the mattress and beckoned Peter to climb on. The light from the coal hole picked Peter out against the military blanket as he scrambled aboard.

'Come on,' the child told him. 'I need to put you back.'

Gently lifting Peter, he crossed the room and placed him on the large silvery web – the biggest one in the room. The child's fingertips tickled gently against the gossamer-thin strands as they bounced against the spider's weight like a miniature trampoline. The boy was careful not to break the threads.

'There you go. Oh, and by the way,' he said, pointing to the web, 'I caught you some dinner. I hope you're hungry? I put him there for you. Don't worry, he's trapped. He can't escape.'

The fly shifted and twisted in his webbed prison, his legs and wings sticking against the fine adhesive lines that anchored him down.

The boy watched as Peter turned and proceeded towards his prey. The spider climbed on top of the insect and there was a sudden shift – an urgent movement – as he bit into him. He proceeded to wrap him in a silken shroud and sat back, waiting for him to die. Once he had, Peter climbed onto the insect and devoured him, piece by piece.

The boy smiled as his friend performed his special eating ritual.

'Nice to see you again, Peter,' he said, whispering down to the spider. 'We've been waiting for you. It's good to have you home.'

CHAPTER 1

SCISSORS

I've never been frightened of spiders. Unlike people, I know they can't hurt me. I had fifteen friends in total, but Peter was my favourite. He loved to crawl up my arms and my legs. Sometimes, when I was asleep, he'd try and tickle me by crawling up my shirt, but he found it hard to get underneath my jumper because it was always fitted so close to my body. I usually wore it when I got up out of bed, but if I was really cold, I'd wear it when I was asleep. My room was always freezing, even when it was bright outside. Sometimes, I'd feel the warmth flooding in through the coal hole above my head. I'd lift up my hand, but I could never reach it properly – I was never quite tall enough.

I hoped that one day the sunshine would be strong enough to stretch down and flood my room with light. You see, I knew what the sun was. I'd written about it in sentences. I knew it was a yellow ball of fire in the sky that helped things grow. Up to that point, I'd never felt it against my face – well, not properly. A few times I'd been lucky; it had shone down through the hole, casting a gridded, golden square against my mattress. Whenever that happened, I'd put both hands inside the square so that I could feel it. I'd leave them there as the sun soaked against my skin. Then I'd lie down, put my legs up against the wall, and position my face inside the golden shape. It made me feel happy – made me feel part of something else, something bigger that was happening outside.

Outside – that place frightened me because I'd never been there. The coal hole was my only glimpse of the world, but I didn't mind the dark, not really, because I was used to it. My friends liked it, too. Spiders preferred the cold, but they really loved dark hidey holes and there were lots and lots down here, especially 'secret' ones buried inside cracks in the mortar. The other spiders were smaller than Peter, so I always thought of him as the leader. There was an Arthur and lots of Georges. There was also an Albert, but I didn't like him very much. He loved to jump out at me. He thought he was clever, thought I couldn't see him, but I always knew he was there, watching and waiting. Albert tried to catch me out, that's why I named him after my father.

Spider Albert would crouch deep inside the cracks, ready to pounce whenever I walked by. He'd sit and wait for flies too. Arthur, the Georges and Peter would do the same. Flies were their food, you see. I'd wait with them because I wanted to help. I'd sit perfectly still so I could catch them for my friends – well, for everyone but Albert, I let him catch his own. I'd wait for a big, buzzy fly to land on something and then…THUD! I'd bring my hand down hard on them. I'd try to stun them so they were still alive when I hung them on the different webs. Sometimes I'd get excited and hit them a bit too hard, squashing them flat. Albert didn't like them almost dead, Peter didn't either, but at least he killed them quickly. Albert was just like my father: he liked to chase and climb on top of them as they struggled. He liked to hurt them, but he wanted them to be really scared before he took them apart.

I thought everyone was like me, that everyone lived with spiders. I'd chase Peter around and he'd sneak up on me, too. I was a little bit jealous of him and the others because they could crawl off whenever they liked. They could clamber off their webs and out through cracks in the bricks. Unlike me, they could climb walls. I tried to copy them once but my feet didn't seem to stick to the bricks as theirs did. They'd mount the wall and scale it as though hanging by an invisible thread, then spend ages climbing until they reached the coal hole. Then they'd go outside and bask in the sunshine; they also knew what it felt like to get soaked in the rain. I imagined them outside, with the wind whistling all around and lifting up the tiny hairs on the backs of their bodies. They could play outside whenever they wanted. I pictured them dancing around in the white stuff that Dad called snow – they were able to roll around in it and build huge snow people.

Or would they build snow spiders? I wasn't quite sure. *Maybe they'd build huge spiders instead of people?*

Once, it had snowed so heavily that the white stuff had fallen in and down the coal hole. I pushed my fingers into it, but pulled them away again quickly – it was freezing! After blowing hot breath against my fingers to try and warm them up, I picked a bit up. I put it against my lips and inside my mouth. I liked the way it melted against my tongue. I'd never thought of my tongue as being hot before but it must have been because the snow melted and turned to water inside my mouth. I wasn't sure what else to do with it, but I soon realised that if I squashed it together, I could make it into a white ball. I liked to draw monsters on paper, but now I had something else to make them from: snow. My snow monsters weren't very big, but I made them arms, legs, eyes, a mouth and even a nose. Although it was really cold in my room, so cold that I could see my breath, my snow monsters never lasted very long. But I enjoyed that day because the snow had given me something different to do other than the homework he'd given me.

It made me sad that my friends could escape and I couldn't. Sometimes I'd feel like one of the flies trapped in their webs. No matter how much I twisted and turned, I'd always wake up inside my room. I wondered how many other boys lived in a room like mine. I supposed that everyone must. He said he kept me there because I was naughty, but I was too scared of him to misbehave. He also hit me a lot and called me horrible names. I'd see him every day, usually in the morning before he went to 'work'. I wasn't sure what that was, but it meant I wouldn't see him again until the light from outside had stopped coming in through the coal hole. He would bring me breakfast when I woke up. He always put it inside a round-shaped thing that was deeper than a plate. I didn't know what it was called until one day he dropped one on the floor and it smashed.

'Look what you made me do, you little bastard! I broke the dish.'

Dish... I thought it was such an odd word for a deeper plate. 'Dish', it sounded like fish! That made me laugh. Fancy eating food out of a fish!

There was another person called Mum, but I didn't know if that was Mum's name or not. Mum would sometimes bring food down, but not as often as he did. Mum would bring me plates of vegetables with meat and gravy, usually cauliflower, broccoli and cabbage. I hated them, but he would make me eat them. Mum would come downstairs, put the plate on the table and leave. Mum never spoke to me and rarely even looked at me. It made me feel sad because I wanted to ask questions, to ask why they kept me down there, but I was never brave enough – I was scared that Mum would tell him I'd asked.

In the mornings, he'd fill a dish with white water and put dry, flaky orange shapes in it. The white stuff would start to smell if I left it too long. One day, it smelt bad before I'd even tried it. My nostrils opened wide when he put it down on the table in front of me and I screwed up my nose. I sipped a spoonful but didn't like the taste. It tasted bad and left nasty, solid blobs that coated my tongue. After he'd left, I wiped them away with the sleeve of my jumper, but I could still taste a sickly tang at the back of my throat. I had a toothbrush and paste to clean my teeth, so I scrubbed them until the taste had gone. Then I washed out my mouth with some water from a jug he'd left on the side and spat the mess into my blue 'spit' dish. With my teeth now clean, I put the breakfast dish on the table but when he came downstairs later that night, he went absolutely crazy.

'Eat it!' he ordered, eyeing the sodden orangey brown food still floating in the white stuff.

'It tastes funny,' I mumbled.

He stopped and turned to stare at me.

'What did you just say?'

Immediately, I regretted it.

'Nothing,' I whimpered as I felt a dead weight ball inside the pit of my stomach. I felt it rise up inside my throat as though it might choke me.

He headed across the room, his brown leather apron swinging from side to side with every step he took. I pushed my back so hard up against the wall that I could feel the rough bricks pressing through my shirt and against my skin. As he raised his hand high above his head, I clamped my eyes tight.

SMACK!

The sound of his hand against the side of my face startled me more than the actual pain. My cheek stung and throbbed as I held my fingers against it. The skin glowed hot beneath my fingers as though I'd just been burnt with fire, like the sun.

'Don't. You. Ever. Talk. Back. To. Me. Again!' he said, shouting out each word with a slap, thump and kick until soon I became a crumpled mess on the floor. 'It's not my fault you're a fussy eater!'

I kept my eyes closed tight because his anger scared me more than the slaps. I didn't even know what 'fussy' meant – we'd not learned that word yet.

'Eat!' he screamed, pushing the rim of the dish into my face. I felt it pressing hard against the bone in my cheek.

His voice had grown so loud that it boomed around the room. It bounced off the bricks, repeating itself as though the walls were whispering, teasing me. My space had suddenly been turned into a room of anger – *his* anger. I felt him grab the top of my arm roughly as he threw me down into the chair and against the table. As he stood over me, watching me, I trembled. Lifting the metal spoon, I held it against my mouth and took a cautious sip.

'Eat!'

I opened my mouth and threw the soggy food towards the back of it, hoping the faster I ate, the less I'd taste. But it stuck against the roof of my mouth, nestled against my tongue and flooded down the back of my throat. I desperately wanted to take a sip of water to wash it down but as soon as he saw my hand reach for the glass he pulled it away.

'No!'

The white watery stuff tasted horrible and my stomach heaved as I continued to shovel it inside my mouth. I felt my throat close up as though it was begging me not to swallow. But I had to – I had to eat because I knew my life wouldn't be worth living if I didn't. I hated vegetables, but he always made me eat them. He said I'd never grow as big as him if I didn't eat my vegetables, but I didn't want to be like him. I'd always hear him before I'd see him, his boots stomping down the ten steps leading to my room. I'd count them in my head to try and prepare myself. I'd hear the latch first – it would lift up on the outside of the door.

CLICK.

The pale green wooden door would creak open, shining light down into my room from above. It glowed against the dirty white walls and his footsteps followed.

CLOMP.

Ten… I jumped up and off the chair.

CLOMP.

Nine… Holding the paper in my hand, I looked for a place to hide my drawings. I knew he'd kill me if he ever found them.

CLOMP.

Eight… I stuffed the paper under the edge of the table, straightened up and looked back down to check the paper wasn't sticking out.

No, all clear.

CLOMP.

Seven… I ran back to the chair and pushed my coloured pencils to one side.

CLOMP.

Six… I sat down.

CLOMP.

Five… I opened up the blue jotter and grabbed the flat-shaped 'carpenter's pencil'.

CLOMP.

Four… I perched both elbows on the table and tried to look as though I was concentrating.

Three… two… one… He was there, standing over me.

'Homework,' he said, clicking his fingers impatiently.

The light from the bare bulb hanging above our heads glinted against the edges of his heavy black-framed glasses. His short ginger hair made it look as though his head was on fire. It wasn't, but his temper always was.

'Homework,' he barked again, waiting for me to hand him the exercise book.

He waved a hand – a signal for me to get up off the chair and let him sit down. Then he took out a blue ink pen and began to mark my work, the nib of the pen scratched along each sentence, marking it with either a tick or a cross. A tick meant supper, a cross meant his belt or something worse. I wanted to look, to peek over his shoulder, but I was too scared.

'Hmm, hmm,' he grunted as he checked through my work.

He was breathing out through his nose noisily, marking each sentence before he moved on to my spellings. The spellings hadn't been too bad today. Although I didn't know what a 'pavement' was, I knew that I'd spelt it right. I practised hard, copying each word out about thirty or forty times. There were only twenty words, but those and the half dozen sentences had taken me hours to write. I prayed that I'd got them all right.

Peter walked along the pavement... that was one.

Albert jumped off the wall... was another.

Pavement... I wanted to ask Dad what a pavement was, but I knew he'd give me a beating, so I kept quiet. Instead, I stood there – my tongue fat inside my mouth – waiting for his verdict, waiting to see what the outcome would be. Everything rested on this – *everything* – especially my food. We had a routine – he wouldn't give me my tea until he had marked everything. I had to get them all right; I *had* to. My stomach churned with both hunger and fear. I was worried he'd hear the noise and go mad, but he was too busy concentrating on my work.

I studied him from behind. His stocky legs were crossed at the ankle and covered in brown trousers. The heavy leather apron he wore was bent against the crease near his hips, making him look much fatter than he actually was. There was a large pouch at the front of the apron; I always kept an eye on that pouch because that's where he kept the scissors. He only ever used them when he was really angry, but these days, he always seemed angry. I had to stay alert. If ever I saw his hand drift near the pouch, I would flinch because that was usually the first sign that he would really hurt me.

Ages before – I couldn't say when because I had no way of

telling the time – it had rained so hard outside that I could hear it bounce. Rainwater flooded down through the coal hole and dripped onto my bed. He came downstairs and noticed my bed was soaking.

'You've wet the bed, you dirty little bastard!' he said, raising his hand to hit me.

Fear caught at the back of my throat as I gasped,

'I didn't, I swear. It was the rain, not me!'

Tears of humiliation stung inside my eyes, but I realised it was no good – he didn't believe me.

'Come 'ere, you little twat.'

I ran across the room to try and escape him, but he became distracted by my work – it was on the table, waiting to be marked.

'Stand,' he ordered. 'I'll deal with you in a minute.'

I knew I was in for it when he turned the page; I noticed he'd drawn red lines through two of my sentences.

Oh no, you've got them wrong! the voice inside my head warned.

Before I could say or do anything, his face grew purple with rage. He stood up so quickly that the chair fell over, clattering hard as it landed heavily against the floor.

'You little bastard!' he screamed as he began to chase me across the room.

Thankfully, I was light on my feet and much too fast for him.

'Come here, you little bastard! If I get my hands on you, I'll KILL you, I swear!' he screamed, baring his yellow teeth at me.

Petrified, I darted from one corner of the room to another to try and escape him. Suddenly, he lunged forward to make a grab for me.

'Come here or I swear I will KILL YOU!' he said, pulling off his belt.

Fear rose like vomit at the back of my throat as I flitted across the room to try and avoid him. He was so angry that there was spit flying out of the corners of his mouth. Some of it remained there at the edges, bubbling up like foam. He was a monster. Lurching forward, he tried to make another grab.

'You little…'

In a rage, he plunged his right hand into the pouch and pulled out a pair of scissors, the type I later found out a tailor or dressmaker would use. Long metal blades glinted in the light as he held them aloft before plunging them towards me as a single closed blade. The scissors sliced through the air, missing me as I continued to shift and dip. He stabbed away angrily at nothing – I was too fast for him. I watched and waited, my breathing becoming short and panicked, as he stopped and threaded his finger and thumb through both handles. On high alert, I was ready for anything.

What was he doing? I wondered as I tried to second-guess what was coming next.

Holding the scissors like a dagger, he threw them at me. Everything seemed to go in slow motion and the shears opened up as they flew through the air. In a total panic, I put up both hands to protect my…

The pain was indescribable as one of the sharp metal points pierced the skin of my hand. His anger and the power of the throw had forced it through skin and gristle, scraping against smaller bones as it came to its final resting point in the centre of my palm. I glanced down in horror – the tip of the scissors seemed so out of place in the middle of my hand that I froze.

'Come here, look what you made me do,' he huffed as he grabbed hold of the scissors and yanked them violently out of my hand.

The sensation of metal scraping through skin and against bone in reverse made me want to throw up. My head and legs felt funny, as though I might fall to the floor. I slumped against the cool wall, gripping the bloodied, throbbing flesh of my hand. Hot tears streamed down my cheeks as he wiped the crimson blade calmly against his apron and tucked the scissors back inside his pouch. Then he disappeared off upstairs to fetch something. He was only gone for a minute when I heard his boots on the stone steps.

Ten, nine, eight, seven… six, five… He seemed to pause and then, *four, three, two, one.* He was hovering over me holding a roll of white fabric in his hands.

'Look what you make me do. Why can't you behave? Why do you make me do these things, eh?'

I winced, but tried not to make a noise as he pulled my bloodied hand towards him and wiped it roughly with an old cloth. But the blood continued to ooze and drip from the open wound.

'Ah well,' he said dismissively, as though I'd just nicked my finger, 'this should do it. I'll use this bandage.'

Bandage… another new word.

I watched as he unravelled the white bandage and wrapped it tightly around my palm. The crimson blood seeped through it again and again, so he wrapped it until soon my hand was swollen with white fabric. To the outside world, I looked brand new. The bandage had hidden the worst of the damage.

'If you hadn't pissed the bed, I wouldn't have to do this,' he hissed.

I wanted to argue and tell him he was wrong, I'd not pissed the bed. I wanted to tell him I'd used my slop bucket, that I *always* used the slop bucket. I wanted him to know that I hadn't wet the bed because it had been the rain, not me. But I knew there was no point because he'd never believe me.

It took ages and he had to bring down some special cream to rub into my hand for the next few weeks, but eventually the scar stopped hurting and my palm began to heal.

'It was a clean cut,' he said one day, checking the scar underneath the dim light bulb. He said 'clean cut' as though it had been a good thing.

The scissors had left me with a scar on both sides of my hand. If I held a pencil in it for too long, the wound to my palm would sometimes ache, but if you didn't look too closely, then you wouldn't have known it was there.

Without thinking, I rubbed the tip of my thumb against the old scar as I waited for him now, waiting for his verdict on my latest homework. The chair legs scraped loudly against the floor as he got to his feet. I watched his apron pouch.

Would he pull the scissors out?

My eyes continued to flit between his hands and the pouch, waiting for him to pull them – to stab me. Instead, he turned, nodded his head and went upstairs to fetch my supper. The frightened breath I'd been holding inside came flooding out as a sigh of relief. I looked towards Peter: he was in the corner, dangling from his web, watching everything from a place of safety.

'It's okay,' I whispered over to him. 'No belt tonight.'

It had been a good day because today, I'd got my spellings right. I felt lucky – I'd escaped a beating and I always got a beating. As long as I kept my mouth shut and ate all my food, I'd be safe – at least until tomorrow.

CHAPTER 2

SLOPPING OUT

I rested my head against the stone floor and counted how many steps Peter took as he ran across my eye line. It was difficult because he had eight legs and they all moved so quickly. I had to count each time he shifted forward and multiply it by eight. I was okay at maths – my father made me practise my multiplications and long division. I had blue jotters for everything: English (that was mainly sentences and spellings), Maths, Science and History. He was really strict about homework. I wasn't sure why; it wasn't like I got to talk to anyone else other than him – well, apart from Peter and the others. It didn't matter though because he was determined I'd use my brain. I loved to draw but I didn't tell him; I was worried if he knew how much I loved it, he'd take all my paper away and then I'd have nothing. I especially liked to draw monsters – ones based on him. I'd draw men with two heads, or three arms and five legs; I'd draw men who were ugly and strange, like him. One time, I drew a monster that was half-man and half-spider. I pictured him living in the cellar in a big crack in the wall, waiting for my father. I imagined the monster wrapping him in a silken shroud and trapping him in a big silver web. I'd watch him struggle and cry out. I decided if it ever happened, I wouldn't help. Instead, I'd sit and watch the half-man half-spider crawl on top and bite hard into his neck. Then I'd watch him die, just like those flies.

He would regularly tell me to copy out sentences I didn't understand, but I was too frightened to ask what all the different words meant. When I was younger, he asked me to copy some spellings. I wrote *ball, dog, beach, hat, gate…* I didn't know what gate meant or any of the others, but I was able to piece them together slowly from sentences he'd given me.

Peter closed the gate.

A gate must be like the door at the top of the stairs, I decided.

George caught the ball.

A ball must be something you could catch in your hands like a spider.

Arthur climbed the tree.

I was dying to know what a tree was, but too frightened to ask in case he hit me. *Tree… tree… tree…* The word rolled around inside my mouth, my lips moving away from my teeth and the letters slipping over my tongue. *Tree*, it sounded a bit like three, but that was a number, and you couldn't climb a number! I did eventually get to see a tree but I didn't know what it was at the time, I only found out much later.

One day, I heard the cellar door open.

'Right,' his voice boomed from the top of the stairs, catching me by surprise. My stomach tightened inside as I pushed my drawings into a secret space underneath the desk.

Ten, nine, eight...

I dipped down to look.

All clear. I couldn't see them.

Seven, six, five, four... three, two, one...

He was standing over me.

'I've decided you're old enough to start slopping out your own bucket.'

I looked over at the silver metal bucket in a corner of the room. He'd usually empty it when it became half-full of pee, shit and toothpaste spit. I didn't have a toilet – I didn't even know what one was. Not then, anyway, although I was about to find out.

'Well, don't just sit there looking useless. Go pick it up!'

The chair legs dragged against the floor as I stood up and walked over towards the bucket. The smell rising from it made me want to be sick. I took short and shallow breaths and tried not to breathe in too deeply.

'Get the bucket. Come on, come on!'

I lifted the handle and glanced over at him.

Was this a trick?

He's going to pour it all over you, the voice inside my head warned.

I had to keep watch; I knew he wouldn't think twice about it. I wasn't sure quite what to do, so I stood there, holding the bucket, waiting for further instructions.

'Follow me,' he mumbled as he headed towards the stairs.

My feet felt stuck as though they'd been glued to the floor.

Was he finally letting me out?

I'd never been out of the cellar before.

He turned, his mouth breaking into a horrible sneer.

'Come on, I haven't got all day.'

I lifted the bucket and followed him slowly upstairs. My legs were trembling as I heaved the slops up, one step at a time. The bucket felt surprisingly heavy and I was terrified I'd spill piss and shit on the stairs, on myself, or, even worse, on him. The first step seemed easy, but the second was a little more difficult. I had to be careful to judge the height of it, making sure I didn't trip, and at the same time watching the water level didn't lift up over the edge.

Three, four, five…

I'd climbed halfway up when I began to feel really scared. Something knocked fast inside of my chest and my mouth felt bone dry. I wondered what was on the other side of the open door, I wondered what he'd do to me: was it a trick?

Be careful, he's going to push you down the stairs or lock you inside another room! the voice inside my head screamed.

Suddenly, my hands began to shake in time with my trembling legs. They felt so quivery that I was frightened they'd fold beneath me.

'Come on, you lazy little shit! Get a move on, I've things to do!'

It was him, his voice booming from the top step.

My arms ached and I was worried I'd drop the bucket. Imagining a flood of piss and shit running down the stairs like a brown river, I shuddered.

He'd kill you. He would actually kill you if that happened, the voice continued.

He was standing there in the doorway, his body blocking out most of the light. The strange thumping continued and my hands felt clammy, as though the handle might slip from them at any moment. I tightened my grip and tried to swallow down the rising terror I felt inside. I grunted with sheer effort as I made my way up the top few steps.

Six, seven, eight…

My stomach turned over as I dipped to one side, trying to look behind him. I needed to see where we were going. I checked his hands — the leather apron hung limply from his body, but his hands were by his sides and nowhere near the pouch.

The scissors, they must still be in there!

I began to panic as my eyes focused firmly on the pouch. Then the voice and another thought flashed through my mind.

What if he has something else, something bigger up there to hit you with?

The thumping inside my chest grew faster. It was so loud, I was certain he would hear it. My eyes strained, still trying to make out what was behind him. But it was no good — I couldn't see a thing. Most of the light had been blocked by him; all I could see was his outline. It looked as though someone had drawn a life-size picture of him and coloured it in with black pencil.

'Hurry up!'

I snapped back into the moment and quickened up the last few steps.

Nine, ten…

I'd done it — I was standing at the top of the stairs. I'd done it before, but never with him standing there, watching me. When I was certain he'd left for work, I'd tried the door a few times before. I'd stretched and tried to wriggle the metal latch on the other side, but it had never come loose. Now I was actually there, standing at the top of the stairs, only this time the door was open.

THUD, THUD, THUD…

My chest heaved as I struggled to draw breath.

My heart. The thudding. It must be my heart!

I'd learnt all about hearts with him in Science.

My eyes scanned the strange new room in front of me – the one that had been hidden behind the door. There was a table, like the one I had downstairs, only much bigger. Lots of chairs, too. Not one, like there was in my room, but lots. I remembered the voices I'd heard above me – voices drifting down through the floor, day after day. There must be other people living here.

One, two, three, four…

I started to count the chairs.

Four chairs and another, taller, chair with a tiny seat and table at the front of it. I remembered hearing a cry.

Who or what sat in the small chair?

'Stop bloody daydreaming and get a move on!'

His voice jolted me. He walked across the room and opened another, much heavier, door. But I was still fascinated by this room – the other world I'd finally been allowed into. I wanted to soak it up, to take in every last detail. The bucket grew heavy and my hands started to burn, but I tried to ignore it. Instead, I turned and stared, trying to absorb as many details as I could. I glanced over to my left: there was another door the exact same size as the one leading to the cellar. It was slightly open. I couldn't see inside from where I was standing, but I could smell it – food. Lifting my head, I breathed in the delicious air. It smelled so good, I could almost taste it. My belly rumbled in agreement.

Yes, it was definitely food!

Delicious smells wafted from behind the half-open door. I made a note inside my head.

If I ever escape, I'll head for that room first. That will be my prize.

'Out here, now!'

It was him – he was actually outside, his feet standing on some square, grey, flat stones. The contents of my bucket swayed from side to side as I followed towards the door. There was a square white-shaped thing on my left; it had two pipes hanging over it and lots of plates stacked up at the side.

'Watch it! Don't spill it, if yer know what's good for yer!' he growled, pointing down at the bucket as the contents sloshed around inside it.

I gulped, unsure what he wanted me to do or where he wanted me to empty it.

My heart pounded as I stepped outside. I wanted to cry – it was the first time I ever remembered coming out of the cellar. The sunlight felt blinding against my eyes and they began to water in protest. I paused on the big step outside the door, partly through fear but also fascination. So many smells and sounds hit me at once. I could hear confused, high-pitched noises, but they didn't sound human. I'd heard them before when I'd been locked in the cellar, but I didn't know what they were or where they were coming from. It wasn't until many years later that I recognised the strange noises as bird song.

The sun was shining; it warmed the skin on my face and it felt good. But I was still scared by so many things hitting me at once, so many things slamming into my senses – in my eyes, up my nose, against my skin, and seeping inside my mind. My cellar walls had trapped me but they also made me feel safe because at least down there I was protected by my spider friends. They were all I'd ever known. Standing here on the back doorstep, I felt uncertain – everything seemed so big, so loud and so different. I glanced all around: there were brick walls out here too, only they didn't have a 'lid' on them. There were no ceilings outside. I lifted my head up towards the blue sky; it was a lighter blue than my shirt, but much, much cleaner. There were clouds too. I knew what clouds were because he'd taught me that's where rain came from – another thing I'd learnt in Science. But I couldn't see any rain now; there was no water at all, just lovely, happy sunshine.

'Get a move on!'

It was him. I started to follow him over towards another smaller building with walls and a door.

'The outside toilet,' he said, waving a finger at it.

The door of the 'outside toilet' was green. I knew my colours because I had a set of coloured pencils that I used for my homework. And I loved my pencils. Although they were meant for homework, I'd secretly use them to draw with. I had about six colours in total – red, yellow, blue, green, black and white – but I'd mix them together to make new colours.

Standing outside the toilet, I watched as he pressed something down. The black latch made a clicking noise, similar to the sound of my door when he came into the cellar.

'In there,' he said, pointing to a round white dish thing with a back circle on top. 'Put it in the toilet.'

So I did as he said and poured the brown slop inside. I wasn't sure what to do next. I noticed a pipe leading up to a square-shaped black box above my head. It had a long metal thread hanging down with a handle on the end.

'Pull the chain,' he said, pointing to it.

I stretched, but I wasn't tall enough to reach. He tutted, leaned over me and pulled the chain hard.

WHOOSH!

The sudden noise was so loud that it startled me. I clamped both hands over my ears and took a step back, which made him laugh. Then I watched as the brown slop swirled around and around until some clear water washed it away and it had disappeared. I stared down in disbelief, waiting for the brown stuff to come back again, but there was only clear water. His hand grabbed the back of my shirt roughly as he pulled me outside.

'Come on, in the cellar.'

We retraced our steps over the grey, square stones, back inside the door and into the room above. I noticed a few more things, but I didn't know what they were. There were some blue and white things fixed to the walls that I later found out were cupboards, and a tall, square, white thing with black circles that was something called a cooker. I also spotted a small window that looked out onto the yard. My feet scuffed along the floor as he pulled me along. I glanced down and saw that the floor was covered in red squares instead of stone.

'Go on!' His hand pushed against the small of my back as he shoved me towards the top of the cellar steps. 'That's enough for one day. Go on, get back down there, where you belong.'

That night, I couldn't sleep. My mind raced with all the new smells and sounds of outside.

'Peter,' I whispered in the darkness. I couldn't see him, but I knew he'd be listening – he was always listening. 'I went outside today. It was amazing! I want to go outside again. When I do, I'll be sure to bring you something to eat.'

After pulling the blanket around me for warmth, I closed my eyes and nestled my head against the flat pillow. I knew then that I had to get out properly – I had to escape from the cellar.

CHAPTER 3

STARLINGS AND THE MOUSE

Time and time again, I tried to wiggle the door open but the latch on the other side always stayed stubbornly locked. It was similar to the one on the outside toilet. I'd wait, and as soon as he'd left for work, I'd be there, shaking the door, trying to knock the latch off. But it never worked.

After my first time outside, he told me I'd have to slop out my bucket every few days. It was a horrible job, but I started to look forward to emptying it out because it meant I'd be able to go outside again and see the sun. I couldn't wait to get back and tell Peter about my new adventures.

'You should have seen it,' I said, settling down next to his web as he twitched against it. 'The room upstairs is called "the kitchen", that's what he called it, and there's a big, white, square thing called "the sink". He told me not to go near it with my slop bucket. The floor is red, too – little red squares. There's lots of doors and chairs, but I'm only allowed out of the door that leads into what he calls "the yard". That's where the outside toilet is.'

Footsteps sounded above my head; his footsteps against the kitchen floor. I inched closer to the web and began to whisper.

'There's another room on the left when you get to the top of the stairs. I don't know what it's called, but there's food in there. I can smell it.'

I smiled because I knew today would be a good day, because today, I'd get to slop out again. I sat and waited.

CLICK!

The latch lifted on the cellar door and his footsteps followed, clomping as he came down the stairs.

STOMP! *Ten, nine, eight… seven, six, five, four… three, two, one.* 'Get the bucket.'

I did as I was told and ran over to it. Heaving it up, I pulled the handle over my right arm and inched sideways up the steps. I decided sideways was safest because it meant I could watch the stairs and the slops as they shifted around inside. I was even getting used to the foul smell – it didn't bother me any more because I knew it was my chance to go out.

It was a beautiful day when I stepped outside and across the square, grey, stone yard. We were walking over to the outside toilet when I happened to glance up: there wasn't a cloud in the sky, just blue everywhere with a ball of sunshine right in the middle. I heard a strange noise, a kind of chirping sound. I looked to my right and noticed a fast-moving black shape coming quickly towards us.

Was it a cloud? No, it couldn't be.

I watched as the black shape soared and then swooped down steeply as though bombing down towards the earth. Then I dropped the bucket on the ground, the contents slopping all around, and ducked behind him as the shape continued to twist and turn. My heart thumped inside my ribcage as the black pattern came alive with fast-moving and changing forms. I saw a circle, then the face of a witch; a long thin knife twisted and turned into a monster. I couldn't tear my eyes away from this weird and wonderful display, but it also terrified me. The monster thinned once more and changed, this time stretching into a long arm that seemed to reach down towards me. I shut my eyes and fell hard against the ground.

'What the...?!'

His face loomed over me, blocking out the sun.

'Get up! Get up now,' he warned.

But I didn't want to stand up because I didn't want the black cloud to get me.

He looked upwards and followed my line of vision. Then he sneered and nodded knowingly.

'Oh, *those*? They're birds, don't tell me you're frightened of bloody birds!'

'Biiirrrdddss,' I said, mimicking the word.

'Yes, birds – starlings. That's what they do, now get up and stop making a show of me.'

'Sorry,' I mumbled as I stumbled to my feet and picked up the bucket. The slops shifted inside, so I looked at the grey stones to check it hadn't spilled.

Birds... I repeated the word inside my head as I looped the handle back over my arm. *Starlings...* Two new words. I thought they were huge flies; they looked like them, only with bigger wings.

I followed him quietly, all the time watching the big dark

cloud as it continued to weave and swim through the sky. The black shape was shot with a glint of silver on its body; all together, they looked like a flying throbbing creature. I couldn't wait to tell Peter.

'In there,' he ordered as I stepped inside the toilet and threw the slops in it. But before I had the chance to turn, he'd slammed the door and locked me inside.

'That'll teach you. You're too soft, you need to toughen up.'

I'd been plunged into darkness again, only this time in a much smaller space. I searched for a light switch but there wasn't one. Instead, I pulled down the lid of the toilet and sat down. It wasn't quite like my chair in the cellar, but it was better than sitting on the cold floor. I glanced all around. There was the toilet, which took up most of the space, and a roll of paper attached to a bar that had been fixed to the wall. I lifted my hand and spun it around and around. Suddenly, it grew out of control and the crispy paper began to peel away.

No! I panicked.

I realised that if I pushed it the other way, the roll pulled all the loose paper back on again even if it wasn't as neat as before.

Phew!

I stared down at my feet: the things on them didn't look like the ones he wore. His had string tying them up, but mine were made of a bendy fabric that had been cut – probably using his scissors – and they stopped around my ankles. Sometimes they slipped off my feet because they were too big. I wondered if he'd given them to me to try and slow me up, to stop me from running away; I wasn't sure.

There were small spots – tiny squares of light – peeking in through a piece of metal that was up in the wall and had about twenty small holes in it. I knew there were twenty because I counted them. It was too high for me to look out of, so I stood on the toilet lid and leaned forward at an angle. Squinting with my left eye, I pushed my right eye close against the holes and peered through them at the world outside. A breeze blew in against my face, making my eye water slightly. I could see the back of the kitchen inside the brick building we'd just come out of and I counted the four walls of the yard. There was a long piece of string with clothes hanging from it that had brown, wooden things fastened at each corner of the cloth holding it on; also, a large metal bin the same colour as my slop bucket, only bigger.

Standing on the toilet lid, I had a very different view on the world. A flash of green shifted in the distance over the top of one of the walls. It swayed to one side and disappeared before reappearing again.

What was it?

I looked again as the tall green thing moved about in the breeze. I could just about see the top – it reminded me of something.

What was it?

Broccoli, that was it! The green tall thing looked like a giant piece of broccoli!

After a while, my legs began to ache so I jumped down. As I did so, I turned, and that's when I spotted something peeking out from behind the toilet bowl: a wooden block with a piece of wire that ran over the top of it. I knelt down and picked it up. The wire had been fitted so tight that when I tried to pull it away from the wood, it snapped straight back, almost trapping my fingers.

SNAP!

I couldn't work out what it was, so I put it down and left it there. Soon, the light had begun to fade outside and the toilet grew dark. I was just wondering about Peter when I heard a strange squeaking noise and the sound of something scratching against the floor. Sitting perfectly still, I waited to see if anything would pass. A short while later, there was a slight movement in the shadows. My eyes strained against the dim light, but I knew it was there – I'd definitely seen the outline of something. It was bigger than a spider, but it was alive and it made a strange noise. I tried to stay awake so I could look out for the creature, but my eyelids grew heavy and I must have fallen asleep. Hours later, I woke with a stiff neck. I'd fallen asleep at a funny angle with my head bent awkwardly against the wall. I opened my eyes and was just beginning to focus when a dark grey thing flitted across the floor in front of my face.

What the…?

I sat bolt upright.

What was that?

I stood up quickly and shook out both legs in case it had crawled up my shorts, like one of the spiders. Thankfully, both legs were clear. Kneeling down, I scanned the floor: nothing. I checked the wooden block thing at the back of the toilet, but it hadn't moved.

I'm not sure how long I'd been sitting there but I heard footsteps and the click of the door latch. It was him.

'Come on, you little bastard, and don't forget your bucket.'

As the door swung open, allowing natural light to come flooding inside, I blinked. I put my hand up against my eyes and cowered beneath him and the sunlight.

'What's the matter? Did the mouse frighten you? Aww, diddums!' he teased as he started to laugh. I didn't understand what was so funny.

Mouse… The mouse, so that's what it had been – a mouse. Another new word.

Before I knew it, he had pulled me across the yard and pushed me back down towards the cellar steps. The door slammed and I heard the sound of the latch fall, locking it from the outside. I was back inside another prison, but at least this one was bigger than the last. I ran down the steps to look for Peter – I wanted to tell him all about the starlings and the mouse.

I didn't have a clock or a watch – I didn't even know such things existed then – so I had no idea of how long I'd been locked in the outside loo. I knew the difference between night and day because light would pour down through the coal hole in the day and a strange white light would glow down it at night. It wasn't until much later that I learned this was a street lamp, something that gave light even when it was dark. I worked out, judging by the light, that it must have been a day since I'd slopped out. It had turned dark before growing light again, so I knew he'd locked me in the outside toilet overnight. I was still sat there thinking about it when I heard the latch and the sound of his feet as he came trundling down the steps.

Ten, nine… I sat at the table and grabbed the carpenter's pencil in my hand. *Eight, seven…* I gulped down my nerves, opened up the blue jotter and looked at the maths on the page. *Six, five… four, three, two, one.*

'Have you finished yet?' he asked, standing over me, peering over my shoulder.

His voice was deep and it boomed around the room. As the

pencil slipped inside my clammy palm, I felt my heart thump. I shook my head. He was so close that I could smell the hot tea on his breath. The steam from the mug in his hand rose and curled in the air as he continued to check on my progress. He stabbed an angry, fat finger against my jotter – it was so unexpected that I pulled the chair away from him.

'No! How many times do I have to tell you? You multiply it, you don't divide it!'

I felt a burning sensation as scalding hot tea seared against my scalp, left shoulder and arm as he threw the mug of tea all over me. As a deep pain soaked slowly into my skin, I gasped for cool air.

'Oh, shut up, and get some work done. It's only a bit of tea.'

That night, I couldn't sleep on my left-hand side because my arm and shoulder felt burnt where the hot drink had soaked me. I gently traced my fingers against my skin, but it had bubbled and felt sore to the touch. Tears streamed down my face and this time, I couldn't – and didn't – want to stop them.

Why did he do this to me? Why did I live down here in the cellar when there was an outside big enough for us all to live in?

Then I heard different voices drifting down from above. I lifted my head from the pillow to try and listen more closely. At first, I thought I must have been mistaken, but then I realised I'd been right all along – I knew what I'd just heard. I'd heard it before but I'd somehow convinced myself I must have been dreaming. But, there was no mistaking it now. I could hear children's voices coming from the kitchen above – other children, like me.

There were other children living upstairs.

CHAPTER 4

THE DANCE

Following that day, I often heard children's voices drifting down into the cellar from the kitchen above. I'd hear them moving around above my head talking, but I never heard them laugh. I did hear one cry, though – I wasn't sure which one it was, but I knew there was definitely more than one child because I could hear different voices. I couldn't be sure how old they were, but I thought they sounded younger than me. What I couldn't understand was why there were other children living above me when I had to live in the cellar.

I remembered the night I'd spent in the outside toilet. The long piece of string across the garden with clothes hanging from it – the one I'd spied through the metal holes. There had been big and small clothes hanging outside that day, but none I recognised as my own. I knew my clothes well; I didn't have many, so I tended to wear them until they were absolutely filthy. Every so often, he'd carry down a large metal bath filled with water. It wasn't warm but it wasn't freezing cold, either.

However, I always felt cold when I climbed out of it. He'd throw in a large block of soap and tell me to wash with it. Then he'd gather up my dirty clothes into a big, cloth ball and take them upstairs.

Sometimes, Mum would pick them up, but not very often. Mum only came down a few times. I had other clothes, ones that I kept in a chest of drawers underneath my bed. My bed was two columns made of brick with a concrete plinth resting on top. The mattress would sit on top of the concrete, and that was my bed. There weren't very many drawers – only two – but they held another pair of short trousers, a jumper, a white vest, a shirt with buttons, pants and a few pairs of socks. But none of the clothes hanging on the line in the yard had been mine – they would have been far too small.

'I think there are children living upstairs,' I told Peter.

I felt my stomach ache as the words left my mouth.

Other children.

'I wonder if he hits them as much as me. I bet he still gives them supper, even when they get their homework wrong.'

I couldn't help but feel bitter towards these children. Why were they treated differently to me?

'I wonder if he locks them in the outside toilet with the mouse.'

I shook my head.

No, I bet he doesn't.

I pushed my face angrily against the cold cotton pillow on my bed.

'I bet he doesn't, because they all live up there and I live down here,' I said, swallowing back my tears. I used the back of my hand to wipe them away with the edge of my sleeve.

No, I bet they don't have to do what I do... I bet they're allowed outside all the time... I bet they get to play with other children, not spiders.

An anger rose inside me until soon I couldn't control it.

'I hate him, Peter! I wish he was dead, then at least I'd be able to leave and you know what? I'd take you with me.'

That night I fell into a fitful sleep. I dreamt that I was chained in the cellar, never able to escape. My father had changed from a man into a monster as I sat in a corner of the room. Strangely, I didn't feel frightened, not any more, because I was sick of the fear. Fear had almost become normal to me, not happiness. When I woke, I realised the dream was trying to tell me something – I'd never felt normal and I'd never felt pure happiness.

A few days later, Dad was sitting down in the cellar alongside me, sharpening my pencils with a pen knife. I was copying out my spellings but I desperately wanted to ask him something I couldn't contain a moment longer. Gripping my chair for extra courage, I cleared my throat. The sudden noise made him look up.

'Can I ask something, please?' I said, remembering to add the word 'please'.

I didn't want him to lose his temper and whip off his belt. He eyed me warily, grunted, looked back down at the pencil and carried on. I watched the pencil shavings as they curled and dropped to the floor – I couldn't be sure if his grunt was a yes or no, but I carried on all the same.

'I want to come out of the cellar. When can I come out of the cellar?' I said, the words leaving my mouth before my courage failed me. As he looked up, his expression changing from curious to one of anger, I steeled myself. I shifted uneasily in my seat, my eyes firmly focused on the pouch at the front of his apron. Then I remembered: he had a knife in his hand.

Oh no, the pen knife! He's got a knife in his hands!

My eyes flitted from the pouch to the pen knife and back again. I watched and waited for him to move, half-poised, ready to bolt from his sitting position.

'Leave?' he asked, his question adding to the tension.

He stood up abruptly so that the coloured pencils spilled from his apron. They landed against the floor and scattered before rolling away into the shadows.

'Leave...?' he repeated, only this time I knew it wasn't a question – it was a trigger, a trigger for his anger.

I gulped.

'You can't leave, this is your bloody home!'

CRACK!

I was so busy watching him, I didn't notice his hand move as it slapped me hard across the face. Then I shut my eyes and waited for the inevitable – for him to kick and thump me – but I felt nothing. Instead, I opened my eyes to see the back of him as he disappeared up the steps and into the kitchen.

THUD!

The cellar door closed with a clatter as the latch fell on the other side. My spirits sank because I knew then that I'd never get out, not if he had anything to do with it. I didn't get any supper that night – it was my punishment for asking the question. Not that I cared; I didn't feel hungry anyway, and I usually always felt hungry. I just felt sick and sad inside, as hollow and as empty as my room.

The following morning, he didn't say a word as he placed

my breakfast on the table. He didn't even say anything later that evening when he sat and marked my homework. Thankfully, I managed to get all my maths right because I'd had a whole extra day to work on them. I decided that all I could do was to try to stay alive, at least until I was tall and strong enough to escape. The following morning, after he'd left for work, I rattled the door again, hoping to knock the latch open on the other side. I'd been doing the same thing for ages but it never seemed to work, and today would be another one of those days.

A few nights later, I got one of my subtraction questions wrong and he went absolutely berserk, even more crazy than usual. I watched as his hand dipped down inside the pouch to pull out the scissors, but I was quick on my feet and fled to the other side of the room. Then he sneered and made stabbing motions through the air as he drew close. I knew he would think nothing of hurting me.

Maybe he wants you to die? Maybe he wants you dead so that he doesn't have to come down into the cellar any more? the voice suggested.

A cold shiver ran through me as though blood had frozen inside my veins.

Yes, that must be it, he wants you dead!

'Come here,' he growled as he held the scissors above his head like a dagger. He brought them down against me but I flitted to one side.

Your chest, he's trying to stab you in the chest!

I was petrified, but I knew I had to defend myself – I had to fight back.

'Don't, please,' I begged, trying to back away from him.

I could feel the icy coldness of the bricks seeping in through the fine weave of my shirt as the roughness of the wall pushed hard against my back. Glancing all around me in a panic, I realised that I'd let him back me into a corner and now he was drawing closer and closer.

'Think you're clever, eh? Well, you're not. You're nothing, you're the shit on my shoe!' He smirked, nodding down towards it.

I saw my chance, grabbed the scissors and tried to hold the blades still. Everything paused and ran in slow motion as he pulled them back towards him; a tug of war, only with scissors instead of rope. I dragged them back, trying to free them from his grip. His eyes widened with rage – he looked like a monster – as he pulled the blades back towards him. The tension gave way as the blades slipped inside my clammy hands, slicing against my skin. There was a searing sensation as I glanced down to see a deep cut and then a flood of blood. Soon, there was red everywhere as my skin opened and crimson blood poured out. There was so much blood that I couldn't work out what or where I'd been cut.

'See what you made me do!' he scolded, as though it was my fault.

I watched as he pulled a cloth from the pouch and began to wipe both blades clean before slipping them inside the apron pocket. The pain – a ribbon of fire – in my hand took a few moments to register before it hit me. A breath-taking sharpness kicked in as I clutched it and ran around the room, screaming. I was almost too frightened to look – my little finger felt as though it was hanging on by a thread. When I finally looked down, I realised that I was right: the scissors had almost sliced all the way through it.

'Come here, let me look,' he barked.

I backed away, not wanting him anywhere near me.

'Suit yerself,' he said, turning towards the stairs.

Minutes later, he had reappeared with another bandage. He grabbed my hand roughly in his and began to wrap it tightly. Although it felt a little better, it didn't stop the pain from burning through. Afterwards, my hand throbbed all night, keeping me awake.

In spite of the scissors – which he used on rare occasions – his usual punishment was his belt. Whenever he thought I'd been naughty, he'd unloop it from the waistband of his trousers, grab me tightly by the shoulder or the arm and hold me still while he whipped me hard across my back, backside and legs. He would always try and hold the belt high up in his right hand so he could get a better swing. At first, I'd attempt to jump so he would miss me but I could never jump high enough and he always managed to catch the backs of my legs with the edge of it. To try and survive the beatings, I'd talk back to myself as though I was another person. I discovered I had another voice within me and it became the only way I could cope with the fear and the beatings. Instead, I would remove myself from my own body and pretend that I was someone else to try and calm myself down.

He can't hurt you, you are invincible! I'd tell myself whenever he pulled off his belt. *You can do this. Soon, it will be you hitting him and then you can get your own back. You will kill him!*

One day, he completely lost his temper. It was bad, even by his standards. I can't remember exactly why, but it would have been because my handwriting hadn't been neat enough. Anyway, he was seething and his face turned a reddish purple as he grabbed and tried to hold me still like a sitting target. But I had other ideas: I moved, doing a special dance I'd invented to try and miss the blows and escape his belt.

SWISH!

The belt whooshed as it sliced through the air towards me. I threw my body forwards so the backs of my legs avoided the swipe.

SWISH!

The belt cracked towards me violently again.

Missed.

SWISH, SWISH, SWISH...

He'd missed again and again.

Grabbing the top of my left arm, he held it in a vice-like grip.

SWISH!

The leather belt whipped through the air at double speed.

Missed.

He can't hurt you, you are strong, the voice insisted.

I needed to believe that I would get through this.

SWISH!

Dance...

SWISH!

Jump...

He held me high up in the air, my feet no longer able to touch the floor, and swung me around like a rag.

SWISH!

Dance...

SWISH!

Jump....

CRACK!

The bone at the top of my arm splintered in his hand as the

leather bit into the soft, fleshy skin on the backs of my legs. My legs buckled underneath me as I jolted with pain. There was a sensation of bone grinding against bone as I folded down to my knees.

'My arm… my arm!' I howled, screaming like a wounded animal.

It made him stop in his tracks. He'd usually just ignore me but I was screaming so loudly, he knew he had to stop because this time he'd really hurt me. Setting me down against the floor, I backed away from him and held my injured left arm protectively with my right. I noticed it was hanging down at a funny angle; it looked all bent, as though it had been put on back to front.

'Please… please…' I begged.

An agonising pain jolted through my body, stealing my breath away.

Gasp!

'Please… please… it hurts so much!'

'What, you think it's broken?' he said, looking down in disbelief. He let go of his belt, dropping it to the floor, and took a step away.

I wasn't sure what he meant by 'broken'. I'd broken a pencil before – the lead had snapped at the tip – but was my arm the same as a broken pencil?

Is that what he's just done to you? the voice asked.

I didn't know or care, I just wanted him to stop.

'Yes, yes,' I insisted. 'I think it's broken.'

'No, it's not,' he argued, straightening up. 'It can't be – I barely touched you.'

For the first time he looked worried and I watched as he ran a nervous hand through his ginger hair, his stubby fingers making each strand stand on end. He thought for a moment, rubbed his left hand across his chin, and looked down at me.

'Alright, stop crying! Now, where does it hurt?'

Tears dripped down from my face and pooled against my shoulders, turning my blue shirt a deeper navy colour.

'Everywhere. It hurts everywhere!' I wailed.

It wasn't a lie – the pain was so bad, it made me want to throw up.

'Alright, STOP CRYING!'

The sharpness of his voice quietened me immediately. I tried to hold my tears inside until soon my chest was heaving with violent, silent sobs.

'I need time to think,' he mumbled as he wandered back over to the chair to sit down. He rested his head in his hands and thought for a moment. I wasn't sure if he would just get up and leave, but instead, he did something completely unexpected.

'You really think it's broken?' he asked me again.

I nodded as I whimpered against the wall.

'It hurts, it really hurts!'

My father rose silently from the chair and trudged back upstairs. I heard the door swing and spotted the glow of the kitchen light as it flickered against the limed walls. He'd gone, but he'd left the door ajar. I didn't dare move: he'd just broken my arm, what else could – or would – he do? Moments later, the door creaked open as the light flooded in and down the stairs. I counted his footsteps.

Ten, nine, eight, seven… six… five… four, three, two, one…

He was standing in front of me, clutching something in his hand. I saw the edge of something metal and remembered the scissors.

No, the pen knife!

I pushed myself away, and that's when I saw it: a set of something in his hands, keys.

'Come on, get up, I'm taking you to hospital.'

Hospital?

I didn't know what a hospital was, but I couldn't believe he was taking me somewhere other than the outside yard.

Maybe this hospital was in the outside yard? Maybe it was somewhere even worse?

My stomach churned as I scoured my mind, trying to remember if I'd ever used the word 'hospital' in a sentence.

Peter went to the park… Arthur climbed a tree… George went inside the house… Albert went to the… Was it a hospital? I shook my head, I couldn't remember.

'What's wrong now?' he asked, still watching me.

I looked up. His face was partially hidden by a shadow cast from the bare single light bulb hanging above his head.

'GET UP. NOW! It's not your bloody legs that are broken!'

I clambered to my feet and followed him upstairs. My feet felt odd as I climbed the steps – steps that were usually out of bounds unless it was slopping-out time. But this time it was different, this time he had to do something.

This time he had to help me.

CHAPTER 5

THE HOSPITAL

The top of my left arm ached with a carousel of pain as I followed him up the stairs and into the kitchen. Instead of turning right towards the back door as we usually did, we headed through another and into a long thin room that had lots of other doors leading off it. We walked through the long room to another door – a much nicer door – which had coloured glass at the top and sides. It looked quite beautiful with the light shining through it, casting green-, red-, yellow- and blue-coloured shapes against the floor. He stepped outside and beckoned me to follow. This outside looked different to the yard: there was a red step leading down onto what I later found out was called a pavement.

Pavement...

I'd learnt that word before.

I was finally starting to put words together with actual things, words and objects joining up inside my head. The outside ground was made up of stones that sat on the ground in a series of bumps. They weren't smooth like the stones in the backyard. There were large buildings on each side made of the same brick as the one we'd just come out of. I looked up at the windows – dozens of them – each one pointing directly out on to the world. I glanced down to my right, the black metal grate of the coal hole by my feet now – my only window on the world. It struck me in that moment how much had been kept hidden from me.

Blood thumped hard inside my ears as my brain tried to absorb everything. I looked up at the light above the coal hole – the one that shed the dim white hue into my room at night. But there was no light now, the large bulb was off. There was fabric of all colours hanging in the different windows and doors. Clouds rose up in the air like the steam from his hot tea, but they were grey and puffed out of big red pots perched on top of the buildings. They were ten times higher than the ceiling in my room. Everything seemed magnified and I felt so small against all the tall things. When I looked up, it made my head swim: the earth seemed to tilt beneath my feet as I swayed at the sheer sight of them. I glanced along the pavement that seemed to go on forever. It stopped at the end, another pavement crossed it, and then it carried on, leading to a new set of buildings that looked exactly the same. The pavement and buildings stretched on as far as my eyes could see.

'Here,' he said, bringing me back into the moment. He was standing beside a dark blue metal thing with windows, seats and four back round things on the outside, with two on either side. 'Get in the car.'

A car – this strange metal thing was called a car.

I did as I was told. He opened up a door as I climbed

in. Holding my damaged left arm in my right hand, I slid awkwardly down into the seat. It made a squeaking noise, similar to the mouse, as my legs shifted against it.

'Sit still and try to act normal,' he ordered, closing the door with a slam.

I lifted my head and sniffed the air – it smelled funny inside. The seats were made of leather, like his apron, and they smelled of dried blood, the exact same as my wounds after he'd beaten me. But there was another smell too. It was overpowering and it seemed as though it was coming from underneath the car. Years later, I discovered that it was petrol. He put the key in at the side and turned it. It clicked and there was a loud roaring noise as he pushed something forward. Holding the large black circle in his hands, he turned it and we pulled away from the pavement. I gripped the edge of my seat with my good hand, both terrified and mesmerised at the same time.

We were moving without walking!

Not only could I see through the window, we were sitting in something that could carry us along.

'You say nothing, you understand?' he said, his voice breaking the awkward silence.

'Yes,' I mumbled, looking down at my lap.

A panic rose inside me.

Where was he was taking me, and what was a hospital?

I'd always dreamed of escaping, but now, sitting here in this strange machine with unfamiliar things whizzing by outside, I felt scared – really scared. But I also wanted him to stop the car because I wanted, no, I *needed* to see everything.

'You keep quiet and don't tell the doctor nothing. If you

say anything, you know what's going to happen,' he warned, waving his fist at me.

But I'd stopped listening because I was too busy staring out the window. I wasn't used to a proper window and this one was amazing because I saw so many new and wonderful things whizzing by us. I recognised something I'd seen before swaying over the wall in the backyard – the tall piece of broccoli – only this time there were loads of them growing at the side of the road.

'You keep quiet. . . ' he repeated, his voice droning on in the background. '. . . and don't say anything to anybody, otherwise you know what'll happen. Just let them do what they've got to do and keep that shut!' he added, pointing a finger to my mouth.

'Yes,' I whispered.

I wanted him to shut up so I could watch the world go by outside – *outside* – I could barely believe I was looking at it. We passed more buildings and more pieces of broccoli. I spotted a group of children who looked about my age, but they weren't stuck inside a cellar, they were playing outside: they were playing together. My stomach twisted inside as I watched them giggle and kick something round along. I noticed one of them clutching his belly and he laughed as he ran after the round thing as it bobbed along the ground.

Why don't they live in a cellar like you? the voice asked.

I took a sly glance at my father – he was looking straight ahead.

Jump out! Do it! Jump out now! It was the voice again.

My eyes shifted to the side, towards the door. I thought about opening it up, of jumping out, but everything was moving by so quickly. At that moment, the car rattled against the road, shaking my arm as I tried to hold it still. I swallowed down the pain. I couldn't jump, I'd only make things ten times worse. I tried to lift myself up, but a deep agony shot down the length of my broken limb, causing me to breathe in sharply.

He turned and looked sideways at me, so I gritted my teeth and gulped a wave of sickness down.

Don't give into it, don't give him the satisfaction.

I looked back through the window to try and take my mind off things. I spotted more buildings like the one we'd just left, more green tall things swaying in the breeze, and people – lots of them – all wandering around outside. There was someone who looked like Mum holding a small child. I saw other children and then an older person bent over and leaning against a long stick. I saw people, so many people – I couldn't believe that so many people lived outside.

CLICK.

His hand pushed something down and we turned. I watched as he threaded the circle through his hands towards the left, realising that whichever way he turned, it was the way the car would go. My heart was hammering and my palms felt so sweaty that I had to wipe my good one against the leg of my shorts. More green things, more people, but all different ages. Lots who looked like Mum, walking with children like me, but they were holding hands. More buildings. A tall red-shaped thing that I saw someone push a piece of paper into. There was a man standing inside a red box with dozens of small windows, holding something against his ear. Another man was walking a creature that wasn't a person: it had four legs, pointed ears and was covered in black and white hair.

Before I knew it, the smaller buildings ran out and had given way to a huge new space. We pulled into it and I noticed lots of other cars, although they weren't the same shape or colour as his. My head was still pounding, trying to process everything I'd just seen; my eyes ached with all the colours – so many colours – and new faces.

'Right, this is it. We're here.'

He pulled a long stick up, turned something and the car stopped making a noise as though it had just been put to sleep. After pushing his glasses up his nose, he climbed out and opened the door on my side. I was frightened: outside was busy, *too* busy...

'Get out!' he roared.

I climbed out of my seat with some difficulty, my arm throbbing as though it was hanging on by a single thread. I felt bone grind angrily against bone, reminding me why he'd brought me here. I gasped; it was so painful, I thought I would pass out with it. He looked at me and I knew that he knew. He saw all the people passing by us and closed the car door behind me. Everyone seemed to be heading in the same direction, so I turned my eyes to follow them and that's when I saw it – the tallest building I'd ever seen. It was absolutely massive, about thirty times higher than my ceiling.

So this is what a hospital looks like?

There were swarms of people. Lots of Mums dressed in blue and walking in a group that he said were called 'nurses'.

Nurses… nurses… I said silently, repeating the word over and over inside my head. I didn't really know what nurses were or what they did, but they all wore a piece of dark blue cloth around their shoulders.

We approached a doorway that all the nurses seemed to be walking through.

'Remember, you say nothing. I'll do the talking.'

I did as I was told and followed him inside the massive building full of windows. It was bright too – just like the outside, only we were now inside. My brain hurt trying to make sense of it all. I was so amazed by all the new sights and sounds that I walked along with my head pointing upwards, trying to take it all in – I didn't want to miss a single thing. There were people standing on corners, chatting and laughing. There were long thin rooms that led to even more doors. My eyes blinked furiously against all the lights – they were everywhere, only these ones were covered, unlike the bare bulb in my cellar. And there were stairs, lots of stairs.

A hand tapped sharply against my good arm, making me flinch.

'Stop that!'

It was him. I faced forwards and we walked on. I concentrated hard, trying to listen to all the different conversations. My nostrils widened because it smelled funny – the hospital smelled funny. My nose twitched: it smelled of soap.

Yes, that was it. It smells of strong soap!

Everything looked clean, too; so clean that the light seemed to bounce off each and every surface, creating even more light. For a moment he stopped to read lots of writing that was on a big board with arrows pointing everywhere and then we turned and entered a new room. He approached someone who was dressed like a nurse, sitting behind a table at the front of the room. I tried to catch him up.

'How can I help?' the nurse asked, smiling up at us both.

I remembered what he'd said in the car and kept quiet.

'It's my son. I think he's broken his arm falling from a tree.'

Tree… there was that word again. I'd written it down in my spellings but I still didn't know what it was. At least now I knew it must be something tall, like steps; something dangerous that I could climb and fall down from.

'Yes, and what's your name?' The person, who looked a bit like Mum but with fairer hair, asked, looking directly at me.

I wasn't used to being looked at; I panicked and quickly dipped behind him to try and hide.

'Oh, he's shy,' the nurse laughed, grinning over at me.

Let me do the talking… His words rattled around inside my head.

'His name is Stephen. It's Stephen Smith.'

'Rightio! If you and Stephen would like to take a seat, the doctor will be with you shortly.'

The nurse gestured over to a line of chairs behind us. Some had other people and children like me sitting on them, but there were still a few that were empty.

'Say nothing,' he whispered out of the corner of his mouth.

I thought how nice and smiley the 'Nurse Mum' had been. Much nicer than the Mum at home – that Mum never even spoke to me, only left me food.

I stared hard at the ground. It was grey coloured, but it wasn't stone. I noticed how much warmer it felt here than in my room. I shifted my gaze to my feet; the things I wore on mine didn't look like those the other children wore – theirs had string holding them on, like his. I let my legs dangle limply from the chair and as I did so, I felt someone watching me. My eyes flitted sideways, expecting it to be him, only it wasn't. There was a little boy sat on the opposite side of the room and he was looking straight at me. I glanced down at my feet again, ashamed, and tried to push them away and out of sight. But the little boy was still staring. He was just like me, only his hair was much shorter and he was wearing long trousers, not short ones like mine. I tried not to stare back at him, but I couldn't help it.

He was so clean.

I bent my fingers against my palm and checked my nails: they were filthy. My shorts were grubby too and so was my shirt. Without realising, I ran a hand through my hair to try and flatten it so that I looked more like the boy opposite.

'John! What have I told you about staring?' a man sitting next to him scolded as he pulled the little boy's arm.

The man looked a bit like him, only he had dark hair. I waited for the Dad to pull off his belt and start whipping the boy, but he didn't do anything. Instead, the child simply looked away. I couldn't believe it.

He would have killed you for being so naughty! the voice gasped.

I nodded.

'Stop that!'

It was him again. I averted my gaze and focused instead on a picture on the opposite side of the wall. It had something called M.E.A.S.L.E.S. written on it, whatever that was. There was a picture of a child with lots of spots. They reminded me of the tiny cuts to my skin the belt buckle would sometimes leave behind. I glanced over at the nurse, who smiled over at me again. I wanted to smile back, but I didn't know if I'd get into trouble so I looked away. We sat there for quite a while, but I didn't mind because the longer we had to wait, the more time I got to be out of the cellar. Eventually, someone called something out.

'Stephen Smith!' a man in a white coat shouted into the room.

Everyone looked up, but no one replied. At first I didn't move, then I felt his hand grab the side of my shirt and pull me to my feet. The man in the white coat noticed and came over towards us, but he didn't seem as happy as the nurse.

'I'm sorry for keeping you waiting. I'm Doctor Brown. Now, if you'd like to follow me…'

Doctor, another new word. But Brown? Brown was a colour!

We walked through a few sets of doors, but they were two doors that swung open and closed together, not one. We followed Doctor Brown down a long narrow room and into another much smaller room with a bed on metal legs, a table, chairs and a window.

'So then, Stephen,' the doctor said, taking a seat opposite me, 'what have you done?'

At first, I didn't know who he was talking to but then I realised he was looking directly at me. I wanted to tell him I'd done nothing – that my father had done this to me – but my throat closed up and it was as though I'd lost the power to speak.

'Oh, right you are. Shy, eh? Well, let's start by asking how old you are.'

There was another moment's silence before Doctor Brown looked to my father for the answer.

'Seven. He's seven years old.'

'Right,' Doctor Brown replied, scribbling something down on a piece of paper. 'And why have you brought him here today?'

I kept my eyes fixed firmly on the floor so that he wouldn't look at me or ask me any more difficult questions. I wouldn't be allowed to answer anyway. Even if I could, I wouldn't know the answers or I'd get them wrong and that would make him angry. My father leaned forward in his chair and clasped his hands together in front of him. I wondered if he'd done it because he was about to tell another lie.

'He fell climbing a tree.'

'A tree?' The doctor nodded knowingly. 'Well, boys will be boys. You need to be more careful, young man,' he said, wagging a finger at me.

Was he angry?

I flinched. The doctor looked confused, but shrugged and carried on writing. I wondered if he had spellings to do, like me. One thing I knew for sure was my father had just told him a lie. I hadn't broken my arm climbing a tree, I didn't even know what a tree was. He'd done this to me – he'd broken my arm and he knew it. I wanted the doctor to ask me what a tree was so that I could say I didn't know, because then he'd know it was a lie. I'd tell him I'd never seen a tree and, even if I had, I wouldn't know because I only ever left the cellar to slop out or come here, like today.

He did it! the voice inside my head screamed. *Tell him, he did this to you!*

But I was too afraid, petrified of what my punishment would be if I dared say a word. Instead, I just sat there.

Doctor Brown wrote a few more things down, gave him a piece of paper and sent us to a different room, where another nurse took something called an X-ray.

'It won't hurt, Stephen. It's just a photograph of your arm,' the X-ray nurse insisted.

This nurse looked like Mum, but was serious like Doctor Brown and not as smiley as the last nurse. But this one smelled lovely, too. I inhaled as the nurse leaned over me to try and place my arm flat.

'Now, I need you to keep still. You think you can do that for me?'

I nodded and smiled back, but only because he wasn't in the room. The nurse had been so kind that I suddenly felt sad, as though I might cry. I wanted to ask what a photograph was, but I knew he was sat right outside the door and I was scared he would hear me. The nurse sent us back to see Doctor Brown, who looked at the X-ray and nodded his head knowingly.

'It's what we call a spiral fracture,' he explained, holding it up against a light on the wall.

I wondered if a fracture was the same as broken.

I thought you'd broken your arm?

Doctor Brown sent us to another man, who wrapped some bandages around it. They had been smeared in some white wet stuff and they smelled funny. They were also freezing cold – as cold as wet bricks. He continued to wrap them around my shoulder and down to my wrist. Then he coiled another, itchier, bandage across my back and across my arm to keep it close to my body.

'You're a very brave boy,' he observed, as my father looked on.

I knew he was watching, warning me not to say a word. I thought I knew what 'brave' was – it was one of the words he'd already taught me. Brave must be that you didn't cry when your father slapped, thumped, kicked or even whipped you. A little word that meant you barely cried when he stabbed you with scissors, or almost cut your finger off. Even if he twisted your arm so badly that it broke, snapping like a pencil. I had to be brave because of all the things he'd done to me. If 'brave' meant all those things then, yes, he was right, I *was* brave. I was frightened that one day he'd hurt me and never stop.

I was brave, but my bravery was because of fear.

Yet, in spite of his lies, the constant cuts and bruises and my newly broken arm, today had been a good day, because today I'd got to leave my room. I'd travelled in a car for the very first time. I'd seen things I'd never seen before, and I'd even been inside a hospital. I'd met more people in one day than I'd ever seen or spoken to in my entire life. Today, I'd also found out two things for the very first time.

My name is Stephen Smith. And I am seven years old.

CHAPTER 6

RELEASE THE DOG

That night, we returned from the hospital. I hadn't eaten, but he still made me do my homework. It was only once he'd marked my maths and I'd got all my questions right that he finally brought me my dinner.

''ere you go, and don't make a mess.'

It was more difficult, trying to eat with one hand, but luckily he'd broken my left arm and my hand was partially uncovered; at least I was still able to wiggle my fingers. The plaster felt heavy, but it was good for catching flies. Not that I was as fast as I'd been before because the weight of it slowed me down.

'Sorry, Peter. Missed that one!' I said, slamming my arm hard against the wall. The impact made the plaster on my arm shudder.

A day or so later, my room had started to feel really cold again. It was dark outside almost all of the time. Even when it was light, it felt grey and gloomy and it seemed to rain constantly — I could hear it bouncing off the pavement. I shivered underneath my blanket and pulled out an extra jumper to try and keep warm. I was just watching my breath form small clouds in the air when the cellar door opened and he came down unexpectedly.

I jumped to my feet.

Ten, nine, eight, seven, six, five, four, three, two… one.

I thought he was bringing breakfast, but his hands were empty. He was wearing the leather apron and it swung from side to side as he grabbed a hold of my good arm and threw me down into my chair. I started to shake.

What have you done wrong? the voice gasped.

I expected him to say something – to tell me – but he didn't speak. As I watched his hands, I was prepared – waiting for him to whip off his belt – but there was no movement, no belt, nothing. He grunted as he leant down and began to study my face on the left-hand side. Then he did the same on my right. Too scared to catch his eye, I stared straight ahead. Then he went back to my left side and started to stroke some strands of hair hanging down around my temple.

I began to tremble; my palms felt damp and my heart thudded loudly. I kept my eyes focused on a solitary brick in the opposite wall. There was a slight tug of my hair as he grabbed it in his hand and lifted it away from my face. He dipped down again to study me. Only this time with his right palm planted flat on top of my head. I felt a sudden pressure as he gripped my skull, pinning me down in my seat. My hair skimmed the tops of my shoulders as he let go and withdrew the scissors from his apron pouch. Swapping hands, he took the shears in his right and grabbed at one of the big metal handles to pull them open. The other blade pointed downwards like a dagger and it hung there as a threat in front of my eyes. I gulped down a rising sense of nausea and he sneered as he looped a thumb and finger through both handles, now just inches from my face. I forgot about the brick opposite and stared hard at the small screw in the pivot of the shears.

Don't panic. Whatever you do, don't panic!

His hot breath soaked against the skin on the side of my neck and he grabbed another handful of hair and lifted it up. Each hair root seemed to pull in the same direction as he traced a finger along my skin underneath. There was a sudden line of coldness – the hard edge of metal – as it rested in a hard line against the skin.

The scissors… He's letting you know they are there, he's holding the blade against your neck!

I gulped as small beads of sweat pricked and then trickled against my forehead.

He's going to stab you, stab you in the neck!

The blade pressed harder and harder before he pulled it away, laughing.

I struggled to breathe as I felt my body burn with fear. Blood pumped furiously inside my ears and throbbed against my brain. The veins in my eyes throbbed as the scissors loomed into view once more, the metal edge glinting in the half-light. The scissors were at the side of my face now.

Run… run! Just run… the voice screamed, as the cold blade slipped slowly down to the side of my neck. He was so close that I could smell his breath and feel its heat as it radiated against my skin.

'Please don't, please don't… I promise I'll be good.'

My voice was barely a whisper as I closed my eyes and

petrified tears streamed down my face. Each breath became more shallow than the last as I struggled to claim them. A trail of snot dripped down from my nose like melted candle wax and traced over my mouth. Mixing with my tears, it quickened its journey and dripped off my chin.

'Please don't… please don't hurt me!'

I started to whimper and my body grew rigid as I braced myself for pain or something even worse. Closing my eyes, I waited for the…

SLICE…

The blades whooshed sharply as they sheared against my ear. I felt something brush past me and then float down towards the floor.

What was it? Hair? A haircut, of course! Thank you! He's giving you a haircut.

I'd had one ages before. Back then, I hadn't been sure what he was going to do to me, then I remembered the hair. It had fallen and rested as soft as breath against my hands. I sat and waited for the next cut.

SLICE!

The scissors were against the side of my skull now; I could feel the cold metal weight of them as they rested against the top of my ear, pushing it down.

SLICE, SNIP!

SLICE, SNIP!

My hair tumbled freely from my shoulders into my lap, gathering against my shorts and thighs. It felt ticklish, but I didn't dare move – I didn't want the scissors to slip in his hand.

SLICE, SLICE, SLICE!

The strands soon multiplied. My hair seemed to be long

and brownish orange in colour. He worked his way around to the back of my head but I still couldn't relax because I knew anything might set him off. The point of the scissors felt sharp. They caught against the thin skin on my scalp as he fumbled around. I winced, felt him readjust them in his hand and carry on.

SLICE!

SNIP!

SNIP!

SLICE!

SNIP!

The cool air caught against my freshly exposed scalp as more and more strands continued to tumble down. The left hand he'd been holding on the top of my head shifted again, this time as a flat palm against my forehead. I saw his face twisted in concentration as he loomed in front of me. He showed me the scissors, opening and snapping them shut with a grin. I trembled as he drew a blanket of hair down in front of my eyes, temporarily blinding me. The strands were so long that the ends prickled against my chin. Even though I couldn't see a thing, I closed my eyes. The blade – the edge of metal – had felt like a pencil drawing a sharp line across my forehead. He held down my hair and sliced through it in one long cut.

S...L...I...C...E!

I opened my eyes to find him standing away from me, admiring his handiwork. Satisfied, he snapped the scissors shut and slid them back inside the pouch. Then he turned and disappeared upstairs. The huge breath I'd been holding inside came flooding out as I started to relax. Then I realised something: he'd not locked the door. The light from the kitchen shone down against the walls and I heard him shuffling around at the top. I counted each step and then he was there, thrusting something into my hands.

'Take this brush and sweep up the mess.'

I didn't know what he wanted me to do. In a temper, he snatched it back and began to 'sweep' up the loose hair into a pile.

'This, you daft bastard! Now, sweep it all together onto this,' he said, handing me something else that was flat and wide. 'And don't be long about it.'

With that, he disappeared. I did as I was told and cleaned up the mess. With him out of the room, I took a chance and ran a hand quickly through what was left of my hair. It felt clumpy in places and much, much shorter than before. It was nowhere near my shoulders now. Using my fingers, I traced around the back of my head and upwards. The bumps on my skull felt exposed as my fingertips ran quickly up and over it like a spider.

Ouch!

My fingers pulled away as I felt a hard ridge near the top of my scalp.

Was it an old scar?

I couldn't be certain, but it felt odd and uncomfortable to touch.

Did you hit your head at some point? Had he?

I tried to think; I tried to picture blood pouring from my head, but there was nothing, no memory, only a blank. I heard the door creak, so I picked up the brush and tried to look busy: he was heading back downstairs. He stood in front of me and grunted as I swept the last few strands up. Then he took the brush from me, turned and left.

Later that day, once he'd left the house, I tried the lock again. Maybe my new haircut had spurred me on, I don't know. Or perhaps now I'd seen the outside – the hospital, the nurse, that boy, the doctor – maybe now I'd seen all those things I wanted, no, I *needed* to see more. I wiggled the door and rattled it violently, but the latch stayed firmly locked. But I was getting taller and stronger by the day. I hoped and prayed that soon I'd be able to smash my way out of there.

I continued with my homework and secret drawings to try and fill the days that followed. Time felt as stretchy as the tops of my socks and there wasn't a moment when it ever seemed to move or go quickly.

I confided in Peter. Already I'd told him about my hospital visit and how much I wanted to escape.

'I wish I could crawl through the coal hole like you, I wish I could get out of here.'

That night, I fell into a fitful sleep. I dreamt I'd shrunk down to the size of Peter – I was still a boy, but with spider's body and powerful legs that could climb walls. I was climbing the wall, climbing up it with Peter. I was almost at the top when I heard something behind me. I turned to see spider Albert, the claws of his mouth bearing down on me. He moved quickly, too quickly for me to try and escape. His jaws opened wide and his claws extended. I cowered beneath him as he bit into my neck, sinking the points in deeper and deeper.

I sat bolt upright in my bed; my blanket had already fallen to the ground. The cold from outside chilled me and a sheen of sweat was covering my body. I shivered violently.

A dream, it had just been a bad dream.

Picking up the blanket, I pulled myself back onto my bed and trembled with fear and a lack of warmth. I *needed* to get out of this room, I *needed* to get out – it didn't matter how, I just *had* to get out. Then I pictured myself at the top of the stairs, waiting for him to open the door. I saw it all so clearly inside my head – my hands pushing against his back as he lost his footing and tumbled down the steps. His skull crunching against one step and then another as he landed, lifeless and heavy against the stone floor. I saw myself running through the kitchen and out through the long room with the nice door and the coloured glass. I'd step onto the pavement outside and then I'd turn left – no, right – and tear along the street. I'd run and run, and I wouldn't stop running until I found the hospital. I'd search for the nice smiley nurse, Doctor Brown or the man who fixed my arm with plaster and I'd tell them – I'd tell them all what he'd done to me. I'd get them to lock him up down here and see how he liked it.

'Get up yer lazy bastard!'

It was him – he was standing over me.

I sat up in my bed, my body still shaking. I must have fallen back to sleep.

'Get up. Get up now!'

The dish with white water and floating orange things was already sitting on the table. I jumped out of bed, picked up the spoon and started to push the food deep inside my mouth. I'd do anything – *anything* – to stop him from hitting me. I'd almost finished when he grabbed my arm, the one with the plaster on it.

'Stand up!' he said pulling me roughly.

I did as I was told and watched as he slumped down in the chair and started to examine my plaster. It was grubby with so much dirt and coal dust that it didn't even look white any more; instead, it was a filthy grey – the same colour as pencil scribble. He dipped down a hand and pulled the scissors from his apron pouch. My throat felt dry even though I'd just drunk all the white water. I felt it cling to the back of my throat as he grabbed my plastered arm and pulled me towards him. He didn't take his eyes from the plaster, not for a moment.

What is he doing?

I feared the worst.

'Stop it! Stay still!'

But it was no good. I was so scared that I thought I might piss myself. He pulled the scissors apart using his fingers and thumb and slid one of the blades deep inside. The outer bit of the metal scraped against my skin and it felt sore as it scored its way downwards, scratching me. I tried not to let him know I was scared because I knew it would make him worse.

The room filled with a strange crunching sound as the shears bit into the plaster. He sliced, snipped and pressed against it until the cast cracked and began to give way. The scissors carved through it, eating it up, bit by bit, until it had opened up to my elbow.

'Stand still!' he snapped again. He was beginning to lose his patience with me as I twisted against the sharp point.

SNIP, SLICE, CRUNCH, CRACK… SPLINTER!

The floor was covered in bits of plaster as he pressed on, breaking the fibres until the old bandage had almost crumbled to dust.

I was frightened, so I tried to think of something else. I remembered what the man had said to me at the hospital – the one who had put the plaster on my arm, the one who'd called me brave.

'This will need to come off in eight weeks, so you'll have to bring him back.'

My father had nodded and I'd felt a flicker of hope that I would get another trip out. But as the days passed, I knew it was unlikely he would ever take me back there again, plaster or no plaster. Instead, he'd left me with it on my arm until it had started to smell. It became so bad that I tried not to move in case the stench escaped and rose up my nose. But now he was cutting it with the very same shears that had almost taken my little finger off. I screwed up my eyes as he worked through the last part, a tight bit around my hand. The metal pressed against the small bones in my knuckles as he struggled to release it.

SLICE, SLICE, SNIP, SNIP… SLICE!

Ouch!

There was nothing but an overwhelming sense of relief when he finally folded the last part wide open. Cool air began to circulate over and around my skin, lifting the small hairs on my arm – it felt amazing. But then the horrible stench followed; it drifted upwards and filled the room with a nasty pong. He held up his hand and waved it around in front of his nose.

'You need a bath,' he said, but I wasn't listening – I was too busy looking at the yellow scaly skin covering my withered arm.

It had changed colour; it looked dead, as though it no longer belonged to me. My arm felt the same, too – as though someone had stuck a spare part on my body. I left it there, swinging by my side, because it felt weak and useless. Too weak to move now that the weight of the plaster had been taken away. He picked up the remains of the cast, walked up the steps and closed the door. But I couldn't take my eyes off my arm as I studied it with revulsion and fascination. I traced a finger over the yellowed skin and wondered if it would ever return to normal.

Moments later, there was a clatter of the tin bath as he knocked it against the cellar door.

Ten... nine... eight... seven... six... five... four... three... two... one.

'Strip off and get in,' he said, resting it down against the floor with a heavy thud. The water swayed up, almost breaching the metal rim. Then he threw in a block of soap for good measure as the tide lifted and splashed me. 'And don't forget to wash, you smelly bastard!'

The water felt tepid to the touch, but the thought of him watching me chilled me more than it ever could. Afterwards, he threw me a small threadbare towel and I shivered because the room was absolutely freezing.

'Get dressed!'

The skin on my arm continued to flake off for days. It looked pretty horrible, as though I'd been burnt, but at least the smell disappeared. It took a while, but eventually, my left arm grew stronger until I was finally able to use it again. I'd spent so long not using it that it felt odd, but soon, and in spite of some stiffness where the crack had been, it was as though it had never been broken at all.

One morning, he came downstairs but he didn't bring any breakfast.

'Slopping out time!' he grunted as he pointed over towards the bucket.

My left arm still ached, but I was right-handed and so able to rest the weight of the handle against that arm to carry the bucket upstairs. It was freezing cold outside as I followed him across the yard and towards the outside toilet. Grey clouds swirled above my head and the sky looked as though it had been scribbled with grey pencil. The air tasted cold and damp, as though it was about to rain. Taking a step backwards, I moved as he opened the wooden door and pointed inside. I walked over to the toilet and poured the slops into it. Standing on my tiptoes, I had just pulled the chain when the door slammed behind me.

He's done it again, he's locked you in! the voice cried.

I slumped down on the floor with my back wedged against the wall.

'Hello?' I whispered through the darkness, hoping the mouse would hear me.

I wasn't scared of him any more because I knew he wouldn't hurt me. He was like Peter: this was his home and I would share it for as long as it took for Dad to unlock the door and let me out. The mouse wouldn't harm me and he knew I wouldn't hurt him. Maybe we could even become friends?

That night, I fell into a chilled and disturbed sleep. The sound of the rain lashing hard against the ground outside kept waking me up. That, and the fact I couldn't stop shivering. I prayed morning would come quickly so I could return to my cellar. My room was chilly, but it wasn't as bitter as the outside toilet.

At least you've got a blanket in the cellar.

I heard the latch scrape metal against metal as it creaked and lifted. I blinked, waiting for him to open the door, but there was nothing – no movement. Unnerved, I scrambled to my feet and waited a few more moments. The hairs on the back of my neck prickled upwards; my senses on high alert – he was up to something. I heard a noise – the sound of footsteps shuffling outside – as the door remained unlocked but closed. My breath grew shallow as I tried to work out where he was and what he was doing.

'Hello?' I called out.

I was shocked at how small and unsure my voice sounded. The door shifted as someone grabbed the latch on the other side.

'RELEASE THE DOG!'

It was him. The door swung open and my heart began to pound. I couldn't see him – I couldn't see anyone, only blinding daylight – so I lifted a hand to try and shield my eyes to give them time to adjust. I took a hesitant step outside, my body trembling, I took another…

WHACK!

There was a sharp blow to the back of my head as his fist connected against my skull. He thumped me hard, so hard that it knocked me off balance and made me stumble forward.

WHACK, SLAP, THUMP!

I backed away from him, holding up my right hand to try and protect myself.

'Get back inside!'

I ran over to the back door, through the kitchen, and didn't stop running until I was at the bottom of the cellar steps. Suddenly, a tall, dark figure appeared at the top, blocking out all the natural light as his silhouette shaded the doorway.

SLAM!

The door closed and I heard him drop the latch on the other side. It was morning, I'd not even had breakfast and I probably wouldn't eat until tonight. I was starving; I needed something to take my mind off the hunger rumbling deep down inside, so I walked over to the table and sat down. There was a gap, two fingers wide, where I hid my artwork. I dipped down and pulled out a stack of drawings. I studied them all, each one more disturbing than the last. Then I picked up a pencil, wiped my eyes and began to draw.

A dog… He'd just called me a dog. I didn't even know what a dog was.

CHAPTER 7

THE ESCAPE

He started locking me in the outside toilet so often that I soon began to see it as my second 'room'. I didn't like it, but at least I knew what to expect now. The following morning, when he unlocked the door, he would always call out the same thing: 'Release the dog!' I made it my mission to find out what a dog was.

At night, I'd lie in my cellar bed, dreaming up ways to overpower him – to kill him and escape the constant beatings. One morning, after breakfast, I sat and waited; waited for him to go to work, so that I could follow my usual routine – wriggling the door latch to try and get it to open. I'd grown quite a bit. I knew because the sleeves on my shirts had begun to creep up my arms as they became longer. For the first time, my shorts really were, well, really short. They fell around the tops of my legs rather than brushing at the edges of my knees whenever I stood up.

Climbing the cellar steps, I expected the usual – a latch that wouldn't lift. I decided I would try it for a little while, do a bit of drawing and then make a start on my spellings and sentences. Taking a step towards the door, I began to rattle the wood. For a while I pushed and pulled at it and was just about to give up when I heard something click on the other side. I stepped back in surprise.

Was it him? Was he back?

I ran back down to the bottom step, my heart hammering, and glanced all around. I'd not pulled my drawings out, so I knew I'd be alright – everything in the cellar looked completely normal. I waited some more, but he didn't appear so I tiptoed back up the steps and pressed my ear against the wooden door.

Nothing.

I pressed it closer and, as I did, I felt something give way: it was the door, it was moving! I stepped back in astonishment.

Was it a trick?

My heart was beating twice as fast, but I couldn't tell if it was from fear or excitement. I waited a little more. I'd dreamt of this moment for so long, but now it was here I was really frightened – I'd never been on the other side of the door without his permission before. Never.

'Hello,' I called weakly.

I paused and waited.

Nothing, only silence.

Threading my fingertips through the small gap between the frame and the door, I curled them around the edge of the wood and stopped.

What if it's a trick? What if he shouts 'Release the dog'? What if he's waiting for you on the other side?

I withdrew my fingers. Terrified, I pictured him standing

there on the other side, shears in his hands, waiting silently. He'd think nothing of slicing my fingers off.

What are you going to do?

I desperately wanted to go outside, but if he was waiting then what kind of punishment would he inflict? I weighed it up inside my head.

If you go out and he's there, he will beat you. But he beats you anyway. If you don't go out, then you might never get the chance to do it again.

I rubbed the heels of my hands against my eyes.

Think, think… You've got to go. If you don't, you'll never know, the voice said, persuading me.

I thought of Peter and the treats I'd promised to bring him from the room – the one that had smelled of food. I *had* to do it – if not for me, then for him. I curled my fingers around the edge of the door a second time and slowly pushed it open. My eyes peeked through the small gap I'd created and scanned the kitchen anxiously. There was no one there. I stopped and listened in case he'd just stepped out of the room. Nothing, there was no noise – I was all alone. My palms were hot and my heart began to pump with excitement as I spied the door to the food room directly on my left. I pushed my hand down on the latch, just as I'd seen him do with the outside loo, and watched as the metal lifted and the door fell towards me like an open mouth, inviting me in. I could smell the food before I'd even seen it. My nose was tracing the air, trying to work out what each delicious scent was. I closed my eyes to try and savour the smell, then took a step inside and began to open them slowly. I was so shocked by the amount of food sitting on the shelves that I gasped out loud – I'd never seen so much food in my life! My stomach rumbled as my eyes took in one thing after another hungrily.

Hurry up! the voice urged.

I gulped down my nerves and excitement.

Stay alert, you don't know how long you've got.

There were metal tins. Lots of them. They all had pictures and writing on the front, which helped me guess what was inside. I picked one up and read the label: *sliced peaches.*

What were sliced peaches?

I shook my head; I didn't have a clue, but they looked pretty tasty judging by the drawing on the front. I sniffed the tin, but couldn't smell anything so I tipped it sideways and searched for an opening. Nothing. I turned it upside down. Nothing, so I shook it hard in my hand. I heard the sliced peaches sloshing around inside but they refused to come out. Frustrated, I placed them back on the shelf. There must be a way to open up the tin, I just didn't know how. I spotted a tall jug similar to my toothpaste rinsing jug down in the cellar. Only this one had a lid on top and something written across the front of it.

'M.I.L.K.'

I sounded the word out aloud.

'Milk.'

I dipped my index finger in and when I pulled it out, it was coated in the white watery stuff that he brought me down at breakfast.

Milk, it was called milk!

Another new word.

I pushed the lid back down and moved it to one side. There was a lump of cheese inside a mesh net hanging down from the ceiling. I lifted it and breathed it in – lovely! I knew what cheese was because he'd sometimes bring me cheese sandwiches. I turned, my eyes scouring the room for a knife to cut myself a chunk of it. I loved cheese but I'd never seen so much before. Usually, he'd bring me thin slithers wedged between two pieces of bread. Taking a knife, I cut one huge lump and then another, but it wasn't enough to satisfy the emptiness – I needed more. I was starving, my hunger increasing the more I saw. There was a loaf of bread, so I ripped off a chunk of that. Noticing a yellow lump on the side, I ran a finger through the middle of it and placed it inside my mouth. I recognised the taste – butter! Taking the knife, I cut away a lump and smeared it against another bit of cheese before swallowing it down.

Delicious!

I licked my lips and then my fingers – I didn't want to waste a single moment.

I glanced around, searching for more to eat. There were other things I recognised – apples and bananas. I'd had those before, but now I could choose. It was up to me, not him, and I was on the hunt for different flavours, for new things to try. There was a tube covered in a brightly coloured paper with a picture of something square and beige on the front.

'N.I.C.E… b.i.s.c.u.i.t.s,' I said, reading the words slowly.

I pulled one of the square things out of the packet and studied it in the palm of my hand. It was coated in silvery white specks. Sticking out my tongue, I rested the tip against it. The silvery white specks dissolved with my spit.

Mmmm…lovely!

I turned the biscuit in my hand and placed a corner of it inside my mouth. It seemed to melt against my tongue, coating it in a sweet-tasting film. I ripped the packet apart, grabbed a handful, and pushed them in all at once. I'd shoved in so many that I began to cough and choke and soon there were crumbs flying everywhere. I grabbed the milk and gulped at it, trying to wash the drier bits down. Then I threw the packet on the floor. With my mouth empty, I ripped off another hunk of bread, pushed some butter and cheese against it, and thrust it in. I'd barely chewed before I was on to the next piece and then the next.

Suddenly, I reached a stage where I couldn't bear to eat another thing. Instead, I felt sick and my stomach was heavy. I turned and rested the knife by the side of the cheese. As I did, I noticed some round, beige-brown shaped circles sat in a little box. I picked one up to take a closer look; it wasn't quite a full circle because it had a slight shape to it and I was surprised how much heavier it felt than it looked. I shook it, like the tin of sliced peaches, and felt something shift inside. Turning it over in my palm, I continued to inspect it. The round thing felt hard, as though it was made of stone. I scratched my head, but that was impossible because there was something inside. I held it up against the light to take a closer look but I couldn't see anything through it. My fingers fumbled as I lifted it higher, trying to find an opening when…

SPLAT!

The beige, circle-shaped thing landed heavily, cracking open as soon as it hit the ground, but I was more fascinated by what had just come flooding out: a runny, see-through thing with a yellow circle in the middle. I pushed my finger into the goo, lifted it up and took a sniff. The runny stuff dripped from my finger like snot. I quickly shook my hand and wiped it against my shorts.

Urgh!

I did the same with the yellow circle, but it dripped and fell down onto the floor in a golden pool. I sniffed my finger again but it didn't smell of anything. When I licked it, it didn't taste of anything either.

What could it be?

I took another and tapped it against one of the shelves. It broke easily, even though it had felt as hard as the last one. I was fascinated. The outside had cracked all around – it reminded me of my arm and the way he'd cracked that. Pushing my thumb and fingers against the splintered opening, I pulled the edges apart and gasped – there was another yellow dot swimming in a small sea of snot! I broke another, and then another. I knew I'd made a mess, but I was far too fascinated to stop. I don't know how long I'd been inside the food room for, but then I heard a noise and stopped dead in my tracks… someone was coming.

Him!

My mouth felt bone dry as I dipped down and picked the biscuits up off the floor. I threw them on the shelf, but it was no good – the ground was covered in the snot stuff and yellow circles. Then I heard the front door click. I didn't have time, I had to go.

Get out! the voice screamed.

Heavy footsteps signalled that someone was coming. I heard them trudge along the long thin room, leading from the front door. There was a clacking sound: two people were coming.

Leave it!

My nerves buzzed like a fly trapped inside my chest; I'd never felt so scared in my whole life. More footsteps, each one grew louder as they drew closer and closer. The door creaked as I pushed it and bolted out and down the cellar steps as fast as I could. I'd just reached the bottom step when I heard a scream: it was Mum.

'Albert! He's been in the pantry. He's broken all the eggs!'

Pantry… eggs?

I thought of the brown circles I'd just cracked open – the yellow dots in snot that I'd left all over the floor.

The light from the kitchen lit up the walls as the cellar door opened.

It was him.

I felt as though my heart had jumped from my chest and inside my mouth as his voice boomed from the top step.

'So, the rats have got out of the cellar, have they?' he shouted, his voice deep and threatening.

I gulped because I knew this was it: I was in for it now. The blades of the scissors flashed through my mind as my skin glistened with fear.

'You think you're clever, eh? I'll show you clever, you little…'

Ten, nine, eight, seven, six, five, four, three, two, one…

His footsteps stomped against each step as he raced down them and into my room. Meanwhile I cowered in the corner, my back pressing against the cold, damp bricks.

He didn't have his leather apron on! I almost wept with happiness. *He's not got the scissors!*

An enormous sense of relief washed over me. It was only a small mercy, but mercy all the same. He strode across the floor, his big, heavy footsteps gathering ground as he towered above me. I trembled as he blocked out the light. Then I watched in silhouette as he slowly clenched and drew back his fist above his head. There was sharpness as his bare knuckles connected with the soft tissue above my jawline. I looked up to see him draw back his fist once more...

THUMP!

A jolt of terrible pain shot through my body as the room began to fade away.

CHAPTER 8

SECRET DRAWINGS

My face throbbed for ages and, although I couldn't see it, I was convinced that it must be covered in deep blue marks like the ones he sometimes left on my arms and body, because it hurt every time my fingers or clothes brushed against my skin. My left eye closed up, but as the days turned into night and back again, it began to open up a little more until soon my face stopped aching.

He starved me for two days and two nights following my escape. The beating I'd been given had been harsh, so harsh that it should have put me off escaping forever, yet it didn't. If anything, it made me even more determined to get out and taste the food again. I also felt a little guilty because, in my rush, I'd forgotten to bring Peter anything back. To make up for it, I helped him catch more flies.

My father examined the door thoroughly after my escape. I realised he was trying to work out how I'd done it, although he never asked me. It was as if he didn't want to admit I was clever enough. Afterwards, every time he left the house I'd rattle the door but it didn't budge. I noticed a crack in the planks of wood and peered through, trying to work out why the latch wouldn't move. That's when I spotted it — a small piece of wood wedged in, holding it down. I tried again and again, but no amount of door shaking would knock it free. Frustrated, I slumped down on my bed and tried to think: there had to be another way.

'I hate him, Peter. Why does he keep me locked down here when the other children live upstairs?'

I felt a pain in my mouth and pushed a finger inside. To my amazement, one of the teeth on my bottom jaw shifted forward and smarted with pain.

Is that your tooth? Why is it loose? the voice asked.

But I didn't know. Even though it was really sore, I was fascinated by the wobbly tooth. I shoved my finger against it and pushed it backwards. Then, grabbing the edge, I wiggled it around.

'Ow!' I said, taking a sharp breath.

It felt painful but I couldn't help myself. I was excited and scared at the same time.

He did this to you when he hit you. He made your tooth loose, the voice reminded me.

I nodded. 'Yes, that must be it.'

When the tooth finally fell out of my mouth, I wasn't sure what to do with it. I turned it over in my hand. It was creamy white and had two small bumps on the bottom. I thought he'd tell me off for breaking it inside my mouth, so I hid it in the cracks of the brick mortar because I knew he'd never think to look there. Over the next few days I got used to the sensation of being able to push the tip of my tongue through the gap in my bottom row of teeth, but I was careful to keep it hidden when I spoke – I didn't want to get into any more trouble.

Not long afterwards, another tooth became loose, and then another. I pushed them all inside the same crack between the bricks. A thread of anxiety ran through me: it was becoming harder and harder to keep all the gaps hidden from him. Whenever he asked me something I'd purposely try and keep my mouth small so that he wouldn't see.

I wondered if the children living above me had gaps in their teeth. Did he hit them too? I wasn't sure because I hadn't heard them very much after the last time. There would be the odd noise or sound of a child's voice, or crying out, but that was it. The more I thought about it and them, the more I started to feel sorry for myself.

You'll never get out.

It was the voice again, only this time it was taunting me.

Frustrated, I spilled my pencils across the table, pulled out a piece of paper from my secret hidey hole and began to draw. I drew a monster with eight arms and eight legs; it looked like a spider, only it had my father's head and his orange hair. Picking up my yellow and orange pencils, I drew big sparks flashing from his eyes – he had evil eyes. I was just about to start on his feet when I glanced at the pencil in my hand. Turning it in my thumb and fingers, I then held it horizontally.

The pencil! Of course!

Running up to the top step, I pushed it through the gap in the door. It was a tight squeeze, but I somehow managed.

Yes! I cheered, almost punching the air in celebration.

I twisted the pencil to the right, placed it against the wedge and tried to push upwards. It shifted the wooden wedge slightly but not enough to make it fall from the latch. Undeterred, I hooked the pencil point underneath and pushed again. There was another slight movement, but the pencil wasn't quite long enough.

Longer, it had to be longer!

I ran back down to the table and searched for the longest pencil I could find.

The white one! Of course! I hardly ever used it.

Grabbing it in my hand, I ran back to the top step and squeezed it through the hole. I twisted and wiggled it around, trying to make the gap a little bigger to give me more space to swing it. Hooking it beneath the wedge, I tried again. This time the wooden block shifted a little more but not quite enough to knock it clear. I tried again and again. Now it was a battle of wits, me against the piece of wood holding me prisoner. I pushed down on the end of the pencil, forcing it up. The wedge jerked as the edge of the pencil grated against the sides of the door, grinding into it.

Push…

The wedge slipped a little more but remained stubbornly in place.

PUSH…

This time I applied more force. I pushed so hard that I was worried the pencil would snap in half and he'd find a piece of it lying on the floor outside. But I knew there was no going back.

P…U…S…H…

I squeezed my tongue hard against the gaps in my teeth in concentration. Suddenly, the pencil shot upwards and the wedge popped out, falling to the floor. I heard it bounce across the kitchen and I shook the door in anger.

He's done this to you, and he'll keep doing it until you make him stop.
I shook and shook until…
CREAK.
The door swung open.
I pulled the pencil out and shoved it deep down into the back pocket of my shorts. I didn't want to lose it in case I needed it again.

Next time… The pencil meant there could be a next time.
My heart soared with hope as I lifted my hand and pulled the pantry door open. Once inside, my fingers moved quickly, grabbing handfuls of whatever I could without pausing. Only this time I left the eggs. Instead, I tore off chunks of bread and dipped them in a jar of jam, leaving the lid on the side. I searched for other bits of food that I could eat quickly – an apple, a banana, more cheese, biscuits. Then I spotted a slab of something pink resting on a plate that had been cut into slices. I grabbed a handful and pushed it inside my mouth.

Hmmmm!
I didn't know it then, but it was ham. I swallowed it down quickly, my tongue still savouring the taste long afterwards. With new purpose, I strode across the kitchen and tried the handle on the back door: it was locked.

Of course, it would be, the voice mocked.
I dragged a chair up against the side near the kitchen window and tried to push it open, but no matter how much I stretched, I couldn't quite reach the handle. I jumped down off the chair and walked along the long, thin room – the one with the nice door at the end. I tried that door handle.

Locked.

I glanced all around, looking for more escape routes, but there was nothing.

Look further, the voice urged.

My hands trembled as I opened up one of the doors leading off the thin room at the front of the building. The room was big and it had a long chair covered in a brown patterned cloth. The floor wasn't stone like it was down in my cellar; this was made from a thick cloth with a swirly brown pattern that felt soft beneath my feet. There were two pieces of brown material hanging down either side of the window and a white net which made it difficult to see outside. I pressed my face up against it and looked anyway. That's when I noticed his car – the one he'd taken me to the hospital in – had disappeared. I breathed a sigh of relief – I was safe, at least for now.

The window handles wouldn't move in this room either so I turned to leave. As I did, I spotted a set of steps running upwards into the ceiling. Although desperate to see what was at the top, I was worried I wouldn't have enough time, so I moved on, deciding to save that bit until next time – if there was one. I wandered over and into the room next door. It was bigger than the last and the floor wasn't covered in cloth but instead had square blue shapes all over it. There was a dark table in the middle with five chairs. Over in the corner were shelves full of what I later discovered were called books and a dark set of wooden drawers placed opposite. There was something made of glass hanging on the wall that seemed to catch the light. It had pieces of coloured glass at the sides, bursting out like sunshine. But it was much too high up for me to take a proper look.

There was another window in this room, but I couldn't open that either. All the windows seemed to be locked or jammed shut. With no way of escaping, I returned to my cellar. I thought I'd left the pantry clean, but when he returned later that evening he knew I'd been out because he found the small wedge of wood lying on the floor.

I heard the cellar door creak open.

Ten, nine, eight, seven, six, five, four, three, two, one…

He was standing before me, the belt hanging limply from his hand.

'Think you're clever, eh? Think you're smarter than me?' he said, whipping it through the air as it cracked loudly.

I gulped and tried to move away from him but I wasn't fast enough. The belt caught me across the backs of my legs, stinging my flesh and causing me to yelp out in pain.

WHIP!

I dodged to one side but he followed.

WHIP!

He missed me again, causing his temper to rise. We continued in this sick game of chase as he lashed out and tried to grab me. Eventually, he caught up and grabbed me by my right wrist. He tried to twist me around to face him when…

CRACK!

I felt a sickening snap inside my forearm, just above my right wrist. I screamed and fell limply to the floor.

'Not again!' he roared.

I whimpered in a heap on the floor.

'I'm sorry, I'm sorry, but I think it's broken… like last time. I think it's broken. I'm sorry, Dad,' I apologised.

Another broken arm meant another trip to the hospital,

only this time it was already dark outside so I didn't see very much through the car window, only shifting shadows in the blackness. By the time we'd pulled up in the car park, I realised it wasn't the same hospital as the one before: the building was different in both shape and height.

'Come on,' he snapped impatiently. 'Get out! Let's get this over and done with, and remember,' he said, lifting a finger, 'not a word from you.'

My right arm throbbed in sickening waves, but I daren't complain. He'd told me all about workhouses as we'd travelled in the car and had even threatened me with one.

'And you don't want to end up in one of those,' he added, his eyes darting over towards mine. 'Remember how lucky you are that I take care of you.'

But I didn't feel very lucky.

Once again, a nice nurse took a picture of my arm and sent me to a different room to have the funny-smelling bandage wrapped around it. The nurse who did it also called me brave. This nurse had a kind face, much kinder than Mum's. But this nurse didn't call me Stephen. No, the nurse called me John, because that's what he'd told the doctor I was called. It was another lie because I saw him hesitate before he'd said the name. I was starting to realise what a good liar he was.

We drove back home in complete silence. Once we'd arrived, he pushed me back down into the cellar without any dinner.

'You don't deserve any, you thieving little bastard,' he hissed, following me down.

As he turned to leave, he marched past my small table. He was just about to climb the stairs when something stopped him dead in his tracks. Pausing, he retraced his steps, stopped and looked down. He stood there for a moment, twisting his head sideways to look at the table. My heart raced inside my chest… he'd found something.

'What the…?' he said, moving over towards it.

My heart was inside my mouth and everything seemed to follow in slow motion as I watched him pull out a corner of paper from the gap.

'Hang on,' he said, talking to himself, 'there's more.'

His fingers fumbled inside the gap: a whole wad of paper came out as he pulled it into the light.

Your drawings! He's found your drawings!

I felt light-headed and dizzy and, in that moment, I prayed the stone floor would open and swallow me whole.

'You did these?' he asked, breaking my thoughts.

I stood there and watched as he began to shuffle through each drawing. He glanced back at me, waiting, for an answer. I nodded reluctantly. He pulled a strange face and I tried to read his thoughts.

Was he angry? Was he upset? I couldn't be sure.

Slowly, he began to nod his head.

'Not bad… not bad. You're quite the little artist, aren't you?'

I wasn't sure if it was a question or not, so I didn't reply. But I felt a small swell of pride rise inside me.

He likes them. He actually likes them! I couldn't believe it. *Maybe now he'll bring you more paper and pens so you can draw lots more pictures for him?*

'You enjoy drawing then?' His question snapped me back into the moment.

I nodded and began to smile. I actually smiled – I smiled at him, but I was careful to smile with a closed mouth to hide all my missing teeth. I was just so thrilled he liked them, thrilled he wasn't angry with me.

Maybe now he's seen them he might let you draw instead of doing maths or spellings? Maybe now he might let you go and live upstairs with the others and ask you to draw for him and Mum?

I dared to hope because I'd finally done something right. I felt like pinching myself.

'Yes, these aren't bad at all. You're pretty good,' he smiled.

I felt so happy, I thought I'd burst. He'd actually told me I was good when I'd always been bad – bad at everything. But not now. Now I'd finally found something that had made him happy, something that made me good. I couldn't believe it. I watched as he studied the last picture, turned it sideways and placed it at the bottom of the pile in his hands. Then he gripped his fingers alongside the edge of the paper and pulled sharply, ripping them in half.

I felt my stomach fall to the floor. My mouth fell open in horror as he continued to rip them until soon, all that was left were small squares scattered across the floor. I wanted to cry. But, I decided in that moment no matter how much he'd upset me, I wouldn't let him know – I wouldn't give him the satisfaction. Instead, I stayed silent.

'Clean it up!' he barked as he turned and climbed the stairs.

I was trembling, but not with fear – I was trembling with rage. My hands shook as I clenched them into balled fists to try and steady my anger. I wanted him to die; I wanted to kill him, to strangle him with my bare hands. My whole body shook. I'd get my revenge when I was big and strong enough. It might take a while, but I'd get him back for this and for everything else he'd done to me. I fell to my knees and began to gather up the ripped pieces of paper into a small pile, the voice inside my head burning with a white, hot rage.

He can hit you, he can beat you black and blue. He can even rip your artwork up into tiny pieces, but as long as you have your pencils and paper you can, and you will, draw more monsters.

The voice was right; I had a head full of them. Monsters like him, only each one was much bigger and scarier than the last.

CHAPTER 9

A CHANGE OF SEASON

It had grown really cold outside and most nights I found it difficult to sleep because a chill would grip me until I couldn't stop shivering, even wrapped inside my blanket. When sleep eventually claimed me, I would be woken by an iciness seeping inside my bones like a frozen, prodding hand.

Even though he'd removed the plaster from it, my left arm throbbed and ached against the damp air where it had been broken – a spiral fracture, Doctor Brown had called it. I climbed out of bed, picked up a pencil and began to draw a picture of a spiral. I traced the tip of my pencil against the paper; it circled around and around as I recalled the way my arm had twisted and cracked at the top. My right arm was still broken and encased inside a grubby plaster. The nurse at the hospital had told him he'd have to bring me back to have it cut off, but I knew he wouldn't – he'd just cut it off with his shears, like last time.

The kitchen upstairs sounded unusually busy. I'd not heard

the children's voices for a while, but over the past few days I'd heard them more and more. I could hear them right now; I imagined them all sat around the table, smiling at each other while I sat downstairs in the cellar all alone. I had no one, only Peter and the others, but they weren't people.

'Something's different,' I whispered across the room to my friend. 'I don't know what it is, Peter, but something's different.'

I'd heard much more noise lately. I'd also heard different noises that morning – unusual sounds from things that I thought might be objects. There'd been laughter, too – actual laughter. Then all the different smells had followed: delicious smells of cooking creeping down through the floor and in through the ceiling of my room. I felt my stomach rumble with hunger. Breakfast. He'd not brought me breakfast today and neither had Mum. Something was different. I'd missed breakfast before, but that had only ever happened when I'd been naughty or I'd escaped from the cellar, and I'd not done that for a while – my broken wrist made it far too difficult to escape.

Then the door creaked open and light flooded along the walls from the kitchen above. I looked up to see his silhouette standing against the light. The voices coming from behind him seemed to hush as he stood there. I couldn't be sure, but I was certain I saw him sway ever so slightly, as though someone or something had pushed him from the side. Then he swayed again, the light quickly shining above his shoulder before disappearing like the sun behind a cloud.

What's he doing?

A streak of terror ran through me as he stomped down the stairs quickly and a little unsteadily on his feet. I noticed something else too: he wasn't wearing his leather apron. My eyes darted over to his hands as he stood before me – no scissors. I waited for him to speak or give me some new spellings, but he said nothing. There was an awkward silence as I waited to see what he wanted.

He hasn't brought you breakfast, either, the voice reminded as I felt my stomach growl.

He had nothing he could feed me but also nothing he could hurt me with.

'Sit down,' he said suddenly, gesturing with his hand towards the single chair.

I saw something glint against the light as he moved; something fastened around his wrist that peeked out from underneath his sleeve – something metal, something new. He was wearing a jumper I'd never seen before. Heavily patterned with different shades of brown, it was horrible.

What's going on?

There was the sound of voices upstairs and of knives, forks and plates being scraped and cleared away. I could hear Mum and the voices of the other children. They all sounded so happy, so normal...

I slumped in my seat as he rested a hand flat against the top of my head.

Is he giving you another haircut?

His hand felt big and hot against my scalp, but I welcomed the warmth down here – any warmth, even if it was from him. I tried not to shake, but I was scared and I was cold. My stomach rumbled and I begged it to be quiet as I swallowed down my hunger. I was starving and wondered when he would bring me something to eat. Just as the thought ran through my mind I heard more footsteps: it was Mum. Dainty feet padded down the steps as a plate of food was placed on the table in front of me. I was surprised – there was more food on the plate than normal.

Maybe it's because you missed breakfast? the voice reasoned.

Suddenly, he spoke: 'What do you say?'

It had taken me by surprise.

'Thank you,' I responded quickly. I looked over at Mum, who refused to smile or even look at me. Instead, Mum turned and disappeared back upstairs quickly.

Not a single word. Mum never spoke; never said a word to me, not even once. I wondered if Mum could even speak. Then I remembered: I'd heard Mum's voice that day telling him I'd broken all the eggs, that I'd been in the pantry. I'd heard Mum shout and call out to the other children. Yes, Mum did speak, just not to me.

My nostrils flared as I tried to keep my eyes focused straight ahead. I concentrated on a single brick in the wall on the other side of the room. I didn't want to make eye contact, not with him. He smelt different today. It took me a moment to realise that the sweet, strong smell was his breath – it smelt kind of sour. I was still looking ahead when he dipped down in front of me, resting all his weight on the backs of his legs. He kept his hand firmly on the top of my head, but shifted slightly as he wobbled and tried to regain his balance. Then he did something really strange. He lifted up his hand. Automatically, I winced and closed my eyes, waiting for a thump or slap. But he didn't hit me, instead he ruffled his hand through my hair. I was so surprised that I opened my eyes to find him there right in front of me, staring straight back. I shifted slightly in my chair. He'd never done it before, but now he was so close that I could really smell his sour, hot breath as it brushed against my skin. Then he did it again.

What's he doing? What's going on?

I glanced over his left shoulder, trying to keep my eyes firmly fixed on the opposite wall.

Don't look at him; whatever you do, don't look at him.

There was a heavy weight as he pressed down on top of my head and staggered to his feet. I carried on staring straight ahead at the wall.

Don't make him angry.

But he wasn't done. He lifted a hand and patted the top of my head before taking a step backwards.

Something's changed. Maybe he's decided to be nice to you after all?

It took all the nerve I had, but I shifted my gaze nervously over towards him: he was definitely swaying. He caught me looking and a slight smile played at the corners of his mouth. My stomach growled, reminding me to eat. I could smell the food and I desperately wanted to tuck straight in, but I was scared.

What does he want?

My eyes darted over towards the plate and he noticed.

'Eat!' he said, pointing down at it. 'Go on, eat it up! Get it while it's still hot.'

Hot? Why would he say that? Usually, he didn't care how or when I ate, or whether my food was hot or cold. He turned away in a slow but exaggerated circle, as though spinning on tiptoes, and climbed each step slowly. He had reached halfway when he paused to look back. I desperately wanted to pick up the knife and fork, to shovel the lot down my throat as fast as I could, but I was frightened it was some kind of trick.

He's waiting for you to start so he can take it off you...

I pushed my fingers underneath the backs of my knees and kept them there, flat against the chair – I wouldn't give him the satisfaction.

'Go on, eat it!'

He sounded irritable and more like himself. In a way it made me feel better – at least I knew what I was dealing with. I leaned forward and picked up my knife and fork.

'That's it!' he said, turning to climb the last few steps.

But I wanted to wait until he was completely out of the room in case this was some kind of sick game. He was never this nice to me, something had changed.

I counted the last few steps.

Seven, eight, nine... ten.

He stopped, turned and looked down from the top step. Then he began to laugh, although I didn't understand what was funny.

'By the way, Merry Christmas, you little bastard!' he said as he threw back his head and roared with laughter.

The door slammed with a rattle and the latch fell.

CHAPTER 10

MEETING MY BROTHER

I continued to hear the other children's voices. The sound tortured me as I sat alone, day after day, in my cramped room. The weather seemed to worsen before it got better, but soon the sun began to shine again. I'd catch glimpses of it hanging in the sky whenever I went to slop out my bucket. One day, I'd just pulled the chain to wash it all away when I turned to find two children staring straight at me. There was a boy, who looked a bit younger than me. He was wearing long trousers and had a short haircut like the boy I'd seen in the hospital. For a moment I wondered if it was him. There was someone else too: it was another child, but this one had fair hair and was dressed a bit like Mum. Its hair was tied in two bunches either side of its head.

I looked at my father and wondered if he would say anything. I also wondered who these children were and why they lived upstairs. I stared straight back and that's when I noticed something else: a large thing I later found out was called a pram. It had something called a baby inside it. The one that looked a bit like Mum went over to the baby and it began to cry. Mum came dashing out of the kitchen door into the backyard. Mum picked up the baby and held it there. Dad glared over. It was obvious he hadn't expected these children to be there or to come outside the back door when I was slopping out. Mum looked at him and ran inside with the baby. The other two children just stood there, staring at me. I didn't know what to say.

Why don't you tell them your name? the voice suggested.

I shook my head; I knew he'd kill me if I said a word – he was always telling me to keep quiet.

'Come on,' he said, suddenly grabbing the collar of my shirt.

I felt the fabric lift up my back and pull out of the top of my shorts as he proceeded to drag me across the backyard towards the kitchen door. The children automatically parted as we came barging through. I waited for him to say something – to hit them like he always hit me – but he said nothing. Instead, as he dragged me, I tried to turn my head sideways to look back at them.

'Eyes forward!' he barked.

I spun around because I didn't want to make him angrier than he already was. He pulled the door open with his left hand and threw me inside. I wobbled on the top step and was worried I might actually topple down, but somehow I managed to regain my balance.

'Get down there where you belong.'

Then the door juddered closed. I was baffled.

Who were the strange children and what were they doing in the backyard?

I heard raised voices. It was him, he was arguing with Mum.

'I told you to keep the children upstairs!' he shouted.

Mum said something back, but Mum's voice was muffled by the closed door. I pressed my ear against the wood to try and listen.

'...the baby... fresh air... They were only playing, not doing any harm...' I caught fragments of the conversation. Then there was a loud clattering noise.

Had he just thrown something or slammed a door?

The following day, the house was pretty quiet when I heard a tap against the cellar door. I took a cautious step up towards it, stood completely still and waited.

TAP, TAP.

There it was again: someone was knocking against the door.

I climbed a few more steps, unsure what I should do. There was a moment's silence before someone tapped again.

TAP, TAP.

Then I heard a voice.

'Hello?' I knew immediately that it was a child's voice. I wondered if it was the boy from the backyard. I inched up the last few steps and sat on the second-to-top one.

'H...H... Hello?' I called.

I was poised, ready to scarper back down in case it was a trick.

Was it him on the other side of the door?

'Hello,' the voice whispered again. 'My name is Andrew, what's yours?'

I remembered what he'd told them in the first hospital.

'Stephen Smith. My name is Stephen Smith.'

'Hello, Stephen, my name is Andrew and I think I'm younger than you. How old are you?'

I scratched my head. I wasn't really sure – I could only go by what he'd said in the first hospital, but that had been ages ago.

'I think… er… I'm seven years old.'

'Seven? No, you must be much older than that because I'm six.'

'There's Jane, too. You saw her in the backyard.'

I thought of the child I'd seen who dressed a bit like Mum, the one with the fair hair.

'Jane?'

'Yes, she's a girl. Her name is Jane and she is four.'

'A girl… four,' I said, repeating him.

'There's Billy, too, but he's only a baby.'

I sat up.

'I saw him, in the backyard!'

'Yes, Mum put him out in his pram because he was crying – Billy's always crying,' Andrew said. 'Anyway, I don't know how old he is because he's still a baby.'

Billy… I said the name silently inside my head.

'Stephen?' Andrew said, breaking my thoughts. 'Why does Daddy keep you down there? Why don't you live upstairs with us?'

Gulping down a lump of sadness that had suddenly become wedged at the back of my throat, I ran a finger up and down the flaking paint of the wooden door that separated me from them.

'I don't know… I mean, I don't know why he keeps me down here.'

I sat and waited for Andrew to say something, to say he was sorry that I was locked in the cellar and not him, only he didn't.

'Well, you must have been really, really naughty to be put down there.'

I nodded even though his words stung me. 'Yes, I must have been...' I agreed, even though I didn't know what I'd done wrong.

I heard a slight scraping as Andrew shifted on the other side of the door.

'I've got to go...' he said, his voice sounding a little panicked. 'I think someone is coming...'

But I didn't want him to go; I wanted to ask him lots of questions. I wanted to ask what it was like to live upstairs and did he hit Andrew and the others as much as he hit me? I wanted to ask him how many times he got to go outside. Did he have a slop bucket like me? I wanted to ask him so much, but he'd already gone.

'Andrew... Andrew...' I whispered, my fingertips tapping lightly against the door.

But it was no good, there was no one there.

A few days later, I was slopping out again when Andrew came out into the backyard. Once again, he stood and stared as Dad made me tip the bucket into the toilet and flush the chain.

'Andrew.'

It was my father.

'Get inside now!'

'But I... I... I've come for my football,' he said, picking up a round-shaped thing. It was a football – the thing I'd seen those boys kicking along the ground.

A football...

Astonished, I watched as Andrew collected his football and dashed back inside. He'd not shouted at or even hit Andrew like he would have done me if I'd answered him back.

Why did he treat Andrew so differently to me? I was much older!

A short while later, I heard a tap on my door. My heart soared: it was Andrew!

I ran up to the top step.

'Hello?' I called quietly.

'Hello...'

'Andrew, is that you?'

There was a giggle, and then he answered.

'Yes.'

I heard someone shuffling. It sounded as though two people were there, not one.

'Andrew, are you alone? Who's with you?' I asked, my heart pounding.

Another giggle.

'Don't worry, it's only Jane.'

I smiled.

'Jane?'

'Yes.'

'What are you doing?'

'Nothing. We've been outside playing.'

Playing... outside?

'What's playing?' I asked.

Now it was Andrew's turn to laugh.

'Playing, you know, playing with toys outside... You do know what toys are, don't you? They are things you play with, silly!'

Scouring my brain, I had a strong memory of a grey elephant and spinning top that my father had once given me. He told me the grey thing was called an elephant. It had a really long nose, thick legs and round feet, with half circles for toenails. I'd loved the elephant so much that I would tuck him up in bed with me at night. I'd talk to him like I spoke to Peter – he was

110

my best friend. Then, one day, Dad came downstairs. I didn't know what was wrong, but he was in a temper and snatched both the elephant and spinning top from me.

'You're not keeping them!' he shouted.

I didn't even know what I'd done wrong, but I never saw either thing ever again. Afterwards, I cried for days and begged him to bring back my elephant, but he never did.

'I had two toys once…' I replied sadly.

'Only two?'

'Yes. An elephant and a spinning top, but he took them both away.'

I heard him gasp.

'But… but… what do you play with now?'

'Peter.'

'Who's Peter?' Andrew asked.

'He's my friend… he's a spider…'

There was a short scream on the other side of the door: Jane – it was Jane. I heard a cry, a scuffle of feet and the sound of footsteps running away.

'Andrew,' I gasped. 'Andrew, what's happening?'

I heard him laugh.

'Oh, it's only Jane. She doesn't like spiders because she's just a silly girl.'

Girl… it was that word again.

I wanted to ask him what it meant, but Andrew said he had to go. I called after him, but there was no one there.

It was ages before I saw him again. By this time, it had grown really warm outside. One day, I'd gone to empty my bucket when I spotted him in the backyard, holding something in his hand. It was threaded with string and he was using it to hit a small ball off the wall. Andrew stopped what he was doing and smiled as Dad marched me past him and over towards the outside toilet. I think he must have been so curious that he used every opportunity he could to get a good look at me. I glanced over again: there was another, much smaller, boy, standing behind him. Billy, it had to be Billy. I looked again. I couldn't believe it: Billy was still only really young, but he was wearing long trousers, like Andrew. In fact, they both had short hair and long trousers – the complete opposite to me. I felt a stab of jealousy as it spread and burned inside me.

Why are they allowed to wear long trousers when you are the eldest?

It was the voice, only this time I didn't have any answers. Billy and Andrew were laughing and chasing each other around the garden. They were shouting and making lots of noise, but he didn't tell them to be quiet. I pulled the toilet chain and as I turned, I spotted Jane as she came running out of the backdoor to join them. When I passed, I tried to keep my eyes focused on the ground because Dad was close behind. But Andrew looked up and spoke.

'You're my brother…' he muttered.

Brother?

The sight of them playing outside in the sunshine, having fun and running around the backyard left me envious. I decided that I hated them, hated them all. How come they got to play outside with toys? How come they got to live upstairs and not in the cellar? How come Andrew and Billy got to wear long trousers when I had to make do with grubby old shorts? How come I was the odd one out? More importantly, how come they got to be happy and I didn't?

And what exactly was a brother?

CHAPTER 11

MAKING MUM CRY

A few days later, I spoke to Andrew again and asked him what a 'brother' was. He told me he wasn't sure but thought it meant we had the same mum and dad. Strangely, it made me happy; happy that I had two brothers, him and Billy. He explained that Jane was my sister because she was a girl, but I didn't know what a girl was.

Andrew laughed, which made me feel both stupid and annoyed.

'I've never met any girls, well, apart from Jane, and I've only seen her,' I argued.

So he explained what a girl was. At first, I found it difficult to understand. I thought of Mum; Andrew said girls were 'shes' and they wore dresses or skirts, not shorts or long trousers like boys. It was the first time I realised there was a difference and I was keen to know more. It also made me feel a bit silly – Andrew was younger than me but he seemed to know lots more because he read something called books.

'I'm really good at reading, so they've moved me on to a different colour. Do you have any books down there?'

'No,' I replied, wondering what colours had to do with books.

I knew it wasn't his fault, or Billy's or Jane's, but I began to resent them all. If we were brothers with a sister then why did I get treated differently? I knew I'd been naughty, breaking out of the cellar to get into the pantry, but that was the worst thing I'd ever done. Also, I'd not done it until ages after he'd locked me in the cellar and I'd lived in the cellar for as long as I could remember.

I realised then that I had nothing to lose: Dad punished me anyway, so I might as well become the boy he seemed to think I was. Afterwards, and spurred on by a new anger, I escaped the cellar time and time again. I would help myself to food from the pantry and even though he tried everything to keep me down there, I always found a way out. One day, he finally tired of me stealing food and fitted a padlock on the pantry door. I tried to shake it free but it wouldn't budge or come undone.

'That'll stop yer!' he announced happily later that evening after he'd found the dislodged wedge on the kitchen floor.

I often wondered why he never padlocked me inside the cellar. Why did he continue to use the wedge of wood to peg me in when he knew I had a way of knocking it out? I thought about it long and hard, but nothing seemed to make sense. Why did he break my bones, take me to the hospital, and have me 'repaired', only to do the same thing again? Why did he even bother repairing me? Why did he teach me how to spell, write and do sums if he wanted to keep me locked in my room? Nothing made sense. I thought about it until my head hurt. Then I realised: I couldn't make sense of it because he didn't make any sense. Instead, I decided to do something else – I'd ask Mum why.

I knew I'd have to wait a while because she hardly ever came down to see me. Even when she did, she would place my food on the table and leave quickly. It seemed to take forever and at one point I thought she would never reappear, but one day she did. I heard the door open and saw the tell-tale light as it crept down from the kitchen above. There were soft footsteps as they padded lightly down each step. Then I spotted her feet, ankles and legs as they revealed themselves before the rest of her came into view. I was sitting in my chair waiting for her to approach the table. I knew I didn't have long. The tea towel was wrapped in her hands as she held the plate and placed it gently down in front of me. She rested a knife and fork at the side and then turned to leave.

Do it! Do it now before it's too late. Ask her!

My stomach turned over as I steeled myself.

'Erm, can I ask something?' I said suddenly. My voice sounded small and tight in the enclosed space but it had caught her by surprise. She spun around to face me, her eyes blinking rapidly, but didn't speak.

Say it again! Go on, ask her!

I cleared my throat nervously as she waited.

'I mean, I want to know why you keep me down here… here in the cellar.'

Mum didn't reply, she just stood there looking at me. Her mouth opened as though she was about to speak, but no words came. It was as though I'd just slapped her. By now, I was fired up. I had questions – so many questions – that I wanted to ask. Soon the words had come spilling out and joined together in one long sentence without a breath in between.

'I want to know why you keep me in the cellar when the others – Andrew, Jane and Billy – get to live upstairs. Why don't I get to live upstairs? Why do I have to live down here? When can I get out? When can I live upstairs like everyone else? Why do I have to stay down here? Why does he hit me all the time and why can't you stop him?

Breathe, the voice reminded me.

I took a huge lungful of air before continuing. 'I hate it down here. I hate being on my own all the time when you all live up there,' I said, pointing up at the ceiling. I looked at her and felt her squirm beneath my gaze. Suddenly, and for the first time, I felt in control. I clambered to my feet and pushed the chair away from the table with authority.

'So when,' I demanded, 'when can I move upstairs?'

I took a gasp of air and allowed it to flow inside, filling up every sac and available space inside my lungs. Then I waited; I waited for her to give me some answers. I stood there looking at her – she had a kind face but she seemed frightened. She seemed as scared as the mouse that lived outside in the dark toilet. I waited for her to speak – to tell me why I had to live down there – but she didn't. Instead, she continued to blink as her brown eyes watched me, her dark, curly hair cropped closely around her face. She was small, only a little taller than me, and as thin as she was delicate. I imagined him hitting her, snapping her in half. She continued to stare blankly as though I'd not said a single word.

'I want to get out of here, Mum. I want to leave the cellar,'

I said, this time more gently. 'It's not fair. It's not fair that I have to stay down here. I know I'm naughty, but I've only been naughty a few times, and I'm sorry. I'm sorry I've been naughty, but if you let me live upstairs then I'll be good, I promise I'll always be good.'

She was still looking, but she'd shifted her gaze from me and was looking straight ahead into nothingness. Her lack of reaction annoyed me and, just like him, I lost my temper.

'Did you hear me? I want to leave! When can I leave?'

Nothing.

Tell her, the voice urged, *tell her what he does to you.*

'He hits me, he hits me all the time,' I said, even though I was certain she must already know.

How could she not?

She must have heard him, she must have heard me – my screams drifting up into the kitchen…

'He always hurts me – but where are you, why don't you help me? I have two brothers and a sister up there… Does he do this to them?'

I was shaking with anger but I didn't care, not any more. I'd finally found my voice and now I wouldn't shut up. I refused to shut up because I deserved to know why.

'Why don't you help me?' I begged, my voice fading to a small, emotional croak.

She looked at the ground and then turned away from me. I couldn't be sure, but I swear I saw her hand lift to wipe something from her face, her eyes? Fired up, I followed her as she headed over towards the stairs.

'When are you going to let me out? I want to get out of here!' I said and I began to cry.

I couldn't help it; I couldn't stand being down there a moment longer.

'I want to leave the cellar. Did you hear me? I want to get out of here!' I shouted the words into her back as she began to climb the stairs.

But it was too late: the door slammed and I heard the catch fall on the other side. Afterwards, I sat there shell-shocked. I'd surprised myself, surprised that I'd finally dared say something, that I'd finally stood up for myself. But a few hours later, I began to worry: what if she'd told him? What would he say when he eventually came downstairs? I pictured him flying into another rage, taking the scissors out of his pocket and lunging forward towards me...

I woke with a start and sat bolt upright in my bed. All that crying must have worn me out because I'd fallen asleep. I glanced up through the coal hole – it had grown dark outside, he'd be here soon. Pushing the blanket away, I ran to my table and pulled out my spellings. I didn't have long – I'd wasted some of the day asleep.

A short while later, I heard the catch and then the sound of his feet on the steps.

Eight, seven, six, five, four, three, two, one...

I gulped; I'd missed the first two because he'd been much quicker than usual.

He knows... He definitely knows you've said something to her. That's it, you're in for it now!

'Homework...' he snapped, holding out an impatient hand.

I waited – waited for him to slap or thump me, only he didn't. Instead, he waved his fingers – a sign for me to get up and let him sit down to mark my work. I stood there, my breath short and shallow, my heart pumping so fast that I thought it might explode.

THUMP, THUMP, THUMP...

I felt the blood pushing and pumping around my body, urging me to get out, to run – run away from him. Still, he didn't say a word. Instead, he grunted and went upstairs to fetch my dinner.

She's not said anything. Mum, she's not told him!

I allowed myself to take a long, deep breath to try and calm the pounding inside my chest. She'd saved me; she had actually saved me from his temper for the very first time. She might not have answered me, but she'd saved me from something far worse – she'd saved me from a vicious beating. I felt so relieved, I almost wept with gratitude.

Maybe she's not so bad, after all?

That night, my thoughts were filled with Mum. Maybe she'd not said anything to protect herself as much as me? I also felt a small glimmer of hope. Maybe she'd become my friend? Maybe I'd be able to talk to her and try and persuade her to let me out?

That night, as I climbed into bed, I felt much happier than I had done in ages because I finally had a friend – I had Mum!

'I think she might help me, Peter. I'm sure I saw her cry. I think she feels sorry for me. Maybe she'll let me go? Maybe she'll take me, Andrew, Jane and Billy somewhere new, somewhere he won't be able to hurt me any more?'

I smiled as I rested my head against the pillow. For the first time, I felt real hope – hope so strong, I could almost hold it in my hands. I'd wait, I decided, wait until next time, and then I'd talk to her again and try to make her understand how I felt.

She'd help me, I was certain she would. She *had* to help me because, besides Peter, there was no one else: no other grown-up in the world knew that he kept me down here in the cellar, no one but her.

'I'll get out, Peter, then we can run – run far away from here and never come back again.'

CHAPTER 12

THE APPLE

As quickly as that small glimmer of hope had started to burn it was extinguished because, after that day, Mum stopped bringing my food down. Not only did she stop bringing food, but I no longer heard her voice through the ceiling. When he took me to slop out my bucket there was no sign of her in the kitchen either, even though my sister and brothers still played out in the backyard. It was as though she'd totally disappeared.

At first, I blamed myself – maybe I'd made her feel so bad that she'd just upped and left? Or perhaps she *had* said something to him after all and he'd punished her? The only thing I was certain of was, as the days passed by and the weather changed yet again, I knew she was never coming back. She'd gone and now it was just me, him and the other children.

I never saw my mother again. If I tried really hard I could still picture her – small and thin, with short dark curls in her hair. But as more days and nights passed, the images I had of her began to fade until all I could remember were small details. Now that she'd gone, he was the only one I'd see. I suppose I knew that I should have missed her, but I didn't, not really. She'd never really bothered with me before and now she'd upped and left – left me with him. I'd hoped she'd be the one to help me escape, yet now she'd gone and I was still alone – as alone as I'd always been.

Meanwhile, I continued to grow, my arms and legs stretching out from clothes that had become far too small for me. My teeth were still coming loose and falling out. I wondered, after I'd lost the first one, if it had set off a reaction inside my mouth and they'd all decided they wanted to up and leave. But I was scared – scared it'd be something else he'd punish me for.

One day, after he'd marked my homework, he brought me a sandwich. I was starving hungry, but as soon as I saw the plate I lost my appetite because he'd brought me an apple too. I waited for him to leave so that I could cut off some chunks of it to suck – I couldn't bite into the apple because my teeth were far too wobbly to be trusted. I waited, but he sat down, pulled out his penknife and began to sharpen my pencils. I watched as the blade carved into the wood and dropped it onto the ground in small curls.

'Eat,' he grunted.

I grabbed the sandwich and tried to nibble it cautiously out of the side of my mouth – the part that still had the most teeth. He noticed, looked over at me oddly and glanced down at the pencil. My lack of teeth meant eating took me a lot longer than it normally would have.

'What's wrong?' he asked, his voice sounding abrupt and

suspicious. He was watching me, but I tried not to make eye contact. 'You not hungry or something?'

I said nothing. Instead, I tried to half suck, half bite the bread, keeping my mouth as closed as I could. He stood up and bunched the pencils in his hand as he rested them down on the table.

'What's wrong with your mouth?' he demanded.

I automatically backed away as he reached his hand towards my face.

'Let me see...' he insisted.

He held my head between his hands and used his thumbs to push up my top lip and take a closer look. Then he did the same with the lower one. I closed my eyes and waited for him to erupt, but to my complete surprise, he remained calm.

'Eat the apple,' he said, sitting back down on the chair.

I looked over at the fruit on the plate: the apple was round, hard, and looked impossible to eat.

'Eat it!'

I jumped inside my skin, grabbed it and held it up to my mouth; the smooth, green surface smelled sweet as I pushed it against my lips.

'Go on...' he urged, observing me, encouraging me to open my mouth.

I angled it against the side of my mouth and bit down as my teeth shook and wobbled in protest. They felt fragile, as though they were made from glass and might shatter at any minute. The first bite seemed the hardest, but once I'd made a hole I was able to grab the rough edges and take smaller, cautious bites. Eating it had felt like another piece of homework, something to learn and try to overcome. In the end, it took me as long to eat it as it did for him to sharpen my pencils. Eventually, all I had left was the single brown stick from the top, which I threw to the back of my mouth and chewed against my big, back teeth.

'You're getting older,' he remarked, breaking the silence between us.

I wasn't sure if getting older was a good or bad thing, but I was definitely getting stronger and taller, and I knew that was a good thing. I hoped soon I'd be tall and strong enough to push him down the steps. Maybe I'd be able to hit him over the head with the chair, or maybe…

'Wait there,' he said, his voice interrupting my thoughts.

He stood abruptly and threw the pencils on the table. I watched as they separated, rolled and scattered across it in different directions. Then he went upstairs, although he didn't shut the door. I was just starting to wonder where he'd gone when he reappeared, holding something. Then I watched as he tore some paper with writing on it and handed it to me.

'Read these pages,' he mumbled. 'They're from the encyclopaedia.'

I wasn't sure what an encyclopaedia was, but I realised it must be some kind of book – the ones Andrew had told me about.

I wonder if this is what he reads.

The pages had pictures of the human body on them. There was a drawing of a man and a woman. The more I read, the more I wanted to learn. I knew what different parts of my body were called, but these pieces of paper allowed me to see inside a body – a body like mine. I read a page about teeth and was shocked to learn the ones I'd lost had been called 'baby teeth'. At this I scratched my head.

But I'm not a baby, I thought, a little annoyed.

The page said children often lost their baby teeth before growing something called a 'second set'. There was something called puberty, too. It explained how hair grew on your body, around your willy and underneath your arms. Once he was out of the room, I pulled the waistband of my shorts away from my stomach and looked down inside my underpants: *no hair*. Then I checked under both arms, but they were smooth and hair-free. The pages said that men, or boys, who'd been through puberty grew hair on their faces. Fascinated, I stroked a hand across my face but it felt soft and smooth – I couldn't imagine having hair on my face like I did on my head.

The next evening, he brought me even more pages down to read. I devoured them all once he'd left, my eyes feasting on the words as I read and reread each piece of paper again and again. These pages had also been ripped from a book, but this time they explained how a car engine worked. There was a bit that had drawings: it explained all about car gears and drive shafts. I remembered the stick he'd pushed forward when he'd taken me to the hospital and how he'd pulled away from the side of the pavement. Now I could finally put a name to it – it was called a gear stick. I'd only been outside in the real world a handful of times, but I was learning about things that I didn't even know existed. Soon, I understood how a car engine worked, even though I didn't know what it felt like to 'play' outside with a football, toys or even other children.

Then he brought me pages to read on different animals. There was a picture of a wolf. I cast my mind back to the creature I'd seen with four legs and black and white hair – it looked similar.

Had it been a wolf?

My eyes scoured the pages, searching for an answer, until finally I found it. There was another picture, only this one looked different to the one I'd seen through the car window because it was covered in golden hair. It also had a much nicer face, although there was no mistaking it was the exact same creature. I read the title at the top: *The Dog*.

So, that's what a dog was!

Slowly, I began to memorise everything, storing all this new information inside my head. Soon, my brain had its very own built-in encyclopaedia. He even brought me down the odd puzzle page that he'd ripped from a magazine. I liked puzzles because I loved the way I had to use my brain to try and solve them. One day, he handed me a book called *The Atlas* and it blew me away. Even though I'd read it with my own eyes, I could barely believe what I was seeing: that there was a whole world outside and it was massive! There were different bits of water called oceans, and creatures lived in these oceans and others on the ground; some could even live in both. I learnt about different places called countries. There were drawings of people with different-coloured skin to mine. The more I read, the more fascinated I became. I didn't know why he wanted me to have all this new knowledge when he kept me locked inside a cellar. If anything, it made me even more determined to escape so that I might be able to explore all these different and exciting places. I imagined travelling to India to pick tea straight from a plant, like the people in the drawings. But India was hot and I was used to living in the cold.

No, I thought, shaking my head, *I'd rather go to the North Pole where it was really cold and build myself an igloo from snow.*

I decided that I would travel to different cold places where people didn't walk but moved around on skis. I pictured myself living in the pages, whizzing down the pictures of snowy mountains. Overnight, it seemed as though a door had been opened inside my brain and now I'd discovered things I could only dream about. Now I needed to know more. Suddenly, my own world had shrunk so small that I felt the walls closing in on me.

Peter was still my friend, of course, but now I dreamt of seeing and meeting other weird and wonderful creatures – different insects, fish, lions, tigers, elephants, goats, cows, sheep... the list seemed endless. But why did he let me read about all of these things when he kept me locked away? Was this another way of punishing me? To show me things but not let me see, hear or smell them?

I rested the piece of paper on the table and wandered over towards Peter's web. Cupping my hands, I encouraged him to climb on. After a moment's hesitation, he lifted his front legs and slowly crawled onto my skin. I smiled down at him as I walked over towards my bed and watched him run up and along my arm. He inched higher and higher, tickling my skin, as he moved along quickly. Worried that I'd lose him up my sleeve, I stuck out my finger on my other hand and let him crawl onto that. He was just rushing along my arm when I heard the cellar door open above me. Guiltily, I dropped my arm down by my side and hoped that Peter would drop down on my bed and scuttle away to safety – I couldn't risk Dad knowing about my friendship with Peter. If he did, he'd take him away from me.

'Go on,' I urged, whispering down to my friend. 'Quick! Run back to your web.'

Ten, nine, eight…

I watched with my heart in my mouth as Peter scuttled off the mattress, down the brick plinth and onto the floor, his legs moving quickly as he shifted across the stone surface.

Seven, six, five…

Four, three, two, one…

He was standing there in front of me, but I was still looking down, watching Peter – I had to know he was safe.

'Urgh!' my father grunted and without warning, he lifted his boot and slammed it down hard on the ground.

I thought my heart would explode with fear.

Peter!

My friend must have sensed the darkening shadow overhead because he'd moved quickly over to one side, but Dad lifted his foot again.

STAMP!

I watched, paralysed with fear, as he chased him around the room, stamping with every other footstep. My heart hammered until I couldn't breathe.

He was trying to kill him – he was trying to kill Peter!

'BLOODY spiders!'

His voice bounced off the walls, echoing around the room, as he stomped his boot down again and again. My eyes scoured the floor, desperately searching for him. I saw a flicker of movement, a quickening of legs as he stopped and then darted to one side and then the other.

STAMP! STAMP! STAMP!

I held my breath, not daring to take another because I had to know he was all right – I *had* to know.

'Got yer!'

He smiled triumphantly as he brought his foot down with a final slam.

I wanted to cry; I wanted to shout out to Peter – to warn him to run – but fear and shock had stolen my voice. Instead, I sat there shaking. My eyes scoured the ground as he lifted his boot. I didn't want to see, but I had to. I watched my father's face as he checked the bottom of his sole – his foot turned away from me – and scraped it hard with sole against stone across the ground. He was wiping him away, he was wiping Peter's body across the floor. A rage burned through me and I began to scream until soon I couldn't stop. I screamed and howled, my cries filling the room. He stopped checking his boot and looked over at me, shocked, as he tried to work out what was wrong. But I couldn't – and wouldn't – tell him. I couldn't tell him he'd just killed my best friend, my only friend in the whole wide world. Soon, huge great sobs wracked my body as it began to convulse with grief.

'Shut up!' he yelled, grabbing me by both shoulders and shaking me.

But I couldn't; I couldn't stop, and I didn't want to. He lifted his hand and drew it up by the side of his face. Violence – his answer to everything.

'Shut up, or I'll give you something to cry about,' he warned.

But I wouldn't. How could I when he'd just killed the one thing – the *only* thing – that I loved?

'I'm warning you…' he said, his hand poised in mid-air.

I didn't care; he could do whatever he liked because nothing else mattered, not any more.

Peter was dead.

'I hate you!' I screamed, the words flooding out of my mouth as a waterfall of tears blinded my eyes. 'You hear me? I hate you, I HAAAAATE YOU!'

PUNCH!

There was a numbness as the knuckles of his fist bit deep against the flesh of my jawline.

'I SAID, SHUT IT!'

He thumped me until I felt delirious with pain. But still, I didn't stop crying – I couldn't. He grunted and angrily unbuckled his belt. It unthreaded quickly, slipping through each loop like a leather snake racing around his waist. He held it in his hand and flicked it until it cracked loudly against the air. Then he began to whip me.

'You're crazy. You hear me, dog? CRAZY! What the hell did I do to be lumbered with you?'

He belted me until he'd used up every last ounce of anger he had inside and then he turned and left me there, a sobbing mess on the floor.

With my eyes still blinded by tears, I pulled myself up onto the bed and lay down, my whole body throbbing in agony. I felt a trickle of blood as it seeped from my left nostril and trailed down towards my mouth. Closing my lips, I let it flood over my chin. Resting my bloodied head against the pillow, I glanced over at the floor where he'd scraped Peter from the bottom of his boot.

My friend was no longer living; he'd become a smear of nothingness. His body, his hair, eyes and legs all gone. He'd killed him.

Bastard! the voice inside my head screamed.

I closed my eyes and blinked away more rising tears. When I finally opened them, my vision was still blurred. I was staring out, looking at nothing, when I sensed something move over in the corner. I blinked and looked harder, my eyes straining against the light. There it was again, a slight movement – a shift in the shadows. I wiped my eyes and sat upright. Something had just moved. I ran over, folded down onto my hands and knees, looked into the shadows and that's when I saw him – Peter. He was moving, crawling back towards me.

He'd missed. The bastard had gone and missed him!

A rush of relief flooded my body as I lifted him, began to cry and then to laugh. I started to laugh like a mad man. I laughed hard and long, and as though I would never stop.

He was still alive – my best friend was alive!

CHAPTER 13

THE SPADE

I felt so happy that the next few days passed by in an unusual blur – a blur of happiness. But afterwards, I found myself worried about Peter's safety. I knew I had to keep him hidden away in his web.

'Just stay away from him. He's a monster, understand?' I whispered as his legs pulled and twitched against the gossamer-thin strands.

I'd expected my father to ask me why I'd been so upset and why I'd spoken back at him for the very first time, but he didn't. He didn't care that I was upset, so why would he be bothered about what had upset me?

Life carried on as usual until, one day, I was passing Peter's web when I noticed that he'd not moved for a few days.

'Hello, Peter,' I said, pushing the side of my finger gently against the web. It caused it to bounce momentarily. He shifted slightly and then hung down by a single, long, silvery thread.

'Stop it!' I laughed, thinking he was playing a game.

I cupped my hand and waited for him to climb on, but he didn't move.

Panicking, I nudged a finger against him and then he fell – like a stone – and landed as a small claw against the floor.

'Peter?' I cried.

But I knew; I knew from the way his lifeless body had landed that it was too late – Peter was dead.

That day, I cried for my friend. Sure, Dad hadn't killed him, but I knew he was to blame. He'd all but killed him – he'd frightened him to death. I'd never buried anyone before, but I'd read about different burials on pages he'd torn from a book. There were ones where they put you on a raft and pushed you out to sea, others where they burnt your body until there was nothing left but ashes and, finally, there were burials where people covered their dead in soil. I couldn't do any of those things, so I tore a piece of paper, wrapped his body in it and buried him deep inside a crack between the bricks. At least I knew Dad wouldn't be able to hurt him there.

Without Peter, I felt so alone. I had other spiders, but they meant nothing to me and I often found myself looking over at his web. When it became too much of a reminder, I demolished it with my hands until there was nothing left. I cried, but I realised there was nothing I could do or say that would ever bring him back. Instead, I sank back into my own company.

Andrew still occasionally tapped at the door, but he never stayed long. I think he was worried he'd be punished if he was found talking to me. It was as if, by association only, I was enough to get someone – *anyone* – into trouble. I wondered why, as my sister and brothers grew older, they didn't tell anyone about me.

A cellar, similar in size and appearance to the one that became Stephen's prison for thirteen years. A makeshift shelf became Stephen's bed. Here you can see the disused coal hole that his 'bed' would have lain over (the black square at the back of the cellar).

(© Author's own)

Above: This is the actual house (pictured in present day, to the left of the photo) where Stephen was locked in the cellar and hidden away.   *(© Author's own)*

Below: Aston Hall Hospital. When Stephen escaped his cellar at the age of thirteen, he had no idea of the horror and abuse that awaited him here.   *(© SWNS)*

Above: St William's School in Market Weighton, East Yorkshire. *(© ITV)*

Below: The courtyard at St William's where boys would be paraded to be chosen for sexual abuse. *(© ITV)*

Above: When Stephen met Gail, he knew his life would change for the better.

(© Author's own)

Below: Stephen and Gail on their wedding day twenty-five years ago.

(© Author's own)

Above: Stephen and Gail on their wedding day, with Stephen's three boys.

(© *Author's own*)

Below: Stephen, Jessica and his boys.

(© *Author's own*)

Above: Stephen, his boys and their girlfriends, daughter Jess and wife Gail enjoying a family get together, something Stephen could only dream of as a boy.

(© Author's own)

Below: Stephen has an incredible circle of friends now.

(© Author's own)

Stephen performing on stage with his band. *(© Peter Stanley)*

Stephen Smith, once the boy in the cellar, performs on stage. He is no longer alone.

THE SPADE

They played outside; they met other people, so why hadn't they said anything?

The books Dad continued to bring down for me made me realise it wasn't normal for a child to live in a cellar. Children normally lived with their mums and dads. Some even had animals, such as dogs or cats – they didn't live with spiders like I did.

One morning, I brushed my teeth and had just emptied my spit into my bucket when he called me from the top of the stairs.

'Come on, slopping out time!'

I grabbed my bucket and began to climb the steps. Then I followed him through the yard into the outside toilet – or 'bog', as Andrew had called it – and emptied the slops into the bowl when the door slammed loudly behind me. I wasn't frightened, not any more. I was used to him and his games. I knew he took great pleasure in locking me in the outside toilet for hours on end until it had almost become normal. Sighing, I nudged the bucket to one side and made myself comfortable – it was going to be a long day and night.

I whispered over to the mouse, praying I'd hear his squeak. We'd become quite good friends and, if I ever had any crumbs in my pocket, I'd trail them along the ground to try and bring him out towards me. I'm not sure how much time had passed, but my bum felt square and cold against the floor and my legs were stiff because I'd been sat with them folded at a funny angle. I moved one and it felt strange – kind of 'fizzy' – inside. It wasn't until many years later that someone told me this prickly feeling was called 'pins and needles'.

I was shaking my leg, trying to encourage the blood back into it, when I heard footsteps and muffled voices on the other side of the door. I listened carefully, pressing my ear against it. The splintered and blistered paintwork crackled against the side of my face as I heard another sound. I was certain there was more than one person standing outside. There was a rattle and the slight movement of the door as it shifted forwards and some light peeked in around the edge.

It's undone. Someone has just opened the door, the voice said, giving a running commentary.

I clambered to my feet and waited; waited for him to call out with his usual shout before giving me a slap and sending me back down into the cellar. However, the door was unlocked but it remained closed. I waited some more; my senses on high alert, watching, waiting, breathing, and trying to second guess what was coming next. But there was nothing – no noise, only the sound of my breath against the door.

What's he doing? Be careful, something's not right.

I waited, each breath becoming shallower and more panicked than the last. My breath began to build up and fire back at me, the warmth of it nestled against my skin as it bounced off the door's surface.

He's waiting for you to open the door. Don't do it! It must be a trap. He's up to something.

My ribcage rattled as my heart hammered against it like a door in the wind, banging against the frame.

Think, think! You've got to be smarter than him. Think!

But no one was talking and nothing was stirring. We'd reached a stalemate and neither of us wanted to make the first move.

Maybe he's already gone? Maybe he's left the door unlocked because he's going to let you go? Maybe…

My mind whirred with endless possibilities. Maybe he had had a change of heart? Maybe with me older and Mum gone, maybe he wanted me to help him with the younger ones? He might even let me live upstairs with them? Maybe I've reached an age where he thinks I've been punished long enough, maybe this is it?

Maybe this is the day I finally get out of the cellar?

Resting a flat palm against the wood, I pushed the door open slightly. The brightness from outside seeped in as a shaft of light, wrapping itself around the edge. I half-expected it to slam shut and when it didn't, I was spurred on to push it open a little more. I wanted to call out, to see if anyone was there, but thought better of it. Taking a deep gulp, I applied more pressure and the door creaked open a little more.

Nothing.

Realising I had nothing to lose, I pushed it wide open, the light from outside temporarily blinding me. I lifted a hand to try and shield my eyes and give them time to adjust. The door creaked open on rusty hinges, but I still couldn't see him. In fact, I couldn't see anyone, just blinding daylight. I lifted my hand higher and took a step outside. One step and then another as I cleared the door...

'RELEASE THE DOG!' his voice boomed loudly.

I jumped even though it hadn't entirely been unexpected. I shut my eyes and winced, waiting for the usual slap around the back of my head. But nothing happened. I began to turn when...

WHACK!

The sickening sound of my body hitting the ground stole the air clean away from my lungs.

WHACK!

The pain seared through me like a raging fire as it travelled up and along my spine, burning everything in its path and flooding my brain with panic. The blow had come from nowhere and was as unexpected second time around as it had been the first. I turned my head to the side and looked up, my lungs crushed and deflated against the concrete ground in the yard. He was standing over me, his solid body blocking out the sun with a huge, darkened shadow. I watched him in silhouette as he lifted something – an object – high above his head. As it twisted, it caught the sunlight just long enough for me to work out what it was he was holding. It was a spade, a metal spade.

I looked on helplessly as he turned sideways, the edge of it becoming sharp as an axe and made a strange grunting sound as he brought it down hard against my spine. I felt it judder against bone – a pain so intense that it caused my eyes to bulge in their sockets. There was a flash of white sparks as they burst and danced around in front of my eyes before the outside yard blurred and I felt myself slip away. My surroundings faded to nothing as I allowed my face to rest against the damp, cold concrete until everything turned black.

CHAPTER 14

THE SHRINK

I remember the sensation of being carried because, as I came to, my legs and arms were dangling uselessly down as though they no longer belonged to me. He didn't speak; instead, he laid me on the back seat of his car before the pain grew so intense that I passed out again.

The next time I awoke, my torso was covered with bandages and I was lying in a bed. It took me a moment to register that I was inside a hospital because I was surrounded by other children – I'd never seen so many at once. A few of them had plaster casts on their arms or legs, but there was one boy in the corner of the room who was a sickly grey colour and looked very ill indeed. I noticed a nurse fussing and buzzing around his bed like a fly.

As my eyes and head began to clear, I sensed that I wasn't alone.

'Say nothing,' Dad's voice warned through the haze of

whatever the doctors had given me. He was there, sitting in a large chair at the side of my bed. Dressed in corduroy trousers and his best shirt and tie, he was playing the part of a concerned parent. 'You hear me? You keep that shut,' he whispered, holding a finger to his lips in warning.

My head felt too heavy, like balancing a big ball on my shoulders, so I let it sink down into the pillow and closed my eyes. I didn't want to look at him.

He did this to you. Tell them, this is all his fault, the voice whispered.

But I couldn't; I daren't. He'd taught me, growing up in the cellar, not to scream. The more noise I made, the worse it would be.

'If you scream, you'll just get more,' he told me time and time again. Instead, I learnt how to scream inside. Scream quietly inside my head, where no one could hear me.

Even with my eyes closed, just the fact that he was sitting there, watching me, left me feeling on edge. I wondered how he'd get out of this one. What excuse would he come up with? What would he say to the doctors to try and explain away those injuries, the worst ones yet?

'Hello,' said a man in a white coat, approaching my bed. He stopped, took my father's hand in his and shook it. 'I'm Doctor Johnson.'

Dad stood and shook the doctor's hand back.

Go on, this is your chance – tell the doctor he did this to you!

But I couldn't. I was scared to death of him. If he could do this to me then he could do anything.

'So,' the doctor said, turning his attention to me, 'tell me, young man, what have you been doing?'

I opened my mouth, but as I did, Dad shot me another warning look – a look that said 'keep quiet' – so I closed my mouth and held it there in a thin line.

'He slipped,' Dad interrupted. 'He'd got the tent out and was playing with his sister and brothers. You know what kids are like…' he chuckled, looking to Doctor Johnson for confirmation. The doctor nodded as if to say yes, he did indeed know what kids were like.

'Especially boys, eh, Stephen?' the medic said, smirking as he shook his head in dismay.

'Anyway, I didn't see it because I was inside the kitchen at the time, but his brothers told me he'd slipped and had somehow fallen backwards onto a tent peg.'

Doctor Johnson raised an eyebrow.

'A tent peg, you say?'

Dad nodded and grinned back at him as though they were the best of friends.

'Anyway, I heard a commotion so I came running out and that's when I found him. He'd split his back open, so I pushed a tea towel against the wound to try and stem the blood, picked him up, put him in the car and drove him straight here.'

The doctor nodded as though he understood. Then he pulled a pen from a pocket on the left side of his white coat and made some notes in a small book.

'An adventurous lad, is he?' Doctor Johnson commented, looking from me towards Dad.

'Oh yes, you know what boys are like. I've three and they're all the same, they're always climbing trees.'

Liar! the voice screamed.

My eyes flitted anxiously between him and the medic. I hoped that Doctor Johnson would be able to tell, that he'd be able to see straight through my father's made-up story.

'Well, we've cleaned up the wound to prevent infection and stitched it up, both inside and outside…'

The doctor slid his pen back into his breast pocket, approached the bed and glanced down at me.

'As for you, young man, you need to learn to be more careful on your adventures! You must have had your poor parents sick with worry. You also need to learn to set a good example to your younger brothers.'

I was astonished. He'd blamed me for all this and the doctor believed him, every single, lying word.

He did this to you. Tell him, tell him!

But I couldn't; I didn't have the courage. Instead, I lay there with my mouth closed, mute and unable to speak.

'Well, Mr…'

'Smith…' he replied, taking the doctor's hand warmly and shaking it for a second time. 'Mr Smith.'

Doctor Johnson glanced briefly down at his notes. 'Yes, Mr Smith. It was a pleasure to meet you,' he said, returning the handshake. 'And as for you, Stephen, no more adventures! You did yourself a nasty injury there. We were able to patch you up this time, but next time you might not be so lucky. Do you understand?'

My father's eyes were on me, willing me to acknowledge everything that the doctor had just said. Every fibre of my being wanted to tell him he'd got it wrong – he'd got me wrong – but I couldn't, I couldn't tell anyone. Instead, I nodded my head glumly.

'Good boy,' he said, satisfied I'd taken his words of warning on board and then he left.

A few minutes later, one of the nurses came over to remind my father that visiting time was over.

'But don't worry, we'll take good care of him, won't we?' she said, smiling down at me.

Her kindness made me want to cry. She was so lovely to me and to him, yet she didn't have a clue what he was like – no one did. He glanced at a metal thing on his wrist, picked up his overcoat that he'd draped over the back of the chair, and turned to point his finger at me.

'You behave yourself.'

The nurse grinned as though he was pretending to scold me, but I knew it was real. He didn't say another word, but then he didn't have to: the message was loud and clear.

I'm not sure how long I was kept in hospital for because I had no concept of time, but I didn't speak or engage with any of the other children on the ward, even when, one day, a boy stumbled over to me.

'What have you done then?' he asked, dragging his leg slowly behind him. He'd clearly broken it because I recognised the tell-tale thick white plaster I'd had on both arms.

'Nothing,' I said, turning myself away from him and onto my side.

'Suit yourself,' he sniffed as he crossed the ward to join the other children over in a corner.

'Now then, Stephen,' another voice said a short while later.

I opened my eyes to find a nurse standing there, the same one who'd spoken to Dad earlier. 'Let's try and get you up and out of bed. Why don't you join the other children over there? They're doing a jigsaw puzzle. Do you like jigsaw puzzles?'

I didn't even know what a jigsaw puzzle was, but I couldn't tell her that so I just shook my head.

'Oh well, never mind, eh. I'll tell you what, why don't you let me brush your hair? It's all knotted at the back.'

With that, she began to plump up my pillows and helped sit me up in bed. Then she disappeared off somewhere. Minutes later, she'd returned with another nurse and they both proceeded to coo over my hair.

'Haven't you got long hair for a boy?' the second nurse remarked.

'It's lovely, isn't it? I'd wear mine down if I had nice hair like you,' the first one agreed as they chatted between themselves.

I thought back to the haircut he'd given me, but that had been ages ago. I couldn't tell how long my hair was; I could only guess by how it brushed against my shoulders.

'He's a proper little rocker,' the second one giggled and they both laughed.

I wasn't sure what they were laughing at or what was funny; I didn't even know what a 'rocker' was, but it was obviously something with long hair like mine. After a bit of tugging, the nurse managed to get the knots, as she'd called them, out of my hair. For the first time in ages I was able to run my fingers through it without them getting snagged and caught up.

'There, isn't that better?' the nice nurse said, sitting away from me on the bed to admire her handiwork.

I liked it in the children's ward because I got to eat nice food and something called puddings. They were served with custard or something cold, called ice cream. I thought back to the way the snow had melted against my tongue. The ice cream was similar but it tasted much nicer.

Of course, it couldn't last and before I knew it, one day he'd arrived to take me home. I was still wearing a bandage to protect the wound, but the stitches had held together well and I was discharged from hospital. If I thought for one moment that his attack would change anything, then I was wrong. My dad simply threw me back in the cellar and let me stew, although he kept up my homework routine – obviously annoyed that I'd missed a few 'lessons'. If anything, he brought down even more pages from books and magazines for me to read, although they weren't necessarily in any particular order. One page would say 100, but another might say 52, or page 65. There was no real order to anything he did. The only consistent thing was he always wore a shirt and tie and the brown leather apron. I'm not sure if questions had been asked after I'd left, but not long afterwards, he told me that I had another 'hospital appointment'.

'You're going to see someone,' was all he would say.

I'd assumed it must be something to do with the scar on my back, but as he drove me to the hospital in the warm weather, I noticed that he didn't seem his usual cocky self.

'Remember, you keep quiet. I'll do all the talking. You say nothing. Understand?'

I nodded to show that I did, even though I sensed this 'appointment', whatever it might be, was somehow different. For one, I hadn't broken a single bone. I read the large sign as we drove past it and into the car park: *Derby Royal Infirmary*. We walked through various doors until we'd reached a desk with a lady sitting behind it. He gave my name, she ticked it off a list and told us to take a seat. This part of the hospital seemed totally different to the place I'd been before when he'd broken my arm and wrist. For starters, this one had comfier chairs that were padded, like the long chair I'd seen in the front room at home. In fact, it felt more like a home than a hospital. There was even a green plant inside a pot that had been put on top of a small table over in the corner.

After a short while, a nurse called my dad through into a room to speak to a doctor. He seemed to be in there for ages and I wondered what lies he was telling them about me. Eventually, the nurse reappeared and asked me to come through to join him. I didn't look at Dad as I entered the room. In fact, I didn't say a word, I just stared at the ground.

'Why do you keep getting into trouble?' a man, who I assumed must be a doctor, even though he wasn't wearing a white coat, demanded to know.

I felt their eyes on me, judging me and waiting for an answer, but I couldn't speak.

How could I with him sitting next to me?

'I see,' the doctor said a little impatiently before resting back in his big black chair. He stared at me so intensely that I wondered if he was trying to see inside of me, like the X-ray I'd had on my arm.

'Alright, Stephen, so why don't you tell me this: why does your dad beat you?'

This question caught me completely off guard.

Had he told him? Had he just told the doctor what he'd done?

I looked over towards Dad for confirmation, but instead he just leapt in with another lie.

'I have to hit him to try and control him. There's something

146

wrong with him, Doctor. He's not all there…' he said, tapping a finger against the side of his head.

The medic sat forward in his chair and it creaked loudly.

'Right, well, I'd like you to go in and see my colleague, a Doctor Robinson, to be assessed. So, young man,' he said, turning his attention away from my dad to me, 'I'd like you to go with the nurse to see him now.'

The nurse stood up and so did my father, but the doctor waved his hand for him to sit back down.

'No, not you, Mr Smith. My colleague will assess the boy alone.'

I was astounded. He always went with me – I was never alone, not when we were outside. Never. Panicked, I turned to him. I didn't know whether to laugh or cry, I'd never seen a doctor on my own before.

'But Stephen wants me with him, don't you?' he insisted, looking at me.

I knew I should have nodded my head. After all, that's what I'd agreed to do – let him do all the talking. But for the first time in my life, I knew I would be free of him, even if only for a few minutes. The nurse seemed a little puzzled as her eyes flitted from him to me and back again. I chose to say nothing and let her guide me out of the room. As she did, I could still hear his voice behind me.

'But I'm his father…' I heard him protest to the doctor.

I was flabbergasted. I'd never heard him sound worried before and there was absolutely nothing he could do about it. Finally, someone had stood up to him and told him what to do. A surge of happiness rose inside me and I felt it flood through my veins like sunshine. It fired inside my stomach, rising high into my chest and heart.

You're in control now. This is your chance. You can tell him; tell the doctor what he's been doing to you. There's nothing he can say or do to stop you. Do it. Do it now!

The nurse led me through the reception waiting area and into a different room, where she tapped lightly at a door. We waited outside for a minute before being called in. Sat inside the room was another, much younger doctor, who was waiting to speak to me.

'Stephen Smith for you, Doctor,' the nurse announced breezily before leaving us alone.

I stood in front of the closed door awkwardly and smiled.

You have to tell him; you have to tell the doctor what that bastard has been doing to you. It's now or never! the voice screamed.

Doctor Robinson, who looked a little younger than Dad, nodded over towards a chair for me to sit down. I imagined my father, waiting outside, straining his neck to try and listen.

Say nothing, I pictured him saying.

But he couldn't control me now, not at this very moment. It was up to me what I said and what I didn't. This was between me and Doctor Robinson.

'Hello, Stephen,' the doctor said finally, leaning in towards his big wooden desk. He had a pile of paper and books stacked in front of him and I wondered if they were anything to do with me.

I opened my mouth and willed the words to come spilling out, but nothing happened.

'Tell me,' he said, lifting a jug of water before pouring some into an empty glass. 'Would you like a glass of water?'

Again, I opened my mouth and tried to speak but it was as though my throat had folded in on itself. Instead, I looked over at him and nodded silently.

'Right you are.' Doctor Robinson smiled, pouring a second glass that he pushed over towards me. 'Don't worry, we've lots of time. Take a sip of water first.'

I did as I was told and felt my throat begin to relax as the ice-cold liquid slid down the back of it.

'So, your name is Stephen, is that right?'

'Yes,' I replied, my sudden voice taking us both by surprise.

'Good, good,' he encouraged.

'And you are…' He glanced down at the top piece of paper on the pile. 'You are twelve years old.'

Twelve? Was I? I didn't know for sure, but I nodded again.

He must know. It's written down in front of him.

I noticed that he was wearing a shirt and tie, like my father, but he also wore a smart jacket. The doctor laced his fingers together and rested backwards in his chair.

'Right, Stephen. I have some puzzle books here that I'd like you to look at,' he said, suddenly standing and walking around to my side of the desk to show me. 'Do you like puzzles?'

I nodded.

'Good.'

He showed me a series of patterns and explained that he wanted me to look at each page and tell me what the missing pattern should be – 'problem solving', he called it.

I looked down at the pages: this was easy! Picking up a pencil, I got to work and before I knew it, I'd finished everything he'd given me.

'Clever lad,' he said. 'And so quick, too!'

Then he handed me another piece of paper.

'Stephen, I would like you to write me a short story. It can be about anything you like. Take your time and when you've finished, let me know.'

The doctor read through some papers as I began to write. I wasn't sure what I should write about, but then I remembered the car manual I'd read, so I wrote a story about cars.

He nodded and began to read it as soon as I handed it over to him.

'Good boy, so you like cars then?'

I grinned and nodded.

'What sort of car do you like best?'

I shrugged my shoulders; I only knew one car and that was my father's, but I hated that because I hated him.

'Never mind, I've some more puzzles for you. Would you like to have a go at these?'

'Yes,' I replied.

By now I was desperate to impress him because I liked this doctor – he seemed much kinder than the first one.

'Tell me, Stephen,' he said as I worked my way through the different pages, 'your father, does he hit you?'

I stopped what I was doing and looked at him, a little startled. *Tell him. Tell him now!*

I swallowed hard and glanced nervously over towards the door. But Doctor Robinson continued to stare at me; he was still waiting for an answer.

'You're not in any trouble, Stephen, and anything you tell me in this room is strictly confidential.'

I must have seemed puzzled because he asked me if I understood what the word 'confidential' meant.

'Not really,' I said, shifting nervously in my chair.

'What it means is anything you say will not go outside these four walls. I just want you to be honest with me. Tell me the truth and you won't get into any trouble.'

I swallowed again as a wave of fear and vomit rose at the back of my throat.

Tell him. Just tell him. Tell him now before it's too late.

He was still looking at me as he repeated the question.

'Does your father hit you?'

Go on. Do it! You might never get this chance again. The other doctor knows, so he must have told him…

My eyes flitted back over towards the door. I needed to be absolutely certain it was firmly closed: it was. I looked back at Doctor Robinson.

'Yes,' I said, my voice sounding small but determined.

He sighed.

'I see. Your father does hit you.'

I took a deep breath – it was now or never, and soon I began to speak without natural pauses as the whole sorry tale came flooding out of my mouth. It was as though someone or something had just burst a dam, a dam of misery.

'He hits me… hits me with a belt… He hurts me all the time. I was here, in hospital, not so long ago. He hit me, hit me with a spade. He'd locked me in the outside toilet – he does it all the time – and then he shouted: "Release the dog!". He calls me a dog, you see. Although sometimes he calls me a rat. Only this time he said "Release the dog!" and then he hit me. He normally punches me, but this time he hit me from behind with the edge of a spade…'

I took a huge gulp of air as the doctor waved his hand to try and slow me down.

'A spade? A children's spade?'

'No,' I said, shaking my head. 'One made of metal that he keeps in the garden, only he lifted it up and turned it to the side, like this,' I added, trying to demonstrate with my hands. 'He turned it on its side and brought the edge of the spade down on my back – that's what cut me, not a tent peg, it was the spade.'

The doctor seemed shocked but waved his hand, urging me to continue. I grabbed my glass of water from the table and lifted it to my lips. As I tried to line it up against my mouth, I realised how much my hand was trembling.

'It's alright, Stephen, take your time,' Doctor Robinson said kindly.

'He'd locked me in the outside toilet, or bog, that's what Andrew said it was called.'

'Andrew?'

'Yeah, he's my brother.'

The doctor dipped forward and checked the piece of paper again.

'How many brothers do you have?'

'Two, oh, and I've one sister.'

He made a note before looking back at me.

'Does he hit them too?'

I shook my head.

'I don't know because they live upstairs from me.'

He seemed a little confused.

'Upstairs? In their bedrooms?'

'Yes, no. Erm, what I mean is they live upstairs in the house. I don't.'

'You don't?' he asked, picking up his pen to write something down.

I shook my head.

'No, I live in the cellar. You know, the cellar downstairs – the one underneath the kitchen. That's where he keeps me.'

I watched as the nib of his pen began scribbling furiously against a piece of paper until soon the page was full of navy-blue writing.

'Just stop right there for a moment, Stephen,' he said, tapping the lid end of the pen against his chin thoughtfully. 'Are you telling me your father keeps you locked in the cellar but your sister and brothers live upstairs?'

I looked him straight in the eye.

'Yes.'

I couldn't be sure, but I'm almost certain I saw a flash of shock register across his face.

'I see… and, erm, what do you do for food?' he asked, writing something else down quickly. 'What do you eat?'

Doctor Robinson continued to take notes as I told him all about the cellar, Peter, my bed, the table, drawers and the coal hole above my head. I even told him how I regularly slopped out.

'That's when he locked me in the outside toilet. He does it all the time. He's usually waiting to hit me when I come out, but the last time was the worst. I wasn't expecting the spade, you see.'

'Yes, yes… I see,' he replied, although it was obvious that he really didn't. It was the horror on his face that had given him away.

His pen continued to work its way across page after page as he wrote everything down that I told him in long, looped handwriting that was impossible to read from where I was sitting.

'He gives me homework, too, like you did just then,' I said, pointing to the pieces of paper he'd given me to look at. 'I have to copy out spellings, do maths and write sentences.'

'So, you read lots of books?'

'Oh yes,' I said proudly. 'I read everything. He brings me different books and magazines down or rips pages from them. Sometimes the numbers on the pages don't match up but I read them anyway. I know all about cars – that's why I just wrote you that story. You could ask me anything about a car engine and I'd be able to tell you how it works.'

The doctor smiled, although I wasn't sure why.

'Yes,' I said, returning to his last question, 'I read and write. He gives me homework all the time, but if I get it wrong, he belts me. He also…'

I was about to tell him about the scissors when he interrupted.

'So why do you steal food, Stephen? Your father said that you steal food.'

I felt nervous; he must have said something – he must have spoken to him. My body began to tremble. The doctor noticed and rested his pen on the table.

'Stephen, is there something wrong?'

'You won't tell? I mean, you won't tell him I've told you all this, will you?'

He shook his head. 'No, I've already told you, anything you tell me is confidential. So, tell me, do you steal food?'

I pushed both hands under the backs of my knees, against the chair, and began to swing my legs nervously beneath me.

'Yes,' I replied. I knew that I should have felt ashamed because even I knew that stealing was wrong. 'But I'm always hungry. Sometimes he doesn't bring me any food; say, if I got my spellings wrong or something, he won't bring me any food down.'

Doctor Robinson picked up his pen and continued to write.

'So you sometimes feel hungry?' he said, guessing correctly.

I nodded. 'I ALWAYS feel hungry,' I said correcting him. 'Even when he does feed me, it's not enough. He gives me really small plates of food, usually whatever's left over.'

'And what about your mother?'

I stopped swinging my legs and looked up at him.

'I don't know. She used to come down, not very often, but every now and then. But one day, she stopped coming and I haven't seen her since.'

He stopped writing, sat back and considered me.

'Do you know where she went?'

'Nope.'

'Do you miss her?'

I paused for a moment – he'd asked me to tell him the truth.

'No,' I whispered in a quiet voice.

'And what about your sister and brothers, how do you feel about them?'

'I feel angry.'

'Why?' he said, taking a sip of water from his own glass.

'Because they know that I live down in the cellar but they don't do anything to try and help me. They know what he's like and even though he's kinder to them, they've seen how he treats me. I hoped they, or Mum, might tell someone, but they never have.'

I didn't want him to think badly of me, but at the same time I needed him to understand – to understand what I was going through.

'So, what do you do in the cellar all day? That is, what do you do when you're not doing your homework?'

I knew the answer to this one.

'I draw. I love drawing, but I hide them from him. If he finds them, he rips them up. But I don't care,' I said defiantly, 'because I've plenty of drawings inside here.' I smiled, lifting a hand and pointing it towards my head.

'And what do you draw, Stephen? What things do you like to draw?'

I searched my mind for the right word.

'Monsters. I like to draw monsters, monsters like him,' I said, nodding over towards the door.

Doctor Robinson stopped writing and pulled out a blank piece of paper. Then he searched a drawer in his desk for a pencil and handed it to me.

'Would you do one for me now? Would you draw me a picture?'

I sat up in my chair because I was excited.

'What would you like me to draw?'

He waved a hand away. 'Oh, anything. You choose.'

With the pencil in my hand, I began to create a new monster from my imagination. I conjured up one with extra legs, big sharp teeth and a huge body. Once I'd finished, I handed it to him.

'Very good,' he said, taking it from me. 'Here, draw me another one.'

I smiled and took a second piece of paper, only this time I made the monster even more frightening than the last, my imagination fired up and ready to explode. The doctor took the second drawing from me and put them underneath the pile of paperwork on his desk.

'So you steal food because you're hungry?'

'Yes.'

'And you're hungry because you say your father doesn't feed you enough?'

'Yes. He tried to lock me in the cellar to stop me from stealing food, but I always knock the wedge out. I do it with a pencil, you see.' I picked up the one he'd just given me to try and demonstrate. 'But don't tell him that, will you? Otherwise, I'll never get out again.'

The doctor shook his head. 'No. No, I won't say a word. Stephen, you are here today because your father told me you steal food and soil yourself, is that right? Do you soil yourself?'

I felt my face flush red as I nodded, a little embarrassed.

'Yeah, but only because I'm frightened of him. I've only ever done it when he's really hurt me… when he really belts me.'

Doctor Robinson put down his pen.

'Right, I see. Well, I think we've done more than enough for one day, don't you?'

Is that it? Isn't he going to help you? the voice inside my head wondered.

I felt gutted — gutted that it was over. *What did he want me to do? Did I have to go back to my dad after what I'd just told him?*

'Er…' I said, unsure what it was he wanted me to do.

The doctor waved a hand for me to stand up, so I did.

'Thank you for your time, Stephen.'

Is that it? Isn't he going to try and help you after everything you've just told him? Is he just going to leave you with him — the monster? the voice gasped in disbelief.

And shockingly, it was right — he did.

CHAPTER 15

THE RAID

'What did you say? What did you tell him in that room?' he demanded to know as soon as he followed me out from the reception. I looked at him, trying my best to remove all expression from my face. I couldn't falter now.

'Nothing, honestly. I didn't tell him anything.'

'You better not have, if you know what's good for you,' he said, clenching his fist.

My face flushed and grew hot and I was terrified that he'd notice – I'd never been a good liar.

'What questions did he ask? What did he ask you?' he pressed, hungry for information.

'Nothing. He didn't ask me anything, he just wanted me to draw him a picture. I drew him a picture, I swear that's all I did – I just drew him a picture.'

I couldn't be sure if he'd believed me or not, but once we were home he whipped me with his belt for good measure.

'You better have kept that shut,' he said, pushing his hand against my face.

With the belt still dangling from his hand, he turned and climbed the stairs. The door slammed, the latch fell and I knew that there would be no tea for me tonight. I wondered if by telling the doctor it would make any difference. Maybe he'd come and rescue me? But as the days and nights followed, I realised nothing had changed.

If he was going to save you then he would have done it by now, the voice mocked.

Utterly desperate, I began to draw more and more. I drew on any blank pages that I could find; I covered my world in new and scarier monsters. My head was a mess: on the one hand I desperately wanted to escape the cellar, but on the other, I felt safe there, even with him living above. This was familiar, this was my home, if you could call it that – it was all I was used to. However, with Peter gone, somehow it felt different. Of course, I had lots of new spiders, including another Peter. The more I read, the more new names I was able to come up with; I now had more spiders than I could actually care to remember. I was surrounded by them, but I'd never felt so alone. Not one of them could replace Peter. Finally, I started to see them for exactly what they were – insects. However, just as I'd begun to lose all hope, several days later, he called me upstairs.

'Come on, time to see the shrink again,' he said in a mocking tone.

We walked outside to the car, but then I noticed someone. There was someone else sitting in the back seat.

'This is Mary and she's the housekeeper,' he said by way of introduction.

I wasn't sure who she was and what a housekeeper was, but I'd never seen such a fat woman in all my life. Twice the size of Mum, she had long dark hair and wore glasses.

'Hello,' she said tightly, gripping a square black bag on her lap with gloved hands.

Dad started up the engine and drove me to Derby Royal Infirmary, where we all sat and waited in reception. Once again, Dr Robinson called me in on my own. I watched my father's face twitch with nerves as his eyes followed me towards the door. Once inside, the doctor gave me more puzzle books to do. Thankfully, I found them as easy as the last ones had been, enjoyable even.

'Clever lad, Stephen,' Doctor Robinson, said taking one from me.

He asked me to draw him some more pictures before returning me to reception and my dad, who was sat waiting for me. We were both told to wait because the first doctor, Dr Robinson's boss, wanted to speak to us all.

'Could you come in, Mr and Mrs Smith?' the nurse called from the doctor's doorway.

I felt my father's beady eyes fixed on me again as we crossed reception and entered the room together.

'Please take a seat,' the first doctor said, pointing to some chairs.

I stared hard at the floor and my throat seemed to close up. With him in the room, I felt mute. His eyes glanced from me to the doctor and back again. I knew what he was doing – he was trying to work out if I'd said anything in the other doctor's room and if so, how much. I tried to recall the word Doctor Robinson had used. What was it again? *Confidential, yes, that was it.*

'So, Mr Smith, I need you to do something for me,' the older doctor said, looking him square in the eye. 'I need you to stop hitting Stephen.'

In that moment my whole world felt as though it had come crashing down around me. The walls seemed to close in as I started to pant with fear, my breath fast and urgent.

He'll know you've said something. He'll definitely kill you now!

My hands gripped the edge of the chair in a panic as my knuckles flashed white. I tried to steady myself; I tried not to faint with terror. I was simply petrified, scared of what else the doctor was about to say.

So much for everything being confidential, I thought bitterly.

I didn't dare look at him or the doctor; I wanted the ground to swallow me whole. I pictured myself sinking to the floor in a shallow puddle. I'd drip through the floorboards and into the safety of the cellar below. Every building must have a cellar like mine. Yet, even though mine was horrible, at least it was familiar; at least I knew what to expect now. But I didn't know anything for sure – instead, I just felt panicked and jittery.

'What did you just say?' It was him. I flinched, expecting him to be looking at me, but he was staring at the doctor. His voice had a hard edge to it and I knew that he was ready to explode at any moment.

'I said, Mr Smith, you need to stop hitting your son,' the doctor repeated calmly.

I glanced out of the corner of my eye just in time to see Dad twist angrily towards me in his chair.

'Why? What has he been saying?' he said, spinning around like a man possessed. 'What lies has he been telling you?'

I held my breath, my heart hammering as fast as a piston

engine. I imagined it bursting from my chest at any moment.

This is it; this is where the doctor says I told him everything.

My body shrank down into the chair as I tried to make myself invisible.

'Nothing, he has not said anything. But what is obvious to me is that this child is frightened of you, Mr Smith. He is frightened of you because you beat him and that,' he said, tapping his pen determinedly against the edge of his desk, 'needs to stop now.'

There was a moment's silence as my father absorbed the words. For a split second, I wondered if it had worked.

Now that the doctor had found out, then maybe, just maybe, it might be enough to stop him.

Without warning, his chair tilted backwards as he scrambled to his feet, startling both Mary and the doctor. I winced, and this time the doctor noticed. I couldn't help it – I knew I was in for a good hiding once he got me home.

Just stick to the same story, it's all you can do, the voice said.

'Mr Smith, if you could just sit…' he said, trying to calm the situation down.

'Fuck off!' Dad roared. He couldn't contain his anger a moment longer. His voice was so big, loud and angry that it bounced off the walls, table and the ceiling. 'Fuck off! And don't you dare tell me how to raise my kids!' he screamed, wagging an angry finger in the doctor's face.

'Mr Smith, I really think you should just calm down. Can't you…'

'Come on,' Dad said suddenly, grabbing me roughly by the arm as he pulled me up and out of my chair. 'I don't have to sit here and listen to this…'

He dragged me over towards the door before turning back to face the doctor one last time, his face purple with rage.

'I brought him to you because he's got problems. There's something wrong with him. That's why I brought him here, not so you can tell me what I can and can't do with my own son.'

My feet barely touched the floor as he proceeded to drag me from the room, the doctor, and down the hospital corridor. We were followed closely behind by Mary, who had kept quiet throughout.

'Dad…' I said, trying to free myself from his iron grip.

'Don't!' He held a finger up against my face. 'Don't you dare say a word!'

The nurse who had shown us into the doctor's room earlier had just turned the corner, so she'd seen and heard everything as he dragged me past her and out through the exit. He was still burning with rage as he threw me in the passenger seat and fired up the car, angrily stamping on the accelerator, causing the engine to roar. Mary climbed into the back seat quietly, and with his foot pressed down hard, we screeched out of the car park and headed back towards home. I looked down at my hands in my lap because I was too frightened to make eye contact with him.

My father never mentioned the doctor or 'the shrink' again. Like me, I think he thought the whole thing had been forgotten.

★ ★ ★

One morning, I was busy drawing at my table when I heard a commotion coming from the kitchen above. His voice was loud and clear. I could hear him shouting and, for a split second, wondered if Andrew or one of the others was in trouble.

'How dare you! This is my house!' his voice boomed overhead.

I pushed my drawings into a new hiding place I'd recently found in the bricks. I didn't want him to rip them up or destroy them.

I sat down and tried to look busy when I heard the sudden creak of the door and saw a tell-tale shaft of light that followed, shining down the whitewashed walls. I waited; waited for the sound of his boots clomping down each step, waited for him to appear in front of me. I was poised, ready to count – ready to try and prepare myself. But nothing happened.

'It's my house, you can't just storm in here and do what you want…' I heard him argue.

What was happening?

I heard more noise and the sound of two or more sets of footsteps upstairs. Then I counted one set coming down the stairs. I moved and looked up. I expected it was him bringing Mary or even Andrew down, even though he'd never brought anyone down before.

'Hello?' a voice called out.

It was female and it was high-pitched. It sounded like Mum; it sounded like Mary. It sounded the same as the nurses in the hospital.

'Hello, Stephen?' the voice called again.

I looked up to see a woman I'd never seen before standing halfway down the stairs. She was wearing a long blue coat, was quite young, and had shoulder-length dark hair. Behind her was a man who had a strange hat perched on top of his head – it was tall and shaped a bit like half an egg. He was wearing a black uniform that I recognised. I thought back to all the pages I'd read. I'd seen someone dressed like him before; I'd read about them.

A policeman! He's a policeman, that's right! the voice screamed.

But why was there a policeman in Dad's house, and why was this strange lady coming down the stairs towards me?

'Come on,' she said, holding out her hand to try and beckon me forward. I began to move, but then I heard his voice and froze in my tracks.

'You can't do this, I have rights!' he shouted and then I saw him as he loomed into view.

I began to move away from her and back into the safety of the shadows.

'It's alright, come with me,' she insisted.

That's when I realised: he was shouting at the policeman, not me.

'Come on, Stephen,' she urged, still holding her hand out. 'It's alright. Everything is alright, but you need to come with me.'

I blinked. For a moment I was stunned, paralysed by what he'd do to me if I left with this woman – this stranger.

'I suggest you keep quiet, sir,' the policeman warned him.

'You've no right, this is my house…' Dad continued to rage.

'Come on, Stephen. Come with me…' the lady said, walking down to grab me by the hand.

I tentatively took my first step. Placing my foot upon stone I knew then – I could feel it in my bones – that this would be the last time I ever climbed those steps.

CHAPTER 16

THE OUTSIDE WORLD

I didn't look at him as I reached the top step. Instead, I kept my eyes forward and focused on the woman. I'd expected to see Andrew, Billy and Jane waiting but there was no one else there, only the policeman, the lady and him.

'Come on,' the lady said, taking my hand in hers.

I followed her out of the kitchen and along the hallway towards the front door. I allowed myself to marvel at the coloured glass one last time, saying a silent 'goodbye' to it as I left.

Where is she taking you? Ask her, ask her!

'Erm…' my voice sounded small and quiet as I struggled to find the right words. I continued to stammer and stumble over them as she opened up the door and turned to face me. 'Where are we going?' I said finally. 'I… I… I… mean, who are you and where are you taking me?'

The lady smiled, not in a friendly way, more in businesslike manner as though this was something she had to do.

'I'm a social worker, Stephen, and you are coming with us.'

Us? What, her and the policeman? I wondered what I'd done wrong and what a social worker even was.

But she offered no more explanation. Instead, she walked towards a car parked on the road outside and opened the door to the backseat.

'Come on, hop in,' she instructed.

I could feel my heart hammering. I'd always wanted to escape, yet now that I finally had I felt uncertain and afraid. I was still in shock as I lowered myself down into the back seat. As I did, I spotted another, slimmer, lady with long brown hair sitting in the driver's seat. She twisted around in her seat and smiled at me. She seemed warmer than the last lady.

'Are you alright, Stephen?' she asked.

I nodded, even though inside I felt sick with nerves.

You're outside! You're actually outside – without him!

I began to tremble. The nicer lady noticed, rested a gentle hand on my shoulder and left it there.

'It's alright, Stephen. We've come to take you away.'

The social worker slid into the passenger seat as the nice lady started up the engine and we began to pull away. My mind raced as the car trundled along the road.

Where are they taking me? What if they're taking me to another cellar?

I looked sideways at the door and for a split second, considered pulling the handle so I could jump out. My whole body quivered with fear. I hated Dad, but at least I knew what he was like and what he was capable of. At least everything was familiar back there, not like this – this was all new. I'd never been taken anywhere by anyone else in my life. I studied the backs of the ladies' heads as we whizzed along and the scenery blurred outside.

Could I trust them? Were they actually taking me somewhere safe or somewhere even worse?

Oh my God! I thought as another thought flashed through my mind. *What if he's sold you? What if these women – whoever they are – what if they've bought you from him?*

My mind went into overdrive as we passed things that were once so unfamiliar that I now recognised from books and my handful of trips to the hospital. I saw trees, houses, people, a big noisy bus. There was blinding sunlight outside and I could feel the warmth of it radiating through the window. There was greenery, too, so much greenery. Grass, more trees, hedges. I took a deep breath and allowed the unique scent of leather car seats, the car engine and petrol to fill my senses. Blinking against the sunlight, I spotted children, Mums and children – whole families walking together. I saw boys running around; two girls holding a long rope while another jumped over it; I saw dogs and an orange cat as it stretched out lazily along the top of a wall.

The car stopped. I looked out of the front windscreen and noticed that the light was red. He'd always stopped when the light was red.

It must be a thing you have to do, I decided as my heart pounded. I was scared stiff. I glanced out of the back window to see if we were being followed.

What if he catches you up? What if he's following you right now?

I twisted again, but I couldn't see his car. In fact, I couldn't see any cars, only the bus.

My hands and legs began to shake at the same time and soon, I couldn't control them.

'Where are you taking me?' I asked repeatedly.

But they wouldn't tell me.

'Don't worry, you're safe,' was all the social worker would say.

But I didn't want to be safe, not if safe meant this. I decided I'd rather be back there – back in my cellar, where I knew every brick, every hiding place, every corner. I'd dreamed of this for so long, but now I'd finally been set free, I realised I didn't like it, it scared me. Things outside frightened me because it was so busy. I didn't want to be out in this world that had different countries and oceans, a world so big that I couldn't even imagine how far it must stretch. I couldn't cope with all the people, the new faces, the sights, the sounds, the new smells... It was too much, too much all at once.

'I w... w... w... want to go. I want to go back,' I heard myself say. I couldn't believe I'd just said the words, but I couldn't help it. 'I want to go back to my cellar, please take me back there.'

The social worker turned to look at me in astonishment.

'Don't be silly, Stephen. We're taking you somewhere you'll feel safe. You weren't safe back there.'

He's sold you. Your father has sold you! the voice taunted.

That was it – the voice was right. He *had* sold me and now I'd go to somewhere even worse.

'Please, please! I'm scared. Please take me back,' I begged.

I couldn't believe how petrified I felt sitting there in the strange car with two strange women. I had pictured my escape so many times but never like this. In my mind, I was running and not stopping; I imagined myself tearing through fields and travelling to different countries. I thought how brave and strong I would feel; I hadn't imagined this, or the very real fear I felt right now.

We drove for quite a while before the younger lady signalled and pulled into a driveway that led to a red brick house with large doors. There was a sign that read: Ashley House.

It's a house, not a cellar, the voice reasoned. *Unless it has a cellar?*

'Come on, Stephen. We're here,' the social worker explained as she climbed out of the car and opened my door. My legs were shaking so much that it felt like my knees were knocking together. One of the women took a step forward and pressed the doorbell. After a while, someone answered.

'We've brought Stephen Smith,' the social worker announced to a lady, who ushered us inside.

I stood over to the side while the older social worker spoke to someone in charge. Then I watched her hand over a brown folder and wondered if it had anything to do with me. But I didn't have much time to think because soon another man was leading me down a corridor. He stopped, turned and headed up some stairs. We walked along another corridor until we'd reached a single door.

'You're in here,' he said, pushing down the handle to open it.

I wasn't sure what to expect, but the last thing I expected was my own bed and my very own window. The room was light, it was too light. My bed wasn't propped on a concrete shelf either. Instead, it stood at the side of the room, where it rested on a metal frame.

'Right,' the man said. 'Well, I'll let you settle in, Stephen, but if you need anything, I'll just be downstairs in the main office.'

I nodded to show that I understood, but I didn't, not really.

What's a main office? I wondered.

I walked over towards the window, lifted a hand and peered through the glass. The room overlooked the garden and I could see trees, flowers and houses that seemed to stretch on forever. My heart began to pound and I grabbed the edges of the curtains and pulled them together. It was too much – I'd seen too many things too quickly. Totally overwhelmed, I ran over to the door and pressed my hand flat against it to make sure that it was closed, then I pulled the curtains so that they completely overlapped to block out all the natural light. Only then could I even begin to relax.

Slumping to the floor, I sat in the gloom. I couldn't stand the light – it was too bright and it was too much. I decided that wide-open spaces didn't excite me any more, they terrified me. It might sound weird, but I felt safest when I was enclosed, enveloped in the dark. The outside went on and on, and that frightened me. Outside was too big and too busy, with too many people. I preferred the dark and the cold – that was the world I was used to, not this. Later that day, another staff member stopped by to see me. I almost jumped out of my skin as he knocked at the door and called my name. For a split second, I wondered if it was Dad and if he'd come to get me.

'Hello,' the man smiled as he popped his head around the corner. 'My name is Colin and I've brought you some shoes to wear. Blimey, it's a bit dark in here, isn't it?' he added, striding over to the window to open the curtains.

'Please… please don't!' I begged, putting up a hand to stop him.

Colin seemed a little shocked.

'Sorry, did you want them closed?' he asked, genuinely concerned.

'Yes. I mean, I don't like the light – it's too bright.'

He nodded his head knowingly.

'That's understandable. Now, I've brought you some proper shoes so you can take off those erm... wellington boots.'

Wellington boots? So that's what the strange rubber things were on my feet.

I used my right foot to push the left one off and then did the same with the other foot. Colin knelt down, picked up a wellington and studied it.

'Someone's cut it down into a makeshift shoe,' he said, staring at it in disbelief. 'Anyway, you won't be needing them any more because I've brought you some proper shoes. Tell me, Stephen, do you know how to tie shoelaces?'

I felt a bit stupid as I shook my head and gazed down at the ground.

'Not to worry,' Colin said cheerfully. 'I'll show you how. You're a smart lad, so it won't take you long to learn.'

He spent a little time explaining how to tie and untie my shoelaces so that the shoes were fastened, but not too tight, onto my feet.

'That's it!' he said, finally satisfied I'd mastered it. 'You look a right bobby dazzler in those.'

I smiled, even though I didn't have a clue who Bobby Dazzler was.

That night, I took my first proper bath in a large tub rather than a freezing-cold dip in a tin bath. It was so big, I was frightened I'd slip underneath the water. So big that I felt I was swimming. Colin had left a bunch of soft, fluffy towels hanging up for me to dry myself with. Then he brought me a pair of striped pyjamas. I'd never worn pyjamas before; this was my first ever pair and I was determined to look after them.

I felt so grateful even if I couldn't express it – I wasn't used to such kindness. But the strangest moment came when I went to brush my teeth. I stepped into the bathroom with Colin and saw other boys there as well. Colin handed me a toothbrush and some paste and told me to brush them at the sink. I hung back and watched the others as they turned on something called taps and held their brush underneath a stream of running water.

So that's what those things had been in the kitchen.

Suddenly, everything fell into place. I waited until the bathroom had cleared and approached the sink. Twisting the tap, I turned it on and held the brush underneath the water before lifting it to my mouth. As I began to scrub, I looked up and that's when I saw him: another boy, who was staring straight back at me. I jumped back in surprise, but as I did so, so too did he.

'Hey!' I said, but the boy did the exact same. I stopped, so did he. I began to brush my teeth, so did he. Then I narrowed my eyes and watched as he did the same. He was wearing the same pyjamas as me too. I looked down at mine and back up, just in time to see him do the same.

'What the…?'

I let go of the toothbrush, held it in my mouth and pointed my finger. He did the same. I pressed it forward a little more and a little more until it came to a halt against something solid. Toothbrush spit smeared and dribbled down the surface. I watched in fascination as it poured down. What was it? A window? *No*, I said to myself, shaking my head. The boy was still there and he did the same. I lifted my other hand and ran it through my hair and watched as he copied.

'Hey, weirdo, are you going to be long?' another boy asked as he came into the room. 'Don't hog the sink and stop looking at yourself in the mirror.'

The mirror. This was a mirror… and this boy? The boy was me?

'Sorry, I won't be long,' I mumbled, feeling flustered and more than a little bit foolish.

I put my head down and scrubbed my teeth as fast as I could, but I found it hard to stop staring.

I was thirteen years old and I had just seen myself for the very first time.

CHAPTER 17

A VISION OF HELL

Of course, I didn't tell the others at Ashley House about the mirror or anything else, even though I knew they were desperate to know where I'd come from. I didn't discuss the cellar with anyone either. As far as I was aware, only the staff and the doctor knew. I felt odd enough in this strange new world as it was – the last thing I wanted to do was draw more attention to myself.

I'd been at Ashley House for two days when Colin came upstairs looking for me.

'You have a visitor,' he said, grinning as he popped his head around my bedroom door. 'He's waiting downstairs in the office.'

My heart froze and my feet felt rooted to the spot. It was him, it had to be – I didn't know anyone else.

'Come on, Stephen. Don't keep the gentleman waiting,' Colin added, trying to hurry me along.

As I placed one uncertain foot in front of the other, I felt like one of the condemned men I'd read about on his way to the noose.

If it's him, you can always make a run for it. Remember the door, just open that and run. You'll easily be able to outrun him.

I swallowed down some bile that had risen and scorched the back of my throat. My stomach churned and my legs felt wobbly as I followed Colin down the stairs. In many ways, it was as though I was going back down there, back down into the cellar, only this time it was my footsteps on the stairs, not his.

Ten, nine, eight, seven, six, five, four, three, two, one… I counted silently in my head to try and prepare myself.

'He's just in here…' Colin said, leading the way.

I gulped. This was it; this was where he started to kick off and tell the staff he was taking me home. I walked through the door expecting find his smug face sitting there waiting…

'Hello, Stephen. It's nice to see you again.'

My mouth fell open. It wasn't him but Doctor Robinson – the shrink I'd seen before at the hospital.

'H… hello,' I replied, a little unsure.

What was he doing here?

The doctor led me through to another room, where he asked me to sit down and pulled out a pile of papers from his briefcase.

'I need you to do something for me, Stephen. I've some more things here that I'd like you to read and write. Don't worry, it's nothing too difficult, just a few standard test sheets.'

I was used to doing tests and having my work marked by Dad. I sat down quietly and worked my way through them all. In fact, if I'm honest, I kind of enjoyed them because I liked to use my brain. The shrink even timed me, although I didn't know then what time was or how it was measured. I didn't realise it, but he had given me various tests linked to MENSA and my score had been well above average for an adult, never mind a thirteen-year-old boy. I had achieved a score of over 150 when the average adult score is normally somewhere between 40 and 140.

'It's incredible, he's exceptionally clever,' I overheard Doctor Robinson tell a man who I later found out was the manager of the unit. 'I'd like to bring someone else in to see Stephen, another doctor. I think he would find him absolutely fascinating.'

Doctor Robinson turned to speak to me.

'Tell me Stephen, what were your parents like?'

I shrugged before saying, 'I told you before, my dad used to hit me and my mum disappeared.'

The doctor didn't seem surprised because he'd heard it all before. Not long afterwards, he left, taking my test papers with him. However, a week later, he returned with an older man who looked like a doctor but was wearing a tweed jacket.

'Stephen, this is Doctor Milner,' he explained as the older man looked over with thinly veiled curiosity.

I didn't smile; I didn't do anything, I wasn't sure why I had to see another doctor.

'Tell me, Stephen,' Dr Milner said, 'I hear you like to draw, would you draw a picture for me?'

I sat down and did him a quick sketch as they sat and discussed something over in the corner of the room. I knew that I shouldn't be eavesdropping, but I heard the words 'exceptionally bright' and even 'gifted'. I wasn't sure if they were talking about me or not.

'Yes, he's hyper-creative and intelligent. The tests prove it,' the shrink told Doctor Milner, who nodded in agreement. 'I knew you'd find him fascinating.'

I wasn't sure how old Doctor Milner was, but he looked to be in his early fifties at the very least. He had leather patches on the elbows of his jacket and was smoking what I later discovered was called a pipe. I'd never seen anyone smoke before and I didn't even know what a pipe was. He puffed on it, tapped and emptied it and then refilled it, repeating the process over again, I sat open mouthed in fascination. Then Doctor Milner led me over to a small table.

'Tell me, Stephen,' he said, pausing to take a long drag on his pipe as he sat there studying me. 'Tell me, why were you kept in a cellar?'

I shrugged my shoulders.

'I don't know, he just kept me down there.'

'I see, and, by him, you mean your father?'

I nodded again.

'Tell me about your parents.'

At this, I rolled my eyes before saying matter-of-factly, 'There's nothing much to tell. My mum disappeared one day and I never saw her again.'

'When was that?'

I watched as a blueish-grey curl of smoke from his pipe rose high into the air. It stretched and then spread out like a long finger.

'Erm, I don't know. When I was ten, I think. But I don't know for sure because I didn't know how old I was. I didn't have a clock down there, you see.'

Doctor Milner nodded, his heavy black-framed glasses glinting in the light as he did so.

'And your father, what did he do to you? Did he ever touch you sexually?' His mouth revealed a row of small, brown, discoloured teeth as he said the word 'sexually'.

I felt my face grow hot.

'No, no, nothing like that. He hit me, he hit me all the time, but he never touched me like that.'

I was shocked and appalled.

How could he even think something like that?

They left together, but Doctor Milner took my sketch with him.

'Very good, very good,' he mumbled as he shoved the paper deep inside his briefcase.

I wondered why he'd found me so fascinating: was it because I'd lived in a cellar?

★ ★ ★

Although I'd refused to tell any of the other boys where I'd come from, I soon learned their stories. Ashley House was a holding unit for boys who had been sent from all over the Midlands. Some had been abused by their families, while others had been sent straight from court after committing a crime, such as burglaries or taking and driving a car away without consent. There were others who had been dispatched there from foster homes because they'd been too disruptive. I wondered if I might see Andrew or Billy at Ashley House, but I never did. Later, I discovered they'd been fostered out. But I never was – the social workers didn't even try. I overheard a social worker say I was too 'feral' to be fostered or adopted. She later explained to me that feral meant I couldn't fit into another family because I didn't know what it was to be part of one. I was upset. I was being punished because of what my father had done to me. I didn't see my siblings again – well, apart from Andrew – but that was many years later.

I knew from the moment I walked through the door at the unit that I was different to the other boys in there. All the staff and both doctors seemed fascinated by me. In many ways, I felt like an animal in one of the zoos I'd read about. For the first week or so, I walked around in a daze. There were people – too many people – and they all talked quickly and at once. Sometimes I had to cover my ears because I could barely concentrate.

I was taken to another room that was different to the others. This one had a large square called a television that stood over in the corner. I was mesmerised by the TV and soon I couldn't stop watching it. TV time was usually rationed, but one evening, one of the staff turned it on so that we could all watch something called *Doctor Who*. It was a programme about a time traveller, and all the kids, myself included, sat there glued to it. There were about thirty boys at Ashley House and most were in a dormitory together. Again, I was the odd one out because I had been given my own room.

'So, where is it you came from?' one of the lads asked as the credits for *Doctor Who* rolled up the TV screen. 'Everyone says you must have come from borstal or something.'

I decided that I wouldn't tell him a thing. By now, I was getting used to batting away awkward questions.

'A social worker brought me here,' I told him.

Nothing more, nothing less.

I already felt like a freak with the staff and the doctor – I didn't want more of the same from the other kids. In a way, to me it felt weirder, much weirder, being kept inside a home with so many children, than being in a cellar on my own.

'I'm here because I stole a car,' the lad told me.

I wasn't sure if I was supposed to be impressed or not.

'Oh right,' I said, shrugging it off as though it was nothing.

My heart would start to race and my mouth would go bone-dry whenever anyone tried to ask me something personal – I didn't know how or where to even begin.

Hi, my name's Stephen. I can't tell the time, but the doctor tells me I'm gifted. Oh, and by the way, I've lived in a cellar for as long as I can remember.

Instead, I sat back, kept quiet and watched how the other boys behaved. I also listened intently whenever the staff gave out times for dinner, TV or bedtime. I used these times to try and work out the numbers on the clock on the wall. I was ashamed to admit that, at thirteen years old, I didn't know how to tell the time.

A week or two after his last visit, the shrink arrived again, only this time he had the social worker with him. The three of us travelled in her car to a hospital where Doctor Milner worked, a place called Aston Hall. The shrink and social worker led me into Doctor Milner's office and the three of them sat in a corner of a room discussing me. Again, I heard the odd couple of words although I couldn't quite work out what it was they were saying. I overheard the shrink say 'hyper-creative and hyper-intelligent', but again I didn't have a clue if he was referring to me or not. Every so often, Doctor Milner would look up from the group and glance over. Eventually, they stopped talking and he crossed the room to speak to me.

'I wonder, Stephen, if you could do something for me?'

I looked up expectantly, waiting to see what it was he wanted me to do.

'Could you draw me another picture? I'll fetch you some pens and a piece of paper. Would you do that for me?'

I nodded; I loved drawing and so I didn't need to be asked twice.

'What do you want me to draw?' I asked, picking up one of the pencils.

'Oh, anything. Draw me anything you like,' he said with a wave of his hand.

Doctor Milner sat on the other side of the big wooden table and watched as I drew him a monster. I drew something similar to Frankenstein's monster – made up from different body parts of people – as he looked on with fascination. I'd never seen or read the book; my Frankenstein monster had sprung from my own overactive imagination.

'Oh, very good. Very good,' he murmured, standing over me. I felt a swell of pride in my chest.

'Tell me, Stephen,' he said, holding up the drawing for closer inspection, 'why did you draw that?'

'You said I could draw anything I wanted, so I drew a monster.'

'I see,' he said, sitting down opposite me again. He rested his elbows thoughtfully against the table and I realised that was why he probably had large leather elbow patches stitched to his jacket. Doctor Milner was staring at me so intently now that I had to look away. I suddenly felt really uncomfortable sitting there with this creepy old doctor, who asked strange questions about my dad and looked at me like that.

'And do you like monsters?'

I thought for a moment and nodded.

'I like to draw them.'

'And what about your father, do you think he was a monster?'

I wasn't sure what to say, so I said nothing. I was worried I'd get into trouble if I said the wrong thing because I felt much happier here, and I was scared I'd be punished and put back down in the cellar.

There was a moment's silence between us that was interrupted by a tap at the door.

'Come in!' Doctor Milner called.

A tall man with blond hair, a small beard and a moustache came into the room. It was obvious that he was a male version of a nurse from the uniform he wore. He stood at the side, towering over me.

'You're in a hospital called Aston Hall,' Doctor Milner explained to me. 'You'll be going to Beech Ward, where you will stay. We will look after you now.'

I looked over towards the shrink and the social worker, waiting for them to say something, to try and intervene, but they remained silent. It was clear that I had no choice in the matter.

'Come on, follow me,' the male nurse said as Doctor Milner nodded towards the door in a signal for me to leave.

I didn't know what to do, so I did as I was told. I'd only been at Ashley House for a matter of weeks, but now I'd moved again – this time to this strange hospital with the strange doctor. I looked at the nurse as I followed him out of the room and along the corridor. I heard a jangling sound as he walked and realised he had a bunch of keys attached to his belt.

'Come on, hurry up! We're gonna look after you from now

on,' he said as he proceeded to unlock, open and then lock doors behind us. 'You'll even go to school here…'

A feeling of dread flooded the pit of my stomach. I couldn't explain it, but it felt wrong – all wrong. I'd gone from a noisy house full of kids to a hospital where the staff unlocked and locked doors as they passed through them.

If this is a hospital then why does he have keys? I wondered.

The male nurse, who I later found out was called Keith Collins, wore a white coat like a doctor, but he didn't seem like any doctor I'd met before. Instead, he was abrupt and aggressive.

'Come on, hurry up, I haven't got all day!' he nagged as I lagged behind.

Suddenly he came to an abrupt halt.

'In here,' he ordered.

I followed him inside another office.

'Stand on there,' he barked as he adjusted a metal weight along a long metal line.

'Why?' I asked, even though I was a little wary of him.

'I need to weigh and measure you for the doctor.'

He made a note of my weight and then told me to stand against a long pole with another sliding piece of metal that he rested against the top of my head. He made a note of that and we left the office. I followed him upstairs to what he called a 'dormitory'. As I did so, I spotted two doors at the side, leading to what I presumed must have been other rooms. The dormitory itself was massive and I felt my heart sink when I spotted all the windows. It was light – *too light*. There were lots of beds, too. I tried to count them quickly.

Ten. I was certain that I'd counted ten beds on one side,

which meant there must be twenty in the room. *Twenty beds in one room!*

'This one's yours,' he said, striding over to the fourth bed on the right. But I wasn't listening, because I was distracted by a strange screaming noise coming from outside. It was the sound I'd expect a pack of wounded animals to make. The dormitory windows were open, but only by about an inch or so because they'd been nailed that way. But they were enough ajar to allow the terrifying screams to come flooding in.

The nurse gestured a hand down towards a small metal locker positioned next to the bed.

'That's where you'll store your things, and down there,' he said, pointing towards the end of the room, 'is the toilet.'

But I wasn't listening. My mind was still preoccupied, my ears following the screams as they drifted in underneath the gap in the window. I walked over to the one by my bed and looked out. What I saw in that moment still haunts me to this day. Outside, there was what can only be described as a cage – a kind of caged tennis court with a wire roof – and it was full of boys and men aged around thirteen to seventy years old. Some were completely naked and openly masturbating. Others wore helmets, presumably for their own safety, as they proceeded to bash their heads off the concrete floor. Some were trussed up in fabric that had tied their hands and arms to their bodies, something I later found out was called a straitjacket. Some spat at each other, while others hit and punched each other. Then there were the other men – the ones who just sat or knelt, rocking back and forth. But it was their screams that buzzed inside my head, like the screams and howls of wild animals.

I felt someone standing close up behind me. I tried to turn, but couldn't. Someone was there, pinning me against the window: it was the nurse.

'You be a good boy,' he whispered, his hot breath brushing against the skin of my ear as he hissed into it. 'You behave yourself, otherwise we'll put you in there with those loonies and you wouldn't want that, would you? A nice boy like you, they'd tear you to pieces.'

CHAPTER 18

MUSIC

The dormitory at Aston Hall felt too hot, with lots of windows open, just not open wide enough. I realised that they had nailed them open only a fraction to stop the boys from throwing themselves out or escaping through the windows on the ground floor. The keys on the nurse's belt clanked and tinkled against each other as he turned away from me and the vision of hell outside.

'Come on,' he ordered, 'time for dinner.'

But I couldn't shake the horror of what I'd just seen from my mind.

'What was that... I mean, who were those people back there?' I asked, my hand still pointing behind me over towards the window. I ran to try to keep up with him as he marched along the corridor.

As he stopped and turned to face me, a sickening leer played on his lips.

'People? They're not people, they're loonies!' he exclaimed.

'And if you don't behave that's where you'll end up – with them lot on Elm Ward.'

'Elm Ward?' I repeated blankly.

'Yes, Elm Ward is where they put the real nutters. Oh, and any lads who don't do as they are told,' he said, stubbing a fat finger against my chest. 'So behave, and don't ask too many questions, otherwise that will get you into trouble,' he said, lifting his finger from my chest to my mouth.

With that, I was led downstairs. He unlocked and then locked doors as we passed through them. Finally, we reached a communal area or 'common room' packed with boys, all of a similar age to me. Some were slightly older, with the eldest being about seventeen years old. I spotted another door that led through to the kitchen, which was where the dining area was. There were the sound and smells of food being served as boys of all ages took their places at a long row of tables: they were serving up dinner. I looked around at the other 'patients'. There didn't seem to be anything obviously wrong with them to say we were all in a hospital, but then there wasn't much wrong with me and I'd been put in there, too.

What sort of hospital is this? I wondered.

No one had any broken bones, bandages or any obvious injuries, I thought as I sat down in a spare seat at the end of a table. I was still thinking about it when someone placed a massive plate of mashed potatoes, pie and beans down in front of me. My stomach rumbled, reminding me that I hadn't eaten in hours. I picked up a knife and fork resting on the table and dug straight in. I'd expected questions from the other kids; I'd expected them to bombard me, asking me where I'd come from, but strangely no one seemed interested. In a way, I felt relieved.

Maybe this place is so mad that you just don't stand out here?

As I was eating, a male nurse came around with a trayful of medicine that he handed out to various kids. I looked at their faces: some had no expression at all, just a vacant stare as though they had no idea where they were. As the days passed, I realised most of them had been drugged with either tablets or a brown syrup – a type of chemical cosh, called Largactil – and we were patients, but we were patients inside a mental hospital called Aston Hall.

I decided to keep myself to myself for the first week or so. At least no one had hit me or broken anything yet.

Maybe it wasn't so bad?

But the constant screams coming from Elm Ward were enough to give me nightmares and keep me on my toes.

One day, a group of older lads approached as I sat reading in the common room.

'So, where did you come from then?' one of the older ones demanded to know.

From the way the others stood back from him and let him do all the talking, I didn't get a good feeling about him. I looked up and then back down at my book – I didn't want any trouble.

'You deaf or summat?' he said, thumping the underneath of the book in my hands so that it closed shut and I lost my page. The others laughed. 'I said, where are you from? Where were you before?'

I watched as he puffed up his chest and tried to make himself seem bigger than he actually was.

'My parents used to beat me up,' I replied, turning my attention back to my book.

The boy pulled a funny face and drew a sharp intake of breath.

'Beat you up, did they? You hear that? They beat him up!' he grinned as the others pissed themselves laughing. 'Aww, and did they hurt you?'

I ignored him.

'Hey,' he said, punching me square in the chest, 'did they hurt you like this?'

The force of his fist made me fall backwards in my chair, but I knew he couldn't hurt me. No one could hurt me – my old man had beaten me so much, no one could even come close.

'Or, like this,' he continued, hitting me in the side of the face.

I knew it was fight or flight time, kill or be killed. I felt a rage build up inside me. I'd had a lifetime of being someone else's punch bag, but not any more. I allowed the lad to punch me for a few more minutes with his weedy fists. He couldn't even come close to the violence and beatings I'd suffered over the years. Then, once he'd used up all his energy, I exploded. My book sailed high in the air as I launched myself at him. It took everyone by surprise, particularly him, as I kicked and punched back as hard as I could. Soon we were a squabbling mess on the floor. The other lads circled us and began to chant:

'Fight... fight... fight...!'

The noise brought two male nurses, who came running over as the group parted to let them through.

'Right, that's it! Break it up,' said one as he pulled me away from the boy. But by now I was a screaming ball of anger and I couldn't help myself. Eager for more, I tried to throw myself back at him.

192

'Stop that! Stop that, if you know what's good for you!'

The group fell silent as everyone felt the threat of what he'd just said. A view of the cage and of Elm Ward flashed through my mind. I stopped immediately and wiped my bloodied nose with the edge of my sleeve.

'That's it, cool down,' one of the nurses said, as he separated and led us to different parts of the common room. The other lads looked over at me strangely; whatever they'd expected, it hadn't been that. I was only thirteen, but I could fight as well as the rest of them.

After that day, I had a bit of name-calling and the odd push or shove in the corridor, but the message must have got through because it soon reached the point where no one bothered me any more. Instead, I became known as the weird kid whose parents beat him up, which suited me fine.

I decided not to tell anyone about the cellar. I'd spoken to the other boys, yet no one, only me, had been locked in a cellar. Most of them had come from foster care or again, as with Ashley House, they'd been to court for stealing cars or starting fires. There was only one similarity between us and that was that no one seemed to have parents who gave a shit about them. I was different in many ways and not only because of the cellar, but because I seemed to be far more educated than the others. The school at Aston Hall was within the grounds and a male nurse would escort us over there in the mornings. But while everyone else was struggling with basic books like *Peter and Jane*, I was reading advanced stuff – books that the adults would read. In fact, I read so much so quickly that within the first two weeks I had worked my way through the entire library, that's how desperate I was to learn. One of the male nurses noticed and decided to bring me in some of his own books from home. He was a decent man, much younger than the others, and he was called Mr Bradbury

'Do you like Tom Sharpe books, Stephen?' he asked me one day as I sat in the common room.

'I've never heard of him,' I answered truthfully.

With that, he pulled out a bag and handed me a couple of books. Sure enough, there was Tom Sharpe's name written on the front cover.

'Let me know if you like them because I've plenty more of those.'

I was so thrilled to have been given a 'present', even if was only a loan of books, that I guarded them with my life. After that, Mr Bradbury brought me in different types of books, written by different authors, including *The Hobbit* by J.R.R. Tolkien, which I read first. I enjoyed it so much that he brought me in some 'harder' occult novels, including some by Dennis Wheatley and another one called *Malleus Maleficarum*. Usually translated as the *Hammer of Witches*, *Malleus Maleficarum* was written by a Catholic clergyman, Henrich Kramer, all about witchcraft. I was fascinated by it, even though large parts had been written in Latin. I didn't know anything about Latin, so I armed myself with a dictionary and began to work my way through the book, looking up words I didn't know or couldn't understand. Afterwards, I developed a real interest in the occult. I had been portraying the devil in my drawings for years, even though I hadn't known that was what he was actually called. I'd just wrapped him up into one huge package and that had been him – my dad.

Mr Bradbury was much trendier than the other male nurses; he had long brown curly hair, was really tall and he wore glasses. He was also the most decent member of staff. I knew that he must have heard my story – the one about being locked in the cellar – because he seemed extra kind to me.

'Tell me, Stephen,' he said, sitting down next to me in the day room one afternoon, 'do you like music?'

I looked up from the book I was reading.

'What's music?' I asked, staring blankly at him.

He reeled backwards in his chair as though I'd just smacked him clean in the face.

'What, seriously? You don't know what music is?'

I shook my head.

'No.'

He gasped out loud in astonishment.

'Right, tomorrow, I'm going to bring you some records in…' He stopped and waved his hands in front of himself, 'Err, I don't suppose you know what records are, either?'

'No.'

'Well, tomorrow, I'm going to bring you some rec… I mean, I'm going to bring you some music in, and Stephen…' he paused and looked me straight in the eye, '…it's going to blow your mind!'

The following morning, I was sat reading in the day room when Mr Bradbury came over. I noticed that he was carrying a large, square, red and cream box in his hands. His knuckles flashed white as he gripped the edges of it. He sat down on a chair by the window opposite the coffee table that was still littered with books. Holding out a flat palm, he pushed them over to one side and then slid the red and cream box onto the table. I watched him plug something in and open some metal catches before lifting the lid.

'Okay, Stephen, this is called a record player. You play records on it. Hang on,' he said, holding up a finger to stop himself. He pulled out a series of flat square things with pictures on the front from a bag.

'Records,' he explained, sliding one from its packet.

I sat up as he placed the shiny black circle on the record player and pulled a lever. The record spun around and around so fast that I found it hard to follow with my eyes.

'Now,' he said, taking a seat next to mine, 'just listen.'

A cream-coloured plastic arm lifted itself and drifted up and along towards the edge of the record before dropping down onto it. There was slight crackling sound from the front as a sudden noise began to flood the room – a wonderful noise, loud, bold and in your face. A noise more beautiful and breathtaking than any other sound I'd heard before. A noise that made me fall back in my chair and close my eyes so that I could absorb and savour every single part of it. I was overwhelmed. It was as though someone had reached inside my chest and grabbed my beating heart inside a clenched fist. For the first time in my life I felt alive, truly alive. If this was music, then he was right, I was hooked!

'Well, what do you think?' he asked a moment after the track – 'Race With The Devil' by the band Gun – had finished.

I'd been staring into the middle distance and listening so intently, it took me a few seconds to register that he was still sitting there.

'Can we play it again?'

Mr Bradbury chuckled and played the rest of the album

– both sides – while I read the record sleeve. The artwork seemed strikingly similar to my own. It reminded me of all the monsters and devils I'd sketched during those cold and lonely years down in the cellar. It was as though, through music and art, something had spoken to me like nothing or no one else had been able to up until now. Instead, I just sat there with my mouth gaping, my mind completely blown.

CHAPTER 19

TREATMENT

After listening to the Gun album on repeat, Mr Bradbury changed it for another, an album by Black Sabbath, called *Vol 4*. Just when I thought it couldn't get any better, he followed it up with Hawkwind's *Roadhawks*. I loved them all, but every time I listened to Gun's 'Race With The Devil' song, my skin prickled because it was as though it had been written about me and him. I sang along:

> *...Strange things happen*
> *If you stay*
> *The devil will*
> *Catch you anyway...*

The music Mr Bradbury had brought in for me changed me in more ways than one, and my interest in the occult and all things devil took a stronger turn, so much so that while the other lads did finger paintings and prints with halves of potatoes, I drew witches, dragons and dwarves living in caves with a kiln.

One day, I'd been standing in school assembly alongside the other kids, including some girls from the hospital's Laburnum Ward. We all faced towards the stage, which had the staff members of Aston Hall school standing along it in a long line. I was minding my own business, tuning out from one of them who had been droning on about nothing, when the headmistress climbed down some steps from the stage and proceeded to walk towards our group. I was just beginning to wonder what she was doing when she appeared and stood right in front of me. Without saying a word, she lifted her hand and slapped me so hard across the face that she knocked me clean off my feet. The other children looked on open mouthed, wondering what I'd done wrong, and so did I. Up until that point, I'd barely had anything to do with her. I was just staggering to my feet when she struck me again. Confused and dumbstruck, I lay on the floor.

What the hell have you done wrong? the voice asked.

But I didn't know. I was just clambering to my feet a third time when she raised her hand again. At that moment another staff member came running over, intervened and led her away.

The headmistress had decided – for whatever reason – that I must be punished and she'd punished me all right, in front of the entire school. But I still couldn't work out what I'd done wrong, until, a few days later, I overheard one of the teachers say the headmistress had called my drawings 'satanic' and said 'someone needed to beat the devil out of me'. By this time, I was so far ahead of the rest of the class that my teachers had pretty much left me to my own devices. Unlike the others, I was allowed to bring in my own books to read and paper and pencils to draw. At some point the headmistress must have seen my artwork and had decided to do something about it. Thankfully, not all the staff members had felt the same. In fact, Mr Bradbury loved my drawings so much, I gifted him around twenty or thirty of them.

'Thanks, Stephen. These are absolutely brilliant!' he grinned as I handed them over.

In return, he fed my thirst for music – all music, as long as it was good. Looking back, I feel blessed that he wasn't a Nolans or Abba fan, because I loved heavy metal and rock. In turn, it became my salvation, my escape from the real world and a place I'd regularly visit through art and music. Mr Bradbury brought me more albums by bands such as Deep Purple, Jethro Tull, Yes and Creedence Clearwater Revival. He opened my eyes to a new and much bigger world than the one I'd previously existed in. Guitars soon became my new obsession, so he brought in an acoustic one for me to practise on. I didn't know how to play it, so he brought me a book of guitar chords and I soon got to work, learning a whole new skill. Soon, my hands moved up and down the fret board. The scars on them were still visible, but at least now I'd discovered something new – something that not only brought joy, but a whole host of new possibilities into my life. For the first time, I felt as though I actually had a future.

Of course, I guarded my record player with my life. I wouldn't leave it alone, not for a second, not even when I went to the toilet – as if it was the Crown Jewels. I was petrified that someone would take it from me, so I carried it and my records with me everywhere I went. Even when I went to bed at night, it was there, right by my side. Everyone knew it was mine and I wouldn't let anyone else other than me or Mr Bradbury touch it.

My other vice was cigarettes. I'd begun to smoke within weeks of arriving at Aston Hall and, after a shaky start of coughs and splutters, I'd turned into quite an accomplished smoker. Everyone smoked at Aston Hall because the staff constantly gave us fags even though we were still children. Looking back, I think they probably did it to keep us quiet. It was the early 1970s, and things weren't so health conscious as they are today. Instead, everyone smoked whenever and wherever they liked. We were given five bob every week, which we got to spend in the tuck shop. I say 'tuck shop', but it was more a shop on wheels – a small wooden trolley, to be precise. However, more importantly, the trolley sold fags. It sold them by the packet and singles, so I spent all my money on them. Everyone smoked at Aston Hall, from boys as young as ten to those aged seventeen. Fights would often break out and I wondered if they gave us medicine and fags to keep us calm and sedated.

The night staff nurse was a man called Mr Swan. Like Mr Bradbury, he was a decent chap who would give me free fags whenever I made him a cup of Ovaltine, which was his favourite. All of us were handed a cup of Ovaltine to drink at night, but I'd make him a cup in the kitchen to earn myself some extra cigarettes. Mr Swan called me Smudger. I have no idea why, but it soon became my nickname.

'Smudger, go in the kitchen and make us a cup. I'll give you a Black Cat if you do.'

It was music to my ears: Black Cat cigarettes were my absolute favourites and his cigarette of choice.

At night, once the lights had been turned off there was talk amongst the boys about something they called 'treatment'. Some lads had only had one, but others had undergone multiple treatments. By now, I'd become good friends with a small group of lads. There was Neil, Robert and Michael. Michael was bald as an egg and extremely sensitive about his lack of hair. He wore a very bad blond wig, which earned him the nickname 'Strawman'. Some of the other lads would try and snatch the wig from his head whenever he passed by, and when that happened Michael would go crazy with rage. I didn't understand what had happened to him or why he had no hair, but I didn't care. He was my friend, so if anyone went near or tried to pull the wig from his head, I would give them a slap.

Most of these lads had been there longer than me and would often talk about how they'd been for treatment.

'But what is it, what happens?' I asked, desperate to know so that I could prepare myself.

I watched as their eyes flitted to each other; no one wanted to say what the treatment was or what happened during it. Whatever it was, I knew it couldn't be as awful as being locked inside a cellar.

'Come on, I mean it can't be that bad, surely?' I said, starting to laugh.

It was Robert who piped up first.

'He touches your knob, Steve. Doctor Milner…he gives you drugs and then he does things to you. He touches you and your knob.'

I looked around the rest of the group for confirmation but their faces and the way they shifted awkwardly told me everything I needed to know. Young lads, barely out of puberty, lost and trapped inside their own personal hell of what Milner had done to them.

'No, you're having me on. He doesn't touch your knob!' I laughed. This had to be a wind-up. 'This is a joke, right?'

Michael looked over at me and shook his head.

'It's not, Steve. He does things to you in the treatment room. He does more to some than he does to others, but nearly everyone in here has had treatment.'

I was stunned, but no one wanted to say any more and then someone quickly changed the subject.

Another lad called Chris had been there almost a year longer than I had, I'd only been there a few weeks.

'Have you ever had treatment, Chris?' I asked him one day as we hung out together in the common room.

Chris's eyes widened. He solemnly laid his playing cards down on the table and looked over at me.

'I've had it three times, but most lads, well, they've only had it once. It depends who he's picked.'

'But how do you know, Chris? I mean, how do you know if Milner had picked you?' I persisted.

'Oh, you know alright. They tell you and then you're not allowed to have any tea.' Chris lifted his hand and tried to demonstrate. 'He puts this wire mask on your face and it sends you to sleep – that's why they don't let you eat anything before treatment in case you're sick and choke on it.'

I stared at him in disbelief, my mouth gaping open.

'Choke? Why? Has anyone actually choked…and died?'

He picked his playing cards back up and stared down intently at them.

'I don't know, but lads, well…' he said, shrugging, a hand to the side of his face, 'they disappear all the time.'

'What do you mean?'

Chris laid a flush of cards down on the table, but he wasn't triumphant and instead just sighed.

'Some lads never come back from treatment. There's stories, too. Stories that some have drowned in the River Trent, trying to escape Aston Hall and Doctor Milner.'

I must have looked completely baffled because he decided to elaborate. He told me about a cart that I'd seen driving around the hospital. It pulled lots of other carts containing food and delivered them to individual wards.

'There used to be a black van that drove around collecting all the dead bodies, but everyone started to freak out when they saw it, so they changed it.'

Now it was my turn to look at him.

'Changed?'

'Yes, they started using these carts to transport food, then fresh linen, and now we think they use them to move dead bodies between the wards.'

I snorted out loud.

'Don't be daft! You're having a laugh, there's no dead bodies. There can't be…' I guffawed, even though I was suddenly starting to doubt everything.

I realised I was in a hospital but Aston Hall was a special hospital where they locked up so-called 'mental defectives' – that's what they had labelled us. The other lads told me that Doctor Milner carried out these treatments to try and work out what made us behave in the way we did. That's why all the boys on my ward were routinely drugged up, so that he could do whatever he wanted to them.

'You heard about Mark though, didn't you?' Chris said, snapping me back into the moment.

'Who's Mark?'

'He was one of the lads here. He was only thirteen, but he did a runner one day – ran off through the woods or something.'

All ears, I sat up in my chair: 'And what happened? What happened to him?'

Chris widened his eyes dramatically as he began to elaborate.

'Well, he was here because he stole cars, that's what he did. Anyway, once he'd cleared the woods or whatever, he must have reached town because that's when he stole a car. He hotwired it or something.'

'And what happened to him? Did they catch him?'

He shook his head.

'Well, that was it, you see. The police spotted him and started to give chase, but Mark put his foot down and went faster and faster. He didn't want to come back here, you see; he didn't want to be brought back to Milner. Anyway, he was so busy trying to get away that he lost control of the car. Well, that's what some people say but I'm not sure I believe it.'

'Why?' I shrugged. 'Why don't you believe it?'

'Because he crashed the car straight into a tree, head-on. I reckon he did it on purpose rather than come back here. You see, Steve, this Mark… well, he'd already had lots of treatments and I just don't think he could face any more.'

A chill ran through me as I thought of Mark and all the other boys who Doctor Milner had drugged up and touched.

I wondered if the doctor would pick me and if so, how long it would be before it happened. That night, I couldn't sleep. When I finally drifted off, my dreams were full of Milner and the horrible things the other boys had said he'd done to them.

As it turned out, I didn't have to wait very long because three weeks after I arrived, I was told that I'd been chosen.

'No tea for you tonight, you're having treatment,' a staff member called Simon Abbot told me. Abbot was a real nasty bastard and I could almost detect the sense of glee in his voice.

'Me?' I asked, double checking that he'd not mixed me up with another lad.

'Yes, Smith, you.'

I knew better than to argue: Abbot and the other male nurse, Collins, were renowned for taking lads into the toilets and giving them a good hiding, so I decided not to argue or answer back.

'Michael,' I whispered over to him in the day room that afternoon, 'Milner's picked me, I'm having treatment tonight.'

The look of pity in his eyes almost killed me more than the fear of having the actual treatment itself.

'What's it like, Michael? What's he going to do to me?'

'It's gonna fuck you up, Steve. He's going to hit you or touch your knob, but there's absolutely nothing you can do about it because you'll be drugged up.'

A few hours later, after everyone else had eaten, I was called to go for treatment. A male nurse handed me two white tablets and an hour later, I was taken upstairs to the treatment room in one of the side rooms – the doors I'd seen – near the dormitories. That first time, I was stripped naked and told to lie down on a mattress on the floor. It had a hospital sheet on it, but underneath the mattress was covered with a thicker, rubber cover.

'Wait there. Doctor Milner will be here soon.'

My heart was pounding as I took in the rest of the room. There wasn't much in it other than a single window, but that had been boarded up and someone had drilled inch-wide holes into the plywood, which forced shafts of light to peek through. That was the only source of light, the rest of the room was dark and gloomy. In many ways, it was like being back in the cellar. My palms felt clammy when I thought of it and my dad, and how he'd beaten me black and blue for years.

Would Milner do that to me now?

My breath became shallow as I heard footsteps approach the room from outside. They grew louder as they neared the door.

It was him. It was Milner!

Maybe this is your new home? Maybe Milner's going to start locking you up here, like he did? Maybe he's waiting outside with Milner? the voice said. It had returned and I wondered if it was because this small, dark room reminded me so much of my former home. Not that it worried me; in fact, bizarrely, I found some small comfort in it. I was so used to small enclosed spaces that they didn't freak me out half as much as wide open areas.

Minutes later, Doctor Milner appeared in the doorway. He was wearing a white coat with a couple of pens tucked inside the breast pocket. As he entered, he pushed something into the room: a white trolley with a tray on top. On that sat a kidney-shaped dish with a needle in it. I watched as he picked up the needle and screwed it onto a plunger and container before filling it with some fluid. He glanced down at me, lying on the mattress, and then back at the needle. Pressing the plunger upwards, he waited until some liquid had squirted out of the top of it, then picked up something else – a wire mask. He opened up the front of it and popped a piece of gauze into it with his fingers. The needle loomed large in front of my eyes as he came over towards me. Even though I was semi-prepared from what the boys had already told me, I was terrified.

Your knob, don't let him touch your knob! the voice screamed.

I flinched as he wrapped a tight rubber tube around the top of my arm and pushed the needle deep into my flesh. He applied so much pressure and had plunged the needle in so deep, I was certain it would come out of the other side. Although I was used to pain, this was something else – this stung as though the injection was burning itself up and through my bloodstream. Despite everything my dad had done to me, I have never experienced pain like it before or since. I waited to see what he would do next, but just as I did, he withdrew the needle and two nurses came into the room and proceeded to tie my hands and knees together with pieces of old, greying bandage. I wanted to fight – to fight them off – but the injection had left me dizzy, light-headed, and without any strength to protest. Suddenly, a loud buzzing started up inside my ears. I shook my head from side to side but it wouldn't go away. Milner came back into sight and placed the wire mask on my face.

DRIP, DRIP, DRIP!

There was a strong smell of chemicals and my nostrils flared as a liquid soaked down onto it.

'Tell me, Stephen,' Milner asked, suddenly looming into view, 'what did your father do to you?'

I tried to answer, but the injection had left me frozen. I felt dead, lying there on the mattress.

DRIP, DRIP, DRIP!

'Did he do anything to you?' he continued, his breath hot against my skin as I felt it cling to my face and neck. His teeth were small, childlike, and stained brown through tobacco. 'Did he do… did he do anything sexual to you?' he leered.

DRIP, DRIP, DRIP!

'N… n… noooo!' I mumbled, my mouth frozen with the chemical as it sank down onto my skin and then underneath it.

DRIP, DRIP, DRIP!

'So, tell me again, did he…'

Milner's voice trailed off as the room faded and everything went blank.

Back in my bed in the dormitory, I tried to move but my legs felt like jelly. I could feel a chafing from where the bandages had rubbed me – where I'd been tied – but other than that, I had no obvious injuries only a banging headache and I felt dizzy. My arm also hurt like hell and didn't stop throbbing for hours.

'What was it like?' Robert asked when I saw him later.

'The injection was the worst part. It really, really hurt…' I said, wincing at the memory.

'But did he, you know,' he said, checking behind him to make sure that no one was listening, 'did he touch you, you know?'

I knew exactly what he meant.

'No, no… Well, at least I don't think so. I passed out. He asked me some questions and then I passed out.'

Robert nodded knowingly.

'Thank God for that,' he said, patting me on the arm before turning and walking away.

But his question left me wondering.

Had Milner touched me? How would I know?

I shook my head. *Of course he hadn't!* But I couldn't be sure, not really.

★ ★ ★

A fortnight later, I was called for treatment again. Unlike before, at least this time I was given a white hospital gown to cover myself with. The last time I'd been completely naked. Once again, I had the deep injection, but I didn't just have one, I had two – one in each arm. I couldn't be sure, but I wondered if they were different drugs; I wondered if he was mixing them and trying out different combinations to see what worked best. Again, my hands and knees were tied together and then Milner placed the mask on my face.

DRIP, DRIP, DRIP!

His ferret-like face zoomed in as he asked me one question after another.

'Did you hate your father?'

I tried to reply, but whatever he'd given me had stolen away my voice.

DRIP, DRIP, DRIP!

'Where did he touch you?'

I gasped a lungful of air to try and answer.

'But he didn't… he hit meeeeeee…'

I felt the pressure of the mask as he pushed it down on my face.

DRIP, DRIP, DRIP!

My eyelids grew heavy and I struggled to stay awake, to try and keep alert to see what he was going to do to me.

You have to fight this, you have to fight him off! Don't let him touch you!

Again, I awoke back in my dormitory bed. My hands and knees had been untied but this time my backside felt sore, as though it was on fire.

'Ouch!' I winced, the pain making my eyes water. My skin smarted as it brushed against the bed sheet. I lifted the bed covers and peeked underneath, but I couldn't see anything.

It's on the backs of your legs – your legs and bum, the voice said.

I turned onto my side, twisted my neck and tried to look down, pulling the hospital gown up so I could see. Staring down at myself, I shook my head in disbelief.

No! You're seeing things, you must be.

My fingers traced along the bright red skin but I flinched underneath my own touch as there, right across my backside and the tops of legs, was something I'd seen many times before. I'd seen it in the cellar, but not here, not until now. As I glanced down at the big, angry red and purple welts covering my thighs and backside, I began to shake. I'd been whipped by Doctor Milner, flogged using a belt or a cane, or something that had inflicted maximum damage to my skin. Milner had done this to me: he had drugged and whipped me like a dog. I didn't think it possible. I'd always thought my father had been the devil, but I'd just met someone far, far worse.

CHAPTER 20

ELECTRIC SHOCK BOYS

However bad things seemed, I kept telling myself that at least I wasn't locked up inside the cage outside Elm Ward. I'd hear them cry and howl all day, every day. I'd see them through the window. They'd be out in all weathers – some naked, some clothed – hitting, biting, punching, spitting and ripping chunks out of each other. Masturbating, and not caring where they were or who saw; they were treated no better than animals in a zoo. Whenever I answered back, nurse Collins would press my face flat against the cool window pane and point me towards the cage with the same warning: 'Be careful, otherwise we'll put you in with the loonies.'

He and others used it as a threat for us to behave. But as time passed and the more familiar I became with the Aston Hall regime, the more I began to rebel. Simon Abbot, the big male nurse, was a particular bastard. We had to clean the floor with huge polishers. When I first arrived, they had heavy manual ones, but soon switched to electric versions. These were still awkward to use and equally heavy. If you didn't clean the floor quickly or fast enough then you'd be punished. Abbot would drag you outside, put a sponge in your hand and make you clean every inch of his beloved car. And if your handiwork didn't meet his exacting standards, you would get an even worse punishment.

One day, I answered one of the staff back over something trivial.

'What did you just say?' Abbot said, spinning around to face me.

'Nothing,' I mumbled, but it was too late.

Before I knew what was happening, I was pinned down by Abbot and Collins. One held my arms behind my back while the other pulled back my head by the hair and poured some of the brown syrup – the chemical cosh – down my throat. Although I tried not to swallow, someone held my nose so that I had to gulp it down just to breathe.

I realised then that at Aston Hall, I could never win, only lose. I'd been there for around four months when I was told I was having another treatment. By now, I was having them so regularly that they'd almost become routine. Sadly, I was one of the few boys – there were twenty of us in total, including Robert – who received treatment at least once, if not twice every week. Once the injection had kicked in, I lay cold and still as a statue as Milner placed the wire mask over my face and dripped the usual chemical onto it. I had no idea what he'd injected me with or why he was doing it, but I thought whatever it was he must be trying to either fix or cure me because that's what they did to you in hospital.

'Did your father touch you sexually, Stephen?'

'Nooooo,' I mumbled.

DRIP, DRIP, DRIP!

Always the same questions and the same answers. I wondered if he thought I'd give him the answer he wanted to hear if he tried different drugs or asked me enough times. Again, I eventually blacked out and woke up groggy in my dormitory bed. However, when I finally came to, this time I realised it wasn't my back or legs that were stinging, it was my anus. A feeling of dread flooded through and I felt chilled to the bone as I realised that someone had done more than just hit me in that room. I felt myself flush with shame.

Fucking Milner! the voice raged inside my head. *The bastard's done something bad to you, he's put something inside you!*

I felt sick to the core as my body flew into full panic mode and my breathing became laboured.

He's done more than touch your knob! the voice observed bitterly as I buried my face in my pillow and began to sob.

Why was I in here? Hadn't I been through enough? Why was I being held inside a mental hospital when my brothers and sister got to live a normal life? At least the cellar wasn't this bad, nothing was this bad. At least my dad had never done that to me. Of course, I never told a soul what Milner had done, but I'm certain that he knew I knew. It was the way I looked at him when he moved in to inject me the following week, the hatred in my eyes.

I hope you die, you sick bastard! the voice screamed inside my head.

My body tensed as he approached and became as rigid as a plank of wood. Soon, the voice kicked in again: *If you could just pretend you're not there… If you could pretend this isn't happening to you, if you could just…*

DRIP, DRIP, DRIP!

A blackness enveloped me and the room faded away to nothing.

* * *

During my treatments I began to suffer the same recurring nightmare: I'd be standing outside in the yard, yet I was unable to escape. There was a thick metal pole that stood in the centre of the yard with another pole that swung from it, like an arm. Attached to the arm was a sledgehammer and it would spin towards me at high speed. I always knew it was coming, and I'd try my best to duck or avoid it, but no matter what I did, it would always smack me in the side of the head, knocking me clean off my feet. I have no idea what Milner did to me during those treatments – he could have quite easily been hitting me or sexually abusing me using force – but I will never know because the drugs he gave me were so strong, they must have been enough to floor an elephant. The only proof I ever had were the marks he left on my body, sexual and otherwise, when I finally came around.

At Aston Hall I soon learned to recognise certain signs. For example, I could always tell when a boy had undergone treatment because the smell of the chemical Milner had dripped on the mask stayed with us all. It lingered in our hair, soaked into the pores of our skin and lived on our breath – I could smell it a mile off. The other thing I noticed was the sandals. I had shoes, as did many of the other boys there, but I could always tell the ones who had been in Aston Hall for a long time because they wore sandals and socks, whatever the weather. If a lad wore sandals then it was a tell-tale sign that he would never get out. It became the dubious badge of honour for some of the longest-serving patients there, so much so that the first thing I did when I met someone was to look at their feet.

One such patient was Harold Spencer. He was the only patient who was allowed to roam freely around the grounds at Aston Hall. Harold was in his fifties, yet he still had the mind and innocence of a child. He also wore the regulation sandals, so we all surmised that he'd been there for a very long time, if not his whole life. As a general rule, we weren't allowed outside unless it was in the school playground or on a supervised walk through the woods, but some of the staff had formed a cricket and football team. Our teams – I was chosen to be a member of both – meant that we could play both sports against boys from other hospitals in the Nottingham and Derby areas. I'd been chosen because they found I had a natural ability and, after spending so many years on my own, I realised I loved to be part of a team because it gave me a real sense of 'belonging'. One day, we were practising for a cricket match when Harold asked if he could join in. A few of the boys began to snigger because he was a pretty useless player, but he was harmless enough and a nice guy so we let him join our team.

One kid – a particularly good batsman – had just knocked the ball for six when Harold cried out that he would catch it. He was fielding, so we all stepped back and allowed him his moment of glory. The ball had been hit high in the air, so Harold had enough time to run and get himself into a good position to catch it as it fell from the sky. Holding his hands high above his head, he clapped them together to try and 'cup' the ball. Somehow he missed and, instead, clapped his empty hands together as the ball continued to crack him full pelt on the top of his head. Immediately, the skin on his scalp split open and there was so much blood that, for a minute, we all thought he must be dead. His knees had buckled upon impact and he had crumpled heavily to the ground, where he lay motionless. There was a moment of silent horror as everyone stood back, unsure quite what to do. Suddenly, Harold's arm stretched to the right and grabbed the ball off the ground. He leapt triumphantly to his feet, blood still streaming down his face, as everyone began to cheer. As the staff ran over to take him inside and have the gash on his head stitched back together again, Harold laughed to himself. Later that afternoon, he begged to come back on the pitch as if nothing had happened and he'd not just had his head split wide open by a cricket ball.

A few days later, we were shipped out by bus to play a different team of boys at another hospital. As we climbed down from the bus and the opposition approached, I noticed that while a lot of them wore their hair long like mine, quite a few had had it shaved at the sides. I thought it was odd, but we formed our teams and later that afternoon, went on to win the match. Afterwards, I wandered over to chat to some of the lads with the interesting haircut.

'So you're at Aston Hall, are you?' one of them said, kicking off the conversation.

I nodded.

'What did you do to end up there then?' his mate interjected.

I looked at them a bit shiftily – I didn't want to tell them about the cellar.

'My parents used to beat me up,' I replied in the well-practised line I trotted out that usually got people off my back.

'That's shit!' one of the lads with the strange haircut remarked.

'Yeah,' I nodded. 'Anyway,' I added, changing the subject before they asked me any more awkward questions, 'what's with the haircut? Is it the fashion here or something?'

Suddenly it was their turn to look uncomfortable. One lad shifted uneasily from one foot to another while his mate stared down at his boots.

'It's the… erm… it's the treatment,' the one looking up said, blurting out the words.

My heart froze at the word 'treatment' – I was so shocked that I gasped out loud, I couldn't help it.

'So, they give you treatment here as well?'

'Yeah,' the lad who'd been staring at his shoes said, glancing up. 'But at least it's not as bad as what they do to you lot at Aston Hall.'

Now it was my turn to look confused.

'Why? And what has it got to do with your haircuts?'

They both looked at me as though it should be obvious.

'They give us electric shock treatment here. That's why we've got no hair at the side – they shave it, see,' the lad who'd been staring at his shoes said, lifting up a curtain of hair to show me how far back the razor had gone. 'They shave it so they can put wet sponges on the sides of our heads.'

I was dumbstruck.

'But why do they use sponges, and what's electric shock treatment?' I eventually managed to ask.

The second lad turned to face me.

'Electricity,' he explained, waving his fingers around in front of him. 'They run it through some wires and into the wet sponges. If they didn't wet the sponges first then the electricity would fry your brain.'

He then made a funny buzzing noise, which made the first one burst out laughing.

'But why do they do that? Why do they put electricity through your brain?' I persisted.

'I dunno,' said the second lad, shrugging his shoulders. 'Maybe they want to jump-start our brains – you know, like an old knackered car.'

Unable to believe what I was hearing, I shook my head. 'Fucking hell!' I gasped. 'And I thought Aston Hall was bad.'

There was a moment's silence and both lads looked at me as though I was completely mad.

'But it is!' the first one chipped in. 'Aston Hall's much, much worse. They might fry our heads here, but at least they don't drug us up!'

When I thought about it later, I realised he was right. Brutal as the electric shock treatment must have been, somehow these boys had felt lucky – lucky they weren't in our shoes, lucky they weren't locked up, drugged, abused and subjected to who knows what else by Milner.

CHAPTER 21

A DEATH IN THE FAMILY

The more I chatted to the friendlier staff, the more I realised that our 'male nurses' weren't actually trained nurses at all – well, not in the full sense of the word. The ones I'd spoken to had taken a job at Aston Hall because it had been the first one they'd got.

One of the day nurses, Mr Kettering, was another one of the decent members of staff. He was in his forties and it was obvious that to him, Aston Hall was just a means of earning money. One afternoon, I was sat reading in a corner when we got chatting.

'So,' I said resting my book down on the table, 'have you always done this job, Mr Kettering?'

He looked at me and shook his head.

'No, I used to work at the Dunlop tyre factory down the road. Then I came here. It was the first job I applied for, the first job I got, so I thought I might as well take it.'

I thought maybe he was an unusual case and the other staff

would have trained for years, but I was wrong. Another nice fella was a male nurse called Pablo. Pablo was Spanish, although his English was superb. I wondered how a Spanish man had ended up working at a hospital in the middle of Derbyshire, so I asked him.

'I fought Franco,' he told me, taking a long drag of his cigarette, 'so I had to leave. I had to escape and get away from Spain before they caught up with me.'

Fascinated, I sat and listened to his life story.

'I was a butcher by trade,' Pablo explained, 'but then I got caught up with it. I fought in the resistance, so when I escaped, I had to find a place of safety and that place was England. This was the first job I applied for, so when I got it, I took it.'

It didn't seem as though working at Aston Hall had been the long-held dream of any of the staff or even a good career move, only a means to an end. I was dumbstruck – I even began to wonder if Doctor Milner had actively employed people who weren't necessarily trained but who were so grateful for a job that they kept their mouths shut about what went on behind locked doors.

The days seemed to drag, although I was having treatment and being injected by Milner, sometimes in both arms, every week. By now, I'd been at Aston Hall about five months. I was always bathed and weighed before the treatments, but only measured once a month. However, one thing remained a constant: my treatments were always carried out on either a Monday or Thursday, or sometimes both, and they were always done around tea time.

'You're having treatment tonight,' one of the male nurses would inform me and that's when I knew that I wouldn't be getting any tea that night. Once I'd been selected for treatment, the staff would keep me in the 'comfy room' where the soft chairs, TV and reading books were kept. The day room was a long room. At one end was the television and on the opposite side was a door leading through to the kitchen and the dining area. There was another door that led through into a corridor, the staff room and the toilets. Through another locked door were the main stairs leading up to the dormitories, which were situated at the top of the stairs on the left.

The treatment rooms were on the right, as I knew better than most because I was part of the select group of around twenty. Milner would treat two boys at the same time, so whenever I was called up for my treatment, a nurse would lead me into one room while another boy would be taken into the other one. It was relentless: new boys would arrive at the hospital a little meek and mild, then they'd go for treatment. It would make them more determined to escape and fight the system, or they would simply withdraw even more. I knew of several lads who arrived, were sent for treatment and never returned – I have no idea what happened or became of them because Beech Ward was always so busy. It was usually full, and lads came and went all the time. Sometimes 'missing' lads' social workers would come to collect them. But the others? Well, I just don't know for sure.

The hospital was rife with rumours that Milner had killed people with his drugs, particularly the patients who never came back. Sometimes, the odd one would reappear after running away, and it was usually a social worker or police officer who would bring them back, kicking and screaming. It became such a regular occurrence that Milner brought in a new rule: anyone being returned to Aston Hall had to be taken straight to his office and not to the ward. I don't know what he did to them, but they were always quiet by the time they reached Beech Ward.

I never seemed to have the same social worker twice after the raid on Dad's cellar, yet my social worker, whenever she turned up to see me, would always be a woman. I never said much to them – what was the point? It was these people who were responsible for me being in Aston Hall in the first place.

After the cricket match at the other hospital, I often thought about the boys with the strange haircuts – the ones we'd played. I wondered whether they'd always been destined to have electric shock treatment. Maybe we'd been destined to be drugged up by Milner, or perhaps it was simply the 'luck of the draw'. Of course, some of the nastier staff – Abbot and Collins, in particular – perpetuated the lie about us being given electric shock treatment, or being thrown inside the cage outside Elm Ward, if we ever misbehaved. At night, visions of the patients on Elm Ward continued to haunt me.

★ ★ ★

Once a month, posh people in suits would arrive at Aston Hall. I'm not sure if they were doctors or inspectors, but they were mostly men. Occasionally, a few women dressed in their finery would turn up. We always knew when we had visitors coming because the staff would make us clean the hospital inch by inch until it was spotless. Although we had to dust and polish the furniture and windows daily anyway, they made us work twice as hard when we had folk coming. We were told to make our beds in a certain way – always with the edges of the sheets tucked in, the blue crocheted hospital blanket smoothed out with no wrinkles. We also had to buff the floor every day; however even that would go up a notch if the posh visitors were coming.

'I want to see that shine, you understand me, Smith?' Abbot barked at me one morning as I buffed the floor, pushing the heavy machine backwards and forwards and across it. 'If I can't see my face in it, you know what's coming.'

I did. It was usually a dose of the brown syrup to quieten me down, or a stint in the toilet, where he and Collins would throw me around and beat me up. Whatever punishment they decided to inflict, it would always end up with my face being pushed against the window to 'look at the loonies', as they called them, drenched in the rain, snow or whatever was blowing outside as they screamed and howled inside their cage. The caged tennis court was their daytime 'ward', then they would be returned to Elm Ward in the evening. Not that they would have known if it was light or dark outside because the windows in the ward were all boarded up. Yet you'd hear screams from inside there, too, only after a while your ears trained themselves to tune out and the horror somehow blended in and became part of the overall background noise.

I'd often stare out of the window in Beech Ward, wondering where my two brothers and sister were. More importantly, I wondered why I had to stay locked up inside here. I could see a line of trees in the distance: woodland. The trees seemed to grow at a funny angle, which made it look as though it was a huge hill. I used to fantasise about getting out and running through the woods to civilisation on the other side. I didn't realise it then, but what others found out to their cost was the

River Trent ran through on the other side. Afterwards, I was told many stories of lads running away only to drown in that river, probably due to the fact that they'd been anaesthetised by the drugs Milner had given them. That's if I could have escaped in the first place: the windows were nailed open only a fraction and often I wondered what would happen if a fire ever broke out. How would we escape? A fire was a very real possibility at Aston Hall because most of the lads smoked and the staff let them. If anything, I suppose I'd settled down into some sort of routine just to try and survive, even if I was still only fourteen and a half years old and this situation was anything but normal.

Soon it was winter and then a seasonal celebration I'd never experienced before – Christmas. I celebrated my first ever Christmas at Aston Hall when Mr Bradbury brought me some more books to read. He told me they were a present because that's what people gave each other at Christmas. I thought back to the time my father had walked down the cellar steps and had ruffled my hair. Mum had given me more food than usual, and Dad had been so nice that it had unnerved me, but he'd only done it that one time because it was Christmas Day, and a time for giving.

One afternoon, I was called out of school. Not that I minded because I found it dull, unchallenging and utterly pointless. For all his craziness, my father had educated me so well that I found school easy – too easy. Another social worker had arrived to see me. I thought it was a usual visit where they would take notes, smile and then leave. However, this one was different. Collins led me through to a staff office, which was along a corridor, about a hundred yards from my school. For a minute,

I wondered if I'd done something wrong, but as the nurse opened the door, I spotted a social worker and another nurse, Pablo, sitting there waiting for me.

'Hello, Stephen. Could you please take a seat?' the social worker said.

My eyes flitted between them.

What had I done? They wouldn't pull me out of lessons for nothing.

I watched as Collins took a seat near me. Out of everyone in the room, he was the one I was most nervous of. I glanced at the social worker as she cleared her throat and paused as though she had something very difficult to say but couldn't quite find the right words.

'Stephen, I'm afraid I've some very bad news for you. We are very sorry to tell you this,' she said, looking over at the two nurses for support, 'but your mother is dead.'

Suddenly I felt three pairs of eyes upon me, watching and waiting for me to gasp or cry out with shock. I knew that's how I should have felt and that that reaction would have been not only expected but entirely normal. Instead, I felt numb; I felt nothing. They continued to stare at me in bewilderment as I sat and shrugged.

'Oh well,' I mumbled.

'But are you alright?' the social worker asked, a little concerned. I could tell she had prepared herself for tears and somehow I'd let her down with my indifference.

I nodded.

'But… but it's your mum, Stephen. You do understand, don't you?'

I nodded again.

'Yes, I do, but so what?'

They all looked a little shocked and surprised, but I knew I couldn't do it; I couldn't fake it and put on a display of grief for their benefit when inside, I felt nothing, just dead and hollow. I thought about Mum and the fact I'd seen her a few dozen times during my entire life before she'd left me.

Why should you grieve? the voice agreed.

But still they continued to stare, watching and waiting for a sudden outburst or show of emotion from me.

'Is that it? Can I go now?' I asked coldly.

The social worker seemed a little horrified but nodded, so I stood up and left the room. I went back to my classroom, but by the time I returned, lessons had already finished. A member of staff escorted me to the common room, where I sat and waited for my dinner. To me, nothing had changed. I didn't feel upset or angry, I just felt indifferent. I greeted the news as if it had been the fate of a long-lost relative. I felt no love or loss towards a woman who quite clearly had felt nothing towards me – a woman I'd called Mum.

★ ★ ★

Afterwards, my life continued pretty much as it had done with a weekly round of treatments from Milner, more drugs, more injections, and a roomful of kids who wanted to be anywhere but there locked up inside a mental hospital.

One morning, on 17 May 1976, Simon Abbot came looking for me. By this time, I'd been at Aston Hall for sixteen months. I thought I must have done something wrong and was in for a good hiding, but this time he had news for me.

'Get your stuff together, Smith, and pack it up, cos you're leaving.'

I turned on the spot.

'Leaving? Why? Where am I going?' I asked, my heart racing with excitement.

You're getting out! You're actually getting out of this hell hole! the voice cheered.

The nurse shrugged his big heavy shoulders.

'How should I know? Just pack up your things because you're leaving now, you're leaving Aston Hall.'

I didn't need to be told twice. Shoving the few clothes I had into a small bag, I packed my clothes, along with my pencils, paper and some watercolour paints that Mr Bradbury had brought in for me. I gathered my drawings, records and most importantly, my record player – a present from Mr Bradbury – together in a big pile. Holding everything in my arms, I was taken to the office, where a slim woman in her mid-twenties was waiting for me.

'Hello, Stephen. My name is Carole,' she said, swishing her shoulder-length mousy brown hair. She blinked up at me through wide-framed heavy glasses in a way that immediately reminded me of Deirdre Barlow from *Coronation Street*.

'Hello,' I replied.

A dull ache throbbed in my arms as they struggled to hold the weight of the record player, but I refused to put it down, even for a moment. I was frightened that if I did, I'd never see it again.

'Wait there, Stephen,' the social worker said, rising from her chair. 'I just need to speak to the other staff and then we can go. I won't be long.'

I slumped down into a chair, grateful to take the weight off my feet and arms. She left me alone, holding everything I owned in the world, wondering where on earth I was being taken next.

At least you won't have to have any more treatments, at least you'll get away from Milner, the voice reasoned.

I nodded. It was true: I would miss the friends I'd made at Aston Hall. I didn't even have time to say goodbye to them, but I knew I wouldn't miss Doctor Milner, some of the male nurses or the treatments. I would, however, miss Mr Bradbury and the kindness he'd shown me – kindness I'd never experienced before in my life.

'Right, that's it,' she smiled, reappearing in the doorway, 'we're all set!'

She had tucked under her left arm a thick file with my name scribbled on the front, a brown handbag over her shoulder and a set of car keys in her right hand.

'Come on, Stephen, follow me. I'm taking you to your new home.'

I clambered to my feet and followed her out of the room, along the corridor and out through the main entrance. On the front steps of Aston Hall, I took a deep lungful of air. It felt good to be outside, to be finally free of Milner and his terrifying drug experiments. In many ways, today had felt the same as the day they'd raided the cellar, only much less scary. I was confident that life could never be that bad again. I'd been locked up and kept in a cellar away from other people for so long and then I'd had to endure over a year and a half locked inside Aston Hall, where I'd been drugged, caned, whipped, beaten and sexually abused. Now I was leaving Aston Hall and the worst was behind me, I decided as I climbed into the passenger seat of the social worker's green VW Beetle. I didn't even look back as we drove along the long path leading from the hospital and back into the real world.

'So,' I began as we turned left and pulled out onto the main road, 'where are you taking me?'

The young woman turned her face away from the road to glance over at me.

'It's a Catholic School called St William's, it's in a place called Market Weighton near Hull,' she said, checking that both sides were clear before pulling out onto another main road.

'And what is it? I mean, what's it like?' I asked, digging for more information.

'Well, it's a bit like a boarding school for boys, so you'll go to school there and you'll live with lots of other boys. I think you'll like it, Stephen. It's a school, not a hospital.'

I felt a small glimmer of hope rise inside me – a school, I was finally going to a proper school, where they had lots of books to read, teachers and genuine lessons. Best of all, I knew there wouldn't be any more needles, treatments or any Doctor Milners.

Yes, I thought, smiling to myself, this was where my life finally took a turn for the better. I'd get a good education, not be given books that were far too easy for me, and I'd learn – I'd learn and then I'd be able to leave and get myself a good job, where no one would be able to lock me up and tell me what to do ever again.

The car continued to journey along the road and we passed dozens of trees and fields on my way to a new and exciting life. Best of all, I was leaving Aston Hall far, far behind.

What I didn't realise then was that I was being taken to a far worse place. I'd effectively jumped from the frying pan straight into the pit of hell – and St William's was that pit of hell.

CHAPTER 22

ST WILLIAM'S

'So, where's Market Weighton?' I asked, bombarding the social worker with more and more questions. I was desperate to know about my new school and my new life.

'It's in a county called Yorkshire, between two places called Hull and York.'

I nodded, although I really didn't have a clue where Yorkshire, Hull or even York were because I'd only ever lived in a cellar and a hospital.

'And is it… nice?' I asked hopefully.

She smiled.

'Oh yes, Stephen. It's very nice. There are lots of boys your age there so you'll make lots of new friends. You'll be very happy there.'

She didn't elaborate much more, but she did let it slip that it was the only place that could take me at that time.

I thought about my old mates back at Aston Hall – Chris,

Neil, Robert and Michael with his ridiculous wig – and I felt a sudden pang of sadness.

Who would stick up for Michael now that I'd gone?

I knew there was very little I could do, but I hoped that the other lads would leave him alone. It was hard enough trying to survive Aston Hall, but to be Michael living inside that hell hole… well, it didn't bear thinking about. A shiver ran through me and I felt a guilty sense of relief that I would never have to hear the haunting howls and screams of Elm Ward ever again.

As we neared a place called Hull, the social worker pointed out a huge bridge that was being built across a greeny blue-coloured river.

'See that,' she said, pointing over to the massive construction that seemed to span the water and hover in mid-air without any obvious support, 'that's the Humber Bridge. Amazing, isn't it? It's very futuristic!'

I nodded. In fact, I thought it was the most incredible thing I'd ever seen in my entire life.

'But it's so massive, what's it for?' I asked.

I knew about bridges because I'd read about them in books and we'd driven over a swing bridge on our way to Hull in a place called Goole – the very first time I'd ever been over one.

'The Humber Bridge will take all the traffic from that side of the water to this. It'll save hours of driving around the edge of the country for those people with cars,' the social worker explained.

'Right,' I said, nodding, although I didn't fully understand because I had no concept of how long it took to drive anywhere.

Having said that, our journey seemed to take forever –

much longer than any of the other journeys I'd made to the different hospitals with Dad. In reality, it had taken us just over two hours to reach Market Weighton. Finally, the social worker indicated, turned and steered her car up a long path towards my new school.

School. I could barely believe I was going to a proper school like a normal lad. For the first time in my life I felt excited instead of afraid. We drove through some large metal gates and past some houses on the left, where I was told the school staff lived with their families. Then I saw an old building that I later discovered was the school chapel. Finally, a large and long white building with dozens of square windows and a dark grey tiled roof loomed into view. The social worker pulled up near a huge stone arch and put on the handbrake.

'That's it, we're here. Come on!'

'But what about my things?'

'Oh, they'll be fine,' she said, sounding unconcerned. 'Come on, let's get you inside first, then you can come and collect your things.'

Against my better judgement, I left my record player and bags of clothes and paints in the car and followed her towards a low office building that stood opposite a grand, much older building. We went to the headmaster's office, where a little man with greased-back hair that looked as though it was stuck to his head was waiting to greet us. I was told he was one of the priests at the school, although he didn't look very much like the priests I'd read about in books because he wore a black suit without a white dog collar.

'Welcome, Stephen,' he said, holding his hands out before clasping them together again in front of him.

The headmaster explained that the school was run by an order of monks known as the De La Salle Order or Brotherhood and that I would be staying in St George's, one of the houses there.

Minutes later, there was a knock at the door.

'Come in,' the diminutive headmaster called out in a surprisingly loud voice.

The door opened and another man stepped in. He introduced himself as Mr Wood, who was one of the teachers at St William's.

'Right then, Stephen, let's go and collect your things from the car and get you settled in.'

I smiled because I was just so relieved I'd be getting my record player back. He turned and left the room, followed by me and the social worker. Together, we unloaded everything from the car, but I insisted on carrying the record player myself. I was determined not to let it out of my sight, not even for a second. The social worker said a brief goodbye as the teacher told me to follow him across a wide courtyard outside. We passed a gym, some toilets and another house called De La Salle. On the right was St George's, which I recognised as the name of the house where I would be staying.

'This is you,' the teacher said, 'this is St George's. Now, follow me.'

We walked through a large room that had a series of shelves on the wall with different things pushed into different squares.

'This is your pigeon hole,' Mr Wood said, pointing to it. 'You can leave your stuff in there.'

But I could tell the space wouldn't be big enough for my record player, even though I'd already decided I wouldn't leave it anyway. Still carrying it in my arms, the teacher led me through to a day room, similar to the one at Aston Hall, only at least here none of the doors were locked.

'You can leave your record player here, Stephen,' Mr Wood said, tapping a hand lightly against a table.

'No, I'd rather keep it with me,' I insisted, wrapping my arms around it protectively.

He looked a little surprised and stood his ground.

'I can assure you, it will be quite safe here.'

I backed away.

'But what if someone nicks it after we've left?' I said, eyeing him with suspicion.

If Aston Hall and my father had taught me one thing, it was to trust no one.

'I can assure you, no one will take it, Stephen. Besides, everyone is in lessons at the moment.'

Lessons, of course. I kept forgetting this was a school, not a hospital. I was safe and the record player was safe. Although I still had a few nagging doubts, I decided to trust the place; after all, it was run by priests, and priests could be trusted, couldn't they? Priests were trustworthy because they were close to God. With my record player on the table, the teacher led me upstairs to my dormitory, which seemed much smaller in comparison to the one at Aston Hall: the new dorm contained just six beds.

'This is where you will sleep,' Mr Wood said before continuing with a guided tour of the school, during which he took me through the rules of the school – lots of rules – but they sounded like a walk in the park compared to Aston Hall.

'So, to conclude: no running, no shouting, no talking after lights out. Just follow the rules and you'll get on just fine,' he told me.

I nodded; it sounded like a good deal to me.

'Right, good you are. Now, it's time to go to school. Come on, follow me, I'll show you all the different parts.'

I followed him around as he showed me all the different departments of the school. First, we visited the painting department, where lads were taught how to paint and decorate to a good standard, then we walked through to the engineering department. As I glanced around the room, a few of the lads looked up from what they were doing to stare at me. It seemed as though they were making long sticks, things I later found out were called pokers. I wasn't sure what these sticks were for and I wondered if they were weapons, sticks to beat people with. Up until that point, my life had been so entrenched by violence that I thought everything could be used as a weapon.

'Who's this then?' a tall man in his fifties wanted to know as he strode over to meet us.

'This is Stephen Smith, Mr Hughes.'

Mr Hughes – who turned out to be another one of the teachers – gave me a cursory glance up and down and then grunted as though I was the shit on his shoe. I decided that I despised him on sight and the feeling was obviously mutual. My instincts later proved correct – he was a real nasty bastard.

After leaving the engineering department, we strolled over to the building department and finally, the farm. St William's had its own working farm, which was run by a Scottish man and his wife, a big, busty blonde who took no prisoners. If I had thought the farm department seemed an easy option, then I was wrong because there were countless cows and sheep to feed, muck out and look after. This school was unlike any other I'd read about or even heard of. Instead of books, which we read in the mornings, the pupils were expected to spend a different afternoon in each department, learning what the teachers described as a 'vocational skill' – they hoped these skills would help us get a job when we finally left. Around 4pm, we would be brought back into the main part of St William's, where dinner would be served.

I soon discovered there was another, separate department – the kitchen department – to which I was duly dispatched. Once there, I was told I'd have to skin dozens of potatoes using a special 'skinning machine'. I spent many an hour at that machine, which looked a bit like a huge tumble dryer, pouring potatoes in to try and remove the skins so they could be cooked, chipped or boiled. When I wasn't 'peeling' potatoes, I was washing dishes – what seemed like hundreds of them. It was menial and mind-numbing to say the least, and nothing like the 'school' I'd expected, nor, indeed, the one that had been sold to me by the social worker. It made me angry because I felt I'd been cheated yet again. St William's took in lads from all over the country and I heard Yorkshire, Geordie and Liverpudlian accents amongst others. I'd not been there that long when a few of the lads approached and asked me where I'd been sent from. It seemed that this was always the first question anyone asked, whether you ended up in a school, a home or even a hospital.

'A hospital,' I said. 'I've just come from Aston Hall, it's a mental hospital.'

I watched as the small crowd of lads backed away from me warily.

'A mental hospital?' one of them asked cautiously, keeping

his eyes fixed on me the whole time as if he expected me to flip at any moment.

I laughed inside. These were hard lads, lads who had robbed places, stolen cars, beaten people up – all so-called badges of honour for being a thug – yet here I was, playing a card that seemed to trump them all.

'Yeah, that's right,' I said, trying on my new character like an old overcoat. If I knew one thing, it was that I'd have to use whatever I could to protect myself here. If Aston Hall helped me do that, so be it. 'Yeah, a mental hospital,' I repeated. 'Tell me,' I said, eyeballing them all, 'have any of you heard of a place called Rampton?'

I asked the question knowing it was the worst kind of mental hospital imaginable, a place where they held the criminally insane. I knew because we'd often spoken about Rampton at Aston Hall, and of it being one of the worst places you could end up. We'd seen it in the news and on television. I knew it was the place where the real nutters went. I watched as their eyes widened in horror.

'Rampton?' the oldest-looking one of the group gasped.

I nodded.

'Yeah, Rampton. Aston Hall – the place I was – well, it was connected to that.'

The look on their faces was priceless and I could tell they couldn't wait to get away from me.

'Okay, right. Well, I suppose we'll see you around then,' the eldest one mumbled as the others stared at each other in wide-eyed horror.

'Yeah, I'm sure you will,' I said, adding a slight menace to my voice for extra effect.

Deep down, I didn't want to be the kid from the mental hospital, but if it helped protect and place me at the top of the pecking order, then so be it.

I soon realised that St William's was far more brutal than Aston Hall because here, there was a real hierarchy, a place where seventeen-year-olds bullied eleven- and twelve-year-old boys. At fifteen years old, I'd had enough of people hitting and beating me. Now it was finally time to stick up for myself and if I let people think I was mental and unstable, then I knew they wouldn't bother me. But if I'd thought the older boys were the ones to watch, I was wrong. The real twisted bastards were the members of staff. The worst was the new headmaster, a man called Brother James, who had been at St William's for a while but had just been promoted to the top position. Religion or no religion, I soon realised he was the devil himself.

CHAPTER 23

HELL ON EARTH

Following my revelation that I'd come from a mental hospital the older bullies – in fact, everyone – seemed to give me a wide berth, which suited me just fine. After we'd had dinner, we were allowed to go and play football outside in the playground. Needless to say, whenever I asked to be on the team, no one ever told me no. The school also had a gym and a swimming pool. We used the gym for PE lessons, but only ever went in the pool if we were told to by Brother James. After a kick-about, we'd usually go back inside and watch television until around 9pm, which was lights out. In spite of all these privileges, lots of boys repeatedly ran away. At first, I was baffled: we had to go to school, but the rest of the day was pretty much a breeze in comparison to Aston Hall. At least they didn't drug us here. Then, only two days after I'd arrived, I heard a strange tale of two boys aged ten and twelve years old.

'Did they run away?' I asked the lad who was busy telling everyone the story as we sat in the dorm one night.

His eyes widened dramatically and then he looked over at me, a little startled.

'I think that's what they want us to believe. More likely, they're dead.'

'Dead?' I gasped, half-laughing. 'Why would they be dead? Did they have an accident or something?'

The lad looked me directly in the eye.

'You've not been here that long, have you, Steve?'

I shook my head.

'You know the double garage, the one with all the sand in it?'

'Yeah,' I replied – I didn't know it well, but I'd seen it.

'Well, they were digging down, trying to hide, when the whole thing – all this sand – collapsed in on them.'

I was baffled.

'But why were they digging – into the sand, I mean?'

'Why do you think?'

As I looked around at the other boys who nodded knowingly, I wanted to ask why two young kids would try and hide in a big mound of sand, but at the same time, I didn't want to look stupid. It wasn't until a few days later that I found out the real reason: they were trying to hide from the headmaster. But there was more to tell.

'Then there was George. He hung himself in the toilets out there in the courtyard,' he said, pointing over towards that general direction. 'Yep, he hung himself because of what Brother James did to him.'

I couldn't keep quiet any longer, I had to know what he was talking about. Brother James, or James Carragher, was our new headmaster.

'What do you mean? What did Brother James do to him?'

The others turned towards me with a look of pity on their faces. It was obvious that they were all aware of something I was not, so the boy decided to enlighten me.

'Brother James and the Black Spider...'

'What, Black Spider the priest?' I asked.

They all nodded as I struggled to keep up with the story.

'Yes, anyway, Brother James and the Black Spider, they choose what boys they want and they, err... Well, they help themselves to them.'

I must have still looked baffled because he decided to continue.

'If you ever get taken to Brother James's office, well, once you're there, you won't get out until he's done things to you.'

He pointed down towards his private parts as he said the word 'things' and I was left in no doubt what he meant: Brother James and the Black Spider were perverts who picked out young boys to sexually abuse. I felt a cold shiver run down my spine. I'd thought Aston Hall was bad, and it had been, but at least I'd been drugged when Doctor Milner had done things to me. A small mercy, but a mercy all the same.

There was more wild talk of boys' bodies being buried in a graveyard in the grounds near the chapel, but by this point, my head was spinning and I didn't know what or who to believe.

The following day, during class, I decided the best thing would be to try and stay in the good books of the teachers. At least that way I'd never have to go to Brother James's office. I found the lessons easy anyway; in fact, I found them almost insulting. The lads at St William's were good lads, but most of them had been denied an education because they came from a dysfunctional family background so most of them were as thick as pudding and barely literate. In comparison, I'd probably had the most abnormal upbringing of them all, yet I was streets ahead when it came to Maths and English. As a result, and, after a couple of months, the Brothers – monks from the De La Salle Brotherhood – concluded it was no good putting me in a class with the others. Instead, it was decided that I would be sent to a mainstream comprehensive secondary school in Market Weighton, where the children of staff members went. I was told it was a great privilege to be chosen to go there, yet I almost shat myself when I was called to Brother James's office to be told the news. As I made my way there, I decided how I could – and would – defend myself should he come onto me. Thankfully, by the time I'd reached the office, Mr Wood was waiting, too. Mr Wood was one of the decent members of staff and he had a son called Simon, who caught the bus to school.

'So, you can catch the school bus with Simon and the others,' he explained.

I was so glad to have escaped Brother James's office unscathed that I almost punched the air in celebration as I left. Not only that, unlike the other poor sods, I actually got to leave St William's to go to another school each day. I hoped that it would somehow help protect me and keep me from the clutches of Brother James. Alas, if I'd thought being shipped out to the local school would be a good thing, it turned out I was wrong because I was not only bullied at my new school for being a social misfit, I also got it in the neck at St William's for being 'a swot' and attending the local comprehensive, so I couldn't win.

One afternoon, I was late back from school. I'd been held down and beaten up by a bunch of comprehensive kids – a gang of them with a chip on their shoulders and a point to prove. I'd tried to defend myself, but there were three of them and they were bigger and years older than me. I'd missed the bus so had to walk two or three miles back to St William's. I was so late that I was greeted by two teachers – Mr Hughes and Mr Baker – who were the sort to punch you in the side of the head just for fun. But now they had a reason and they were determined to use it. As soon as I walked into the school grounds they were there, waiting for me.

'Look at the state of you, Smith!' Mr Baker roared.

I glanced down at my hands, legs and arms and realised they were smothered in cuts and bruises.

'What time do you call this, boy?' Mr Hughes demanded as he grabbed hold of my hair and led me into a nearby room.

Once inside, they closed the door and proceeded to set about me, kicking and punching me as a punishment for coming home late, bloodied and dirtied. The irony was breathtaking. If I'd thought the kids at the comp had given me a good seeing to, it seemed a walk in the park in comparison to the beating these two grown men gave me.

From that moment on, I never felt safe again. I was always poised, ready and on high alert, waiting to be attacked. Often, I'd attack first, usually because I felt it was my best form of defence: attack or be attacked. Inevitably, I found myself fighting all the time, and soon, I was summoned to Brother James's office – the last place on earth I wanted to be.

It was 7pm when a staff member came to find me to let me know that Brother James wanted to see me. My throat felt bone dry and it seemed to close up in fear as the palms of my hands prickled with a nervous sweat. I slowly made my way over to his office and, standing outside, I stopped for a moment to try and prepare myself. I thought of Dad – it was his fault that I was here, his fault I'd been put in Aston Hall and now St William's, his fault I was now going to have to try and fend off a grown man, and a pervert to boot.

Lifting my hand, I knocked twice on the door. It was still shaking as I withdrew and let it dangle by my side.

'Come in!' Brother James's voice boomed from the other side.

Tentatively, I opened the door and peered inside, even though every fibre of my being was telling me to bolt, to run the other way.

'Ah, Stephen! Come in, come in, and close the door behind you,' Brother James instructed me breezily.

So I did as he said, but remained standing by the doorway and as far away from him and his desk as I could get. I watched, my whole body now trembling, as he got to his feet and came over towards me.

'Come,' he said, his hand on my shoulder, guiding me across the room.

My eyes darted all around, looking for a way to escape. There was a small window with blinds, but it was closed. The only way out was back through the door, but Brother James was standing there between it and me. My heart thudded inside my ribcage like a fist punching a brick wall.

'So, tell me, you clever boy – *my* clever boy,' he smiled, correcting himself as though I was his property, 'how are you finding your new school?'

I wasn't quite sure what to say. I thought I'd been called there to explain why I got into so many fights, not to talk about my new school. This question threw me.

'It's okay, I suppose,' I replied, shrugging my shoulders. I knew that I should have told him about the bullying at both schools, but I just wanted to be out of there and away from him as quickly as possible.

'Good, good,' he said, smiling. With that, he began to walk around me, like a shark circling its prey. 'You do know that you are the first boy from St William's ever to attend the local comprehensive school, don't you?'

But I wasn't really listening. Instead, I was watching him, keeping my eyes focused on him all the time until he disappeared from view somewhere behind me. I panicked – I wanted to turn, to see where he'd gone, but I didn't want any trouble, I just wanted to leave.

'No, I didn't know that,' I mumbled, my heart racing as I waited for him to reappear in my eyeline.

'Yes,' Brother James said, clasping his hands in front of him in glee and grinning as he circled me once more. 'That's why you are my clever boy, my special boy.'

I felt a hand suddenly grab me from behind and push my head upwards as a second snaked its way down into my underpants. I began to struggle, but I was fifteen years old and although strong, I was no match for a grown man. The more I struggled and tried to pull away, the more he fought back. I felt his breath against the skin on the side of my face and then his voice as he whispered in my ear.

'Don't ever forget, I have the power of life or death over you. Now, be a good boy and do as you're told. Understand?'

But I shook my head because I didn't understand. I didn't understand what I was doing there inside the head teacher's office with his hand down my pants, groping me. I felt sick, sick to my stomach that it was happening. The same thing had happened with Doctor Milner, of that I was certain because I'd woken up sore, but at least he had anaesthetised me against the horror of it.

'Get off me, get your hands off me!' I screamed, wriggling and squirming in his arms as he tried to hold me still.

'Just be a good boy and do as I say,' he insisted.

That evening, I left his office tear-stained and shell-shocked. I didn't know why he'd picked me or why this kept happening to me.

What have you done to deserve this? the voice asked, but I had no answers.

Actually, I did – I was 'his clever boy', that's what he'd called me. My cleverness had marked me out in more ways than one and now I was not only the target of bullies, I was Brother James's target.

★ ★ ★

After that day, I became part of his group and once there, I quickly discovered who the other members were: it was a club, not entirely exclusive, but one that no one wanted to be a member of. We were Brother James's prey and there was no one we could talk to and absolutely nothing we could do about it. Whenever I found myself trapped inside his office alone with him I would try and distance myself from what was happening. I'd switch off my mind from my body so that I could keep it purely to myself. Instead, while he did the most despicable things, I'd find myself trying to level objects up against each other to allow my mind to disengage. I'd shift my line of vision so that the edges of chairs would be level with the edge of the table, or so the door handle would line up with the bottom of a picture frame, anything to escape that room. To this day, smells still remind me of his office. The table always smelt of polish whenever he pushed my head down. My nostrils would flare as I smelt the ink of the ribbon in the typewriter placed on his desk. The room was a mixture of fear and body odour, the terror of pubescent boys forced to do things – unspeakable things – against their will.

Looking back, I know I should feel anger, and in many respects I do, but I cannot change what happened. If I could change one thing it would be the flashbacks and the sexual knowledge I had that no boy should have to carry for the rest of his life. My mind is still plagued with images I'd rather not have to re-live or see.

A week or so later, Brother James told me and five others that we had to go swimming. It sounded fun until I realised that he wanted us to swim naked. Still relatively new, I went along with the flow – I knew there would be safety in numbers, plus, I'd never been swimming before in my life.

Maybe people swam naked all the time? After all, you didn't have a bath with your clothes on.

We arrived at the swimming pool and were told to strip off in the changing rooms. Brother James threatened that if we didn't get in the water, he would throw us in. I wasn't sure if he was joking or not. Even though I was shivering, I jumped straight in. I couldn't swim properly because I'd never been taught, so I made sure that I stuck to the shallow end. It felt odd, standing there naked with the other boys, but I wasn't sure what swimming entailed so I just kept quiet. In the end, we had a bit of a laugh although I could feel Brother James's eyes on us the whole time. At the end of the session, I climbed out with some of the others and that's when I realised he had followed us into the changing room. I rushed to get dressed as quickly as possible so that I could make a quick escape. Guilt overwhelmed me as I heard the voices of two other boys, the ones he'd presumably caught. They hadn't been fast enough to escape in time, avoiding his clutches.

A short while later, I received a visit from a social worker. It was never the same one twice yet always a woman. By this time, Brother James had been sexually abusing me in his office at regular intervals. I knew there was no one I could tell at the school, but surely the social worker would listen? Yes, I convinced myself, she'd listen and she'd make him stop molesting me and the others in his special 'group'. As we sat down to discuss how I was getting on, I took a deep breath – I knew it was going to be embarrassing and awkward to tell her, but that would be the hardest part. Once that bit was out of the way, things would get easier.

'So,' she said, looking up from my file resting on her lap, 'how's things? Are you enjoying St William's?'

I looked down at my hands and picked at some loose threads of skin around my fingernails.

Tell her, just tell her, then it will be over. She'll make it stop, the voice urged.

But I was frightened. The others said that Brother James made boys 'disappear'. What if he did that to me? I was desperate to say something, but what could I say? Would she even believe me? I'd already been through so much and I thought that once I'd been 'rescued' from the cellar I'd be safe but, if anything, I felt even more vulnerable now than before.

Tell her, tell her!

I shrugged.

'It's okay, I suppose,' I said, casting my gaze to the floor.

'Good, good,' she said breezily, ticking something off on a piece of paper. I'd told her exactly what she'd come to hear and now she'd 'seen' me, she was free to leave. 'Well,' she added, 'I better be going, but someone else will be along to check on you again soon.'

After she left, I looked at myself in the mirror.

Coward, the voice scolded, *you coward!*

But I was petrified of what Brother James would do if I did tell. No, I just had to survive it, I reasoned. I was fifteen, only one or two more years and then I'd be out of there for good. That night, as I rested my face on my pillow, I thought of Dad and how I'd kill him for what he'd done to me. I'd punch him, I decided. No, punching him would be far too good. I'd hit him over the head with a rock, bash his brains in. No, I wouldn't be able to see the fear in his eyes, the fear I'd felt for fifteen long years, fear at being locked up inside a mental hospital, drugged and abused by the head doctor; the fear I felt now, daily, watching and waiting for Brother James to make his next move. No, I decided, I'd stab him – stab him right in the heart – and then I'd twist the knife for maximum pain and watch him writhe and perish on the floor like a dog, the blood and life draining from him.

Soon, Brother James was molesting me at least once a week. All the boys would dread going to the school swimming baths because he would wait for us when we got changed. He told us the story of a lad who had died running along the side of the school swimming pool – the same one he'd had us naked swimming in.

'He slipped and went straight through a glass window. That's why you should never run, boys.'

Back in the dormitory, the others had a different take on it.

'He's told us that to stop us running away from him, not just larking around. But…'

The lad broke off his story and looked around to check that no staff were listening. We leaned in to hear the end: 'I heard he died because someone threw him through the window, not because he slipped and fell.' Then he tapped the side of his nose knowingly.

'But why would someone throw him through a window?' one of the older lads at the back piped up.

The storyteller looked over to him and then took in the rest of us: 'Because he was running away from someone. He was running away from them because he didn't want them to touch him. When he refused to do what he was told, they picked him up and threw him straight through the window.'

I shook my head in horror. Surely, this was just a tall story, but so many things had happened here that I wasn't sure what was false and what was the truth anymore.

Not long afterwards, and as a rare treat, a group of us were told we could go and build a tree house – a kind of adventure playground – in the woods. The teachers seemed to think I was the smartest of the lot so they put me in charge. I didn't care either way, but I knew one thing: we'd need an axe to cut the wood to build one. So I duly went to the office to ask if we could borrow one but stopped dead in my tracks when I spotted Brother James lurking in a corner.

'Come back later, Stephen. We'll dig you one out and...' one of the teachers started to say.

Brother James held up a hand and stopped him mid-sentence.

'No, I'll tell you what. Come to my office tonight and I'll have it waiting for you.'

I felt my stomach flip with fear. What had started out as a good day had now taken a turn for the worse. But Brother James must have forgotten, because when I returned to his office later that night after seven o'clock, I stumbled in on him and a lad called Brian. Brother James was on his knees with Brian standing before him. Both had their trousers around their ankles and Brother James had Brian's penis in his mouth. I'd always known that I wasn't unique, but to witness Brian being abused by that bastard was disgusting. The pair of them separated as soon as they spotted me and quickly pulled their trousers up. Poor Brian looked completely mortified as the head teacher shoved him out of the room quickly. Then he turned to me and warned me not to say a word to anyone.

'Remember the sand pit...' he said, and I knew exactly what he meant.

I turned to leave.

'Do not say anything. Not a word,' he reminded me as I turned to open the door. 'Remember, I have the power and discretion to sort you out. Besides,' he laughed with a wave of his hand, 'no one would believe you.'

Brian refused to meet my gaze whenever he passed by in the corridor after that. It was as though if we didn't talk about it, it hadn't actually happened. But the image of him and Brother

James had burned itself inside my mind and now I couldn't shake it off. I didn't tell any of the others what I'd seen, but they must have known something was wrong by my sombre mood that evening. My trembling hands must have given me away. I started to shake and soon I couldn't stop. Those bastards had done this to me! Soon I was a nervous wreck, my body on high alert the whole time. It was exhausting. Brother James had raped me – he'd raped a whole load of us – yet there was no one I could turn to.

Not long afterwards, I was called to the headmaster's room, but instead of just Brother James, there was another man there, one I'd never seen before. Tall and heavily built, he spoke with a posh accent. The man – a visitor to the school – had short dark hair and was wearing a suit. Both he and Brother James overpowered me, held me down with force, and brutally raped me. Shaken, I fled his office.

Needless to say, our adventure tree house never got built.

CHAPTER 24

A PAEDOPHILES' SWEET SHOP

I never got over what had happened to me inside Brother James's office. Seeing other lads also being abused caused me to panic even more: there were no boundaries here. None.

A few weeks later, a social worker took me out for the day to buy me some new clothes. I decided I would tell her what had been happening at St William's, waiting until we were clear of the school and in the safety of her car.

'They touch us there,' I blurted out quickly before I lost my nerve.

'What do you mean?'

'Brother James... he does stuff to me and the others. He does dirty things to us, sexual stuff. He interferes with us. And the others, well, the teachers, they bash us around.'

The social worker listened, but her face didn't change. I waited for something, a look of shock, horror, revulsion – anything.

'I don't believe it! Brother James is a lovely man, and you

could get yourself into a lot of trouble saying such disgusting and horrible things about a man of God!' she insisted.

I watched as she indicated and began to turn the car around. 'Where are we going?' I asked.

'I'm taking you back,' she told me. 'You don't deserve anything, making up nasty stories like that about other people. I've never heard such nonsense in all my life!'

I tried to protest, I tried to make her listen, but she wouldn't. Instead, she drove me back to St William's, kicking and screaming.

'But you have to believe me. Ask anyone, they'll all tell you what he's like. He's a pervert!'

The car pulled up sharpish outside St William's, causing the tyres to screech. On hearing my protests and the general kerfuffle, Hughes and Baker – the two thugs who masqueraded as teachers – appeared at the car door and dragged me out. After one of them had spoken to the social worker, I was taken into a nearby room, where they gave me a good pasting, punching me square in the face as punishment for making a 'scene'. I realised then that if she didn't believe me, no one else would.

One summer's day, it was decided the lads would go out and play a game of football in the courtyard outside. I usually joined in, but that day, I wasn't in the mood. Brother James had been raping me at regular intervals and I felt constantly sore and hypervigilant, waiting for the threat of an attack. Always on high alert, I was well aware of the danger of being grabbed, used and abused at any moment. Instead, I drifted into the corners and away from the others as they shouted, hollered and kicked the ball to each other.

At one point I peeled away to a quieter part of the courtyard so that I could have a sneaky cigarette. I was just lighting it when I overheard Brother James talking to a friend of his, who I'd seen hanging around the school, as they sat on a bench outside. The lads had nicknamed this stranger 'Sailor John' on account of his cream cable-knit jumper that he seemed to wear in all weathers and even now, in the sweltering midday sun. I'd seen him around St William's before, but unlike Brother James's other friends who all wore suits, drove Jaguars and spoke with a posh accent, Sailor John seemed a bit more common. Whether John was his real name or he was a sailor, or it was just the jumper he wore, I have no idea. Both were facing away from me, sitting on the bench, watching the lads play football. From afar, they seemed totally absorbed in the game, but the reality was that they were sitting there discussing one of the boys, totally unaware that I was behind them, listening in.

'Look at him!' I heard Sailor John observe gleefully.

I watched as they laughed and nudged each other with their elbows as they continued to discuss and nod over towards a lad called Sam. Sam was only fourteen or fifteen, but he had an athletic build and because it was a boiling hot day, he'd taken his top off to play football.

'Ooh, he's nice!' Sailor John continued, turning towards Brother James as the two of them smiled and giggled in unison as if on a day out at the fair. I was still hiding in the stone archway, but moved a little closer so that I could listen.

'Yes, he's really nice. He's the one for me, I'll have that one,' Sailor John decided, as if choosing a cake in the window of a baker's shop. 'Send him round to me later.'

At this I gasped, backed away into the shadows of the archway, and stubbed my cigarette out. I knew I had to try and warn Sam, but how? I couldn't just walk out and past the men because they would know I'd been listening. Instead, I crouched down and listened as they discussed poor Sam in a more sexually explicit way.

Eventually, the football match was over and the two men stood up and wandered off inside, following the lads into the dining hall. I ran over, looking for Sam, but there were so many kids, I couldn't find him. I felt scared and guilty all at the same time; I had to warn him that they were coming for him. Afterwards, as the dining room started to clear and the crowd thinned to only a few stragglers, I spotted a mate of Sam's still sat at a table, so I ran over.

'Have you seen Sam?' I asked urgently, grabbing him by the arm.

The lad seemed a bit freaked out. He pulled away from my grasp and looked up at me oddly.

'No, he's gone.'

My heart began to pound.

'Gone? Gone where?' I gasped.

His mate, a ginger kid, just shrugged.

'I dunno. One of the staff came to get him,' he said, standing up from the table.

'But why? What did they want?'

He shook his head.

'How should I know? I just heard he had to go and see someone.'

That night, Sam disappeared and no one saw him for a couple of days. Even though I never told a soul, his disappearance was coupled with talk.

'Brother James wanted to see him,' one of the lads said later, confirming my worst fears.

Like so many others before him, Sam had been put into a special single room for two long days to give him time to recover from whatever had been done to him. Afterwards, when I finally did get to see him, I couldn't look him in the eye. Ghostlike, he was a shell of his former self. He never said a word about what happened and no one ever asked. We didn't have to – we all knew what he'd been through because we'd been in similar situations ourselves. Sam grew quieter and quieter until finally, he withdrew into himself.

After that day, I never saw him play football ever again.

Dunstan was another friend of Brother James. He was in his fifties and British, although one of the boys later told me he had something to do with South Africa. Before then, he hadn't been a regular visitor to St William's but, suddenly I began to see him more and more. One day, I was in a room where our clothes were kept. I was just sorting out my uniform when I heard someone come into the room and stand by me. Then I turned to find Dunstan standing right behind me. I stood in horror as, without a word, he unzipped his trousers and told me to put his knob in my mouth. When I refused, he belted me until I was black and blue – he wouldn't let me escape that room until I had masturbated him. Afterwards, I felt horrible and disgusted but, in many ways, it was just one more thing on a long list of abuse that had now become my 'normal'.

Not long afterwards, Brother James took me out to an air raid shelter situated near the chapel at St William's. I suppose I knew what was coming and by now, I lived in fear of him and what he might be capable of. On more than one occasion he'd told me about the boys who had died in the sandpit. I couldn't be sure if it was just talk, but he convinced me that this was how boys would be dealt with – the ones who didn't do as they were told.

'There are cliffs nearby and you or I could be blown off the edge of them quite easily by the wind.'

He said it in a voice that left me in no doubt what he meant – an accident that would be no accident. It had been a veiled threat, maybe a false one, but I was still a kid and all I knew was thanks to both the authorities and my own father, this so-called man of God had absolute power over me. In short, he frightened the life out of me. I'd heard stories from the others about lads dying and I honestly believed, rightly or wrongly, that if I spoke up then Brother James might harm me.

Once we'd arrived at the shelter, Brother James pushed me into the darkness and I felt his hands on me as he pulled me towards him. Then he yanked both my trousers and underpants down roughly. I was absolutely terrified. I fought him to try and claim my own body back, but he easily overpowered me. As I struggled he grabbed my head and hit me repeatedly before pinning me down and raping me violently. My mind drifted into a self-survival type of trance to try and remove itself from him and the air raid shelter. This was just another attack in a long list of abuse I'd already suffered, but I had trained myself to switch off from the situation, this time by focusing on a pile of rubbish that had been thrown into the shadows. Through the gloom I spotted a couple of old school desks, some wooden chairs that had been stacked together, a pile of red bricks, and a couple of hessian sacks, straining at the corners to try and contain all the rubble they held.

You're just like that rubbish. That's how he treats you – like something he can just use and throw away, the voice said, mirroring my thoughts.

My life had become so unbearable that I couldn't see a future now, not any more, just a sickening carousel of sexual and physical abuse.

Ironically, and in spite of what Brother James and the Black Spider were doing to the boys, we were forced to attend church at 7am every morning. The church was in the top left-hand corner of St William's and just after dawn we would be marched over there in our best bib and tucker. If you weren't deemed to be presentable enough, you would cop for another good hiding. The church always felt freezing inside, even in the height of summer, although I couldn't be sure if it was the temperature or the Black Spider – the priest in the pulpit – that left me chilled. Sometimes we'd have a visiting guest priest, but more often than not, it would be the Black Spider, preaching down to us about God.

'You are blessed for God protects you. He looks after you and protects you from harm…' he droned on and on.

It might have been laughable, had it not been so heartbreaking. Here, we had these so-called religious men telling us how lucky we were when they were sexually abusing us on an almost-weekly basis. I'd never been strongly religious, but that day I decided if this was how God protected you, then he could shove it and his religion where the sun didn't shine.

It was always the same with Brother James: he'd call me to his office to tell me what a good boy I was and how privileged I was and then he'd grab and molest me. On one occasion I struggled so hard, he beat my head off the wall in his office repeatedly, almost knocking me unconscious. Then he crushed me to the floor, pinning me down so that he could brutally rape me once more.

After the football game, I'd often see men – visitors to the school – sitting on the bench, choosing (I presume) who they wanted to rape or abuse in a bid to fulfil their sick and perverted desires. St William's, it seemed, had become a sweetie shop for visiting paedophiles – a shop that Brother James held the key to.

Every night, I'd go to bed thinking of how I was going to kill my father. I held him fully responsible for my being there, trapped inside this hell hole. I thought about escape, but the police always seemed to catch up with those lads who did. Often we'd see the cop cars bringing them back, kicking and screaming, only to be placed straight back into the arms of Brother James – we'd hear them too, begging not to be returned to the school.

'They do things to us here,' I heard one boy protest as the police car pulled up outside one evening. The officer ignored him and proceeded to drag him over towards Brother James's office. 'They do things to us that they shouldn't. They touch us, they touch our knobs and do dirty things to us – that's why we all keep running away.'

But the copper seemed far from impressed and certainly wasn't taking him seriously. Looking back, things were so different in the 70s when children were not believed as they would be today.

'Alright, son, now come on, stop lying. You're in enough trouble as it is. Now be a good lad and come quietly.'

I decided that I would tell the social worker again, whichever one turned up for my next visit. My chance came sooner than

I thought when a week or so later, one arrived to see me. I was led to the day room by a member of staff and waited until he had left us alone.

'Come and sit down, Stephen,' the female social worker said, wondering why I was still standing near the door. She nodded towards a chair opposite hers.

I went over and sat down, but leaned inwards so that she was close enough for me to whisper. She seemed a little startled and rested back in her chair to try and create a distance between us. I double-checked, glancing over both shoulders to make sure that the coast was still clear, and then I stared at her.

'I haven't got long,' I said, the words sounding a little more dramatic than I'd intended, 'there's something I need to tell you.'

'Go on,' she murmured, her interest suddenly spiked.

'It's about this place, St William's. They do stuff to us, they interfere with us. Brother James, he does things to me,' I said, shifting awkwardly in my seat, 'stuff I don't like. He does...' I took a gulp for courage so that I could say the word out loud. 'He does sexual stuff to me...'

The social worker, who had by now leaned in to listen, raised an eyebrow and backed away sceptically.

She believes you, doesn't she? the voice said, causing a panic to rise inside. Surely she believed me? There was no one else I could turn to.

'I see,' she said, a slight colour rising in her face as though she was embarrassed for me.

I waited for her to say something... anything.

'You do believe me, don't you?' I asked, breaking the silence. 'They do it to all of us. If you don't believe me, ask the others. Ask them what they do to us.'

Another silence. I was finding this beyond excruciating, but watched as she picked up her pen.

'Well, yes, but you would say that, wouldn't you? You'd say anything to get out of here and so would the others.'

I felt my body shrink back down into my seat, crushed with horror and disbelief.

'You don't believe me, do you?' I mumbled.

The social worker looked at me properly for the first time.

'No, Stephen, I don't. I think you should be grateful to be living here in a place as good and as caring as St William's.'

She ticked something on a piece of paper on her lap, shuffled the page inside a file and I knew that was it, our conversation was effectively over.

'So, besides your silly story, how are things…?' she added as though we'd just been discussing the weather.

Devastated, I turned away from her and shrugged. There was nothing left to say.

I tried to convince myself not to lose hope. After all, every visit to check on me brought with it a new social worker. Yet, in spite of this, each time I told a different woman (they were all female for some reason, and eight in total), not one of them believed me. Instead, I was told to stop 'telling stories'. I believe I had also been marked down as a troublemaker. I'd been given a label and now I knew I'd have a job to try and get anyone else to listen, never mind believe me.

One morning, I was collecting some clean sheets from the laundry when I heard the door slam behind me. It was Sailor John, he had followed me inside. He moved quickly, trying to make a grab for me, but this time I put up a struggle – I was sick of people touching me and treating me like a piece of meat.

Inside my head, something snapped. I knew no one else would help me and I would have to keep fighting to try and protect myself.

'Get off me, leave me alone!' I hollered, hoping this would be enough to fend him off, but he seemed determined.

I tried to swipe his arm away as he grabbed at my trousers and attempted to pull them down.

'Just bend over and keep quiet!' he ordered.

But there was no way I was going to let him do that to me.

'Fuck off! Leave me alone, you fucking pervert!'

I continued to scream and shout. I'd heard the sound of footsteps and I knew that one of the female members of staff – a woman called Audrey – would be working nearby. She was ironing in her room, one that contained all the laundered linen. I could hear her radio playing a tune in the distance, so I picked up some spare crockery she kept on one of the shelves and threw it as hard as I could at the ground.

'Leave me alone! Get off me!' I screamed, throwing anything and everything I could. I even managed to kick over a chair.

Sailor John's face turned ashen as he panicked and pulled up his trousers. After zipping himself up, he made for the door. As he grabbed the handle, he turned to face me.

'I'm not finished with you,' he warned.

I didn't care – I just wanted to get away from him as fast as I could. But Audrey never came. In fact, when I stepped outside, I couldn't see anyone, only the back of Sailor John as he fled down the corridor. Still, I'd done it, I'd escaped his clutches. However, my victory proved short-lived.

Not long afterwards, we were staying at a holiday cottage in Leversham on the Yorkshire Moors, between Whitby and

Pickering. It was meant to be a holiday for all the boys in my dorm, and it had been, until Brother James came looking for me and led me to an upstairs bedroom, where he brutally raped me. A day or so later, I was allowed out to go fishing. It was one of my favourite things because it enabled me to escape into a peaceful solitude far away from the sexual perversions of Brother James and Sailor John. I was standing down by the stream thinking of nothing in particular when I heard a voice as someone approached from behind.

'No, you're doing it all wrong. Here, let me help.'

I turned to find Sailor John striding over towards me and I immediately froze. He noticed and saw his chance. Circling his arms around me, he told me that he would teach me how to 'hold the rod'. But his big clammy hands clamped over my private parts before pushing down into my trousers and pants as he began helping himself to me. Humiliated and ashamed, I ran all the way back to the cottage, but there was no one to tell, no one to confide in, nothing anyone could do because Brother James and his pals seemed to have absolute control. I could try my best to fight them off, but they were grown men and I was still a boy, trapped and unable to escape. Afterwards, the 'holiday' became a sickening merry-go-round of sexual abuse. Towards the end, myself and another lad, Eric, were taken up to the bedroom, where we were force-fed brandy and whisky.

It was the first time I'd tasted alcohol and it completely knocked me sidewards. I didn't realise it then, but it had been used as an alcoholic cosh to leave us in a stupor and therefore more compliant as both men raped us throughout the night. They also made us do despicable things to one another. The following morning, I felt deeply hungover, sore and ashamed, but Eric was in a real state and he couldn't stop crying. We were both deeply traumatised by the rape, but also what we'd been forced to do to each other for the pleasure of those sick bastards.

If anything, the abuse of me by these men made me even more determined to assert my own heterosexuality but, gay, bisexual, or straight, the abuse they inflicted on us was utterly inhumane. I was determined not to let them tarnish every area of my life. Soon, it was the new term and one day at school, I plucked up the courage and asked a girl at my mixed comprehensive out on a date.

'Fancy going to the pictures with me on Saturday? *Exorcist II* is playing at Pocklington Picture House.'

The target of my affections – a lovely girl called Alison – grinned and nodded.

'Yeah, I'd love to.'

We arranged to meet later the following day and held hands as we headed in to see the film. Not that we saw very much because we were too busy kissing on the back row. In fact, we got so carried away, by the time we ran to the bus stop we'd missed the last bus.

'Steve, my dad's going to kill me!' Alison gasped, as we searched for a spare two pence and ran over towards the red phone box so that she could call home.

Soon, a dark green Humber car pulled up, its headlights picking us out like two convicts in a line-up, as we stood there, waiting for him. A man in his forties leaned over and wound down the passenger window, angrily.

'Get in, Alison!' he said shooting me a warning look before opening the passenger door.

She turned to look at me and then back at her father.

'But what about Steve?' she asked, grabbing the top of my arm to try and pull me in.

He took one look at me and pulled a disapproving face.

'No,' he said firmly, 'not him, just you.'

Alison looked over at me apologetically.

'Steve, I'm so sorry.'

I smiled.

'It's fine, honestly. You get in the car.'

She grabbed the door handle and hesitated.

'But what about you? How will you get home?'

'I'll be alright,' I told her gently. 'Now, go on, your dad's waiting.'

The middle-aged man sitting behind the wheel glared at me once more before turning back towards the road, his fingers tapping impatiently along the top of the steering wheel.

'But I'll see you at school on Monday?' Alison checked.

'Yes, I'll see you then.'

Satisfied, she climbed into the passenger seat, closed the door and the car roared off into the night, leaving me standing there. I looked up at the sky: pitch-black. With nothing else for it, I turned and began the six-mile walk back to St William's along the darkened country road. I hadn't been walking very long, only about half an hour, when a police car pulled up alongside me.

'Hello, son. What are you doing out this late at night on your own?'

I stopped and turned to talk to the officer through his half-open window.

'I missed the last bus.'

He nodded.

'Right, and where is it you're heading?'

'St William's? In Market Weighton.'

I couldn't be sure because it was dark and the only light on the road was coming from the headlights at the front of his car, but I'm almost certain I saw him flinch.

'You want a lift, son?' he asked kindly.

I nodded, knowing I was already in trouble, but surely, if a police officer brought me back, it wouldn't make it much worse? In fact, it might even help protect me from a good beating or the wandering hands of Brother James and his pals.

'Thanks,' I smiled, climbing into the passenger seat.

As the car trundled along, the bobby looked between me and the road.

'So, how long have you been there?' he asked, making conversation to try and pass the time.

'A year or so…' I mumbled.

'So, why are you there?'

'My dad used to hit me.'

He tutted and nodded knowingly.

'I see.'

I turned to face him.

No, you don't see, not really, the voice chipped in. *Tell him! He's a police officer, tell him. He'll have to listen to you, then he'll have to do something.*

I'd not met any coppers on my own before, but this one seemed really friendly. He'd laughed when I'd told him how Alison's dad had picked her up and left me standing. His sense of humour made him seem more approachable somehow, and I hoped and prayed that he might actually listen to me. I took a deep breath and began to tell him what had been happening to us at St William's.

'No,' I replied, looking directly at him, 'you don't see, because they hit us there. In fact, the beatings are the least of our worries. One of the Brothers, he touches us, interferes with us. Him and his mates, they do stuff to us... sexual stuff.'

The officer squirmed in his seat and refused to meet my gaze.

'I see,' he said, keeping his eyes firmly focused on the road ahead.

'You don't believe me, do you?' I said, exasperated. 'You don't believe any of us because we've been labelled "bad lads", but it's true. They do stuff to us and no one will help us.'

He ran a set of fingers along the top of the steering wheel as he gripped it with his other hand.

'I do believe you. We all know about it, we know what goes on at that place, but there's nothing we can do about it, son. Nothing.'

I spun back to look at him.

'But you're the police, there must be something you can do – lock them up or something?'

He shook his head.

'Nope, we don't like to get involved. It's nothing to do with us. The lads back at the station, they've all heard the stories, taken boys like you back there, kicking and screaming, but it's not a police matter, son. I'm sorry, but it's nothing to do with us,' he said, shrugging and lifting up an open palm.

And that was the moment when I finally gave up. All hope flew from me; it had dive-bombed away as swiftly and violently as the starlings I'd seen out in the backyard all those years before.

CHAPTER 25

RACE WITH THE DEVIL

After I'd told the copper and he'd refused to do anything to help, I realised that I was doomed: for the rest of my time at St William's, I would be left to my own fate. Of course, the abuse didn't stop – if anything, it intensified. Life continued but all I could do was count the days down until I could finally leave. I'd been broken and abused, but focusing on the future was my only way out of this hell hole.

I was sixteen years old when Mr Wood came looking for me one afternoon. He was carrying a brown paper envelope in his hand; inside it were my exam results.

'Are you nervous?' he asked, grinning, although I could tell by the look on his face and the fact the envelope had already been torn open that I shouldn't be. 'Look,' he added, thrusting a piece of paper in my hand, 'you've got six O levels, all As and Bs!'

I tried to raise a smile, but in truth, I didn't really give a toss – I just wanted to leave St William's.

'Stephen, we are all so proud of you. As for me, well, I'm really pleased. No one here has ever passed an exam before!'

He was still smiling, basking in my so-called glory, when he handed me the envelope and left. I glanced down at it and secretly fumed. My name had been written on the front but it had been addressed care of the school, so they had got to it first. I couldn't even have that one thing to myself. Brother James, his mates and the teachers had invaded every part of my life – they couldn't even do me the common decency of letting me open my own exam results. As the teacher had said, I'd achieved high grades in Art, History and Geography. The last one made me chuckle. I'd been locked in a cellar for thirteen years, yet I knew the geography of the world to O-level standard. I'd only failed one subject and that had been Maths. I smiled, secretly proud. My father, the bastard, had beaten all those sums into me day after day. I'd been starved and punished whenever I got them wrong, yet in spite of all of that, I'd just failed my maths O level. How sweet that small revenge tasted, like two fingers up at him.

Not long afterwards, I was busy reading in my dorm when a staff member came looking for me. I completely froze because I presumed it was my turn again – my turn in Brother James's office. Was he going to do to me what he'd done to Brian? Would someone else be witness to abuse as I had been to his?

'Does he want to see me on my own?' I asked, my voice beginning to falter. The thought of it left me sick.

'No, there's a social worker waiting to speak to you.'

It was a cold day outside – October time – so I pulled my coat tightly around me and followed him over towards the day room, where the social worker sat waiting for me.

'Hello, Stephen. Come and sit down,' she said, patting a soft chair next to hers.

Was I getting out? Had she come to take me away?

Mr Hughes – one of the brutal teachers who regularly beat me up – was sat beside her. I eyed him warily as he stared over at me.

Was I in trouble?

I cast my mind back. But I hadn't been involved in a fight for a few weeks and, as far as I could remember, I'd done nothing else wrong.

What did she want, and why was the teacher staring at me so intently?

The woman glanced down at the file in her lap and lifted her pen from the top of it. Turning it sideways in her hand, she rested her elbow on her knee and her chin against the top of her knuckles.

'Stephen, I'm afraid I have some bad news for you...' she began.

Bad news? What could be any worse than being kept here with these perverts at St William's?

I wanted to laugh out loud.

I waited for her to elaborate, my eyes searching hers, trying to work out what she was going to say next. She looked over towards Mr Hughes, who leaned forward and clasped his hands together as though in silent prayer.

'It's your father,' she said finally. 'It's your father, he has died.'

Died? Dead? How could he be? How could he die on me when I'd been waiting for years to get my own back on him?

'He had a brain tumour,' she continued, her eyes sad and expectant as though waiting for me to break down right there and then.

'A brain tumour?' I repeated in a monotone voice.

The social worker nodded.

'Yes, he'd been ill for quite some time and was in hospital. But we've just received news that he's sadly passed away,' she said, casting her eyes downwards as though to afford me a space to allow the news and personal grief to sink in.

'And what about them?' I asked suddenly. 'What about my brothers and sister?'

She looked momentarily flummoxed as though not expecting that question. I watched as she quickly flicked through the papers in her file, trying to locate the right piece of information.

'They still live with Mary,' she said, reading it aloud.

'Mary? What, Mary the housekeeper?' I asked incredulously.

'No, Mary your stepmother.'

At this I was dumbstruck; the social worker watched as my mouth fell open in shock.

'Yes, your father... well, he married Mary. Didn't you know?'

I shook my head and reeled back in my chair. So, the old bastard was dead, but he'd married her before he died. How convenient! It transpired that once Dad had remarried, he'd somehow become 'respectable' once more and so my siblings had been returned to him. Yet, as usual, I'd been left to rot.

Mr Hughes stood and I automatically flinched, expecting him to grab me from my seat. Right now, in front of the social worker, he was on his best behaviour, though.

'Are you alright? Would you like a cup of tea, Stephen?' he asked with fake concern.

I shook my head, tears pricking at the backs of my eyes. But they weren't tears for him, my dead father, they were tears of anger. Tears that death had claimed him before I could. He'd been the devil alright, but the devil had just run out of life. Now the devil was six feet under where he belonged. No, he was deeper than that, he was in the pit of hell with all the other evil bastards of this world! My only regret was that I hadn't put him there myself.

I heard a voice speaking to me, piercing my thoughts, ripping through the wall of anger I felt building up inside.

'I said, are you alright, Stephen? Is there anything we…' It was the social worker again. She gestured over to Hughes, who looked pathetic standing there, holding a mug, 'or I can get you?'

I shook my head as Hughes placed the cup of hot, sweet tea down on the table in front of me. Then I looked at it, shook my head and pushed it away as though it had been laced with poison.

'No, I'm absolutely fine,' I insisted.

And in many ways, I was. He was dead. The bastard was finally dead!

Why are you angry? the voice wondered. *You're finally free of him.*

It was right. If anything, I should throw a party. I should celebrate the fact that he could no longer hurt me.

I glanced up at the young social worker and thought what a strange job she had. I'd been taken from him – the devil – and put in Aston Hall and now St William's for my own protection. But what kind of protection was it to throw a child, a boy, from one danger into the path of another? How could they think we could be protected by God when we were being abused and used like worthless pieces of meat? How ignorant could the social workers and the police be after they'd been told time and time again by different boys about what really was happening here? They'd have to be stupid not to see the bigger picture. Yes, they'd have to be all of those things and more – they would have to be incompetent – and they were. The fact we'd told them what had been happening, and the fact they'd chosen to ignore us, made them as guilty as our abusers in my book. My eyes remained stubbornly dry and without tears. I refused to shed a single one for the devil – the devil who had just run out of luck.

'I just want to ask you one thing,' I said, breaking the deathly silence in the room.

'Yes, of course, Stephen. Ask me anything, what is it you want to know?'

I ignored Hughes, still sitting there next to me, and looked her directly in the eye.

'When am I getting out of here?'

CHAPTER 26

THE PET SHOP

Outside, it was freezing cold. A blanket of snow covered the ground at St William's, making it almost picture-postcard pretty, even though the reality couldn't have been further from the truth. Christmas came and went. I'd celebrated my first ever Christmas at Aston Hall when Mr Bradbury brought me some more books to read. Then I'd had two more at St William's. The first I'd spent at Mr Wood's house with his son. He and his wife had tried their best to give me a normal day with presents. They bought me a set of pyjamas and some socks and then we'd had turkey with all the trimmings. In spite of their very best efforts, I still felt very much like an outsider. To me, there was nothing worse than trying to join in someone else's family day when you don't have one of your own. For all their kind and best intentions, I ended up feeling even more lonely than I would have if I'd spent the day alone in my dormitory.

My second Christmas at St William's was a different day

entirely. For whatever reason, Mr Wood decided not to repeat his invitation to me again. Instead, Mr Hughes – the nastiest bastard of all the teachers – had obviously drawn the short straw and been made to work, looking after us all. His resentment was evident and, even though it was only my third Christmas, it felt like the longest day of my life. Plus, none of us got a present that year.

A few weeks later, I was reading over in a corner when a staff member told me to go back to the dormitory and gather my things together.

'Why?' I asked suspiciously.

'Because the social worker's on her way over later today. That's it, you're leaving St William's.'

I almost dropped my book in shock.

'What? Really? Now?' I asked.

'Yes,' he laughed. 'Really. Now, hurry up about it.'

In my rush, I threw the book down and it clattered, open-paged, to the floor. I ran so fast up to the dorm that my feet almost didn't touch the floor. Needless to say, I had my things packed within minutes and I couldn't stop smiling. However, my joy was short-lived when the same staff member popped his head around the door.

'Brother James wants to see you before you leave. He's waiting for you now, down in his office.'

'Does he?' I replied, my voice edged with a barely suppressed rage.

By the time I'd reached Brother James's office I was ready for him. I also knew I had to be careful, I couldn't fuck it up now. No, I just had to get out of there – get away from the place.

Then you can tell everyone what he did to you, the voice reasoned.

I knew it was right. I had to control my temper – keep a lid on it – if I stood a chance of getting out of St William's for good. Taking a deep breath for courage, I composed myself and tapped lightly against his door.

'Come in!' the voice on the other side called out.

Bastard, I thought as I watched his face spread into a sickly smile as he crossed the room to greet me.

'Stephen, my clever boy. Come in, come in…'

I knew it was forced… I knew, better than others, what he was capable of.

'So, I hear you're leaving us?' he said, continuing with the small talk.

'That's right,' I said as I gripped my hands together in a single fist behind my back.

One smart move from behind and I'll punch you in the nuts, I thought as he began to circle me. However, this time, instead of keeping my eyes facing forwards, they followed him as I began to turn – I wasn't going to let him out of my sight, not even for a second. Older and wiser now, I knew what the slippery bastard was capable of.

'Stephen,' he said, finally getting to the point of why I'd been called to his office, 'I hope that you can be trusted. That is, I trust there will be no mention to anyone outside of what has been happening here.'

I couldn't believe the sheer audacity of the man. Brother James, the one who had raped me throughout my time at St William's, was actually asking me to keep quiet? I eyeballed him and that's when I knew for the first time in my life that I had the upper hand: he was running scared, scared of what might happen to him if I blabbed. I already had, not that he knew that, yet no one had believed me. *Why would they believe me now?* I held my mouth firmly shut because I knew I'd soon be free. I was leaving St William's for good. From now on, I'd be able to make my own decisions and, for the first time in my life, I would be in control of my life. There were so many things that I wanted to say, but couldn't. I had to leave first, and then I could shout from the rooftops if I chose to.

'The thing is,' he said, circling me a second time, his feet treading the same well-worn path around me. 'The thing is, if there is any mention of anything that has been happening here, well, you could find yourself...' he rubbed a thumb against his fingertips as though he had something nasty stuck to them. 'The thing is you could find yourself back here, or somewhere far, far worse.'

He was threatening me; Brother James was telling me to keep my mouth shut and if I didn't, he'd make sure that I was punished. The rage I'd tried to contain suddenly came rushing to the surface and I knew that I couldn't contain it a second longer.

'Oh, don't you worry,' I hissed through gritted teeth. 'You're never going to see me again, mate.'

Brother James nodded.

'Good, good,' he smiled, relief washing over his face.

No, I thought, *once I'm out of those doors, you will never find me again.*

'Well, I suppose I should wish you luck then, Stephen,' he added.

Taking it as my cue to leave, I marched over towards the door – I couldn't get out of there quick enough. I was just turning the handle when Brother James spoke again.

'Good luck, and goodbye.'

I turned one last time, but I didn't smile and I didn't thank him. I didn't even say goodbye. I just opened and then slammed the door, safe in the knowledge that I'd never have to see the perverted bastard ever again.

The social worker helped me carry my things down to the boot of her car and slammed it shut with a satisfying thud.

'Right, let's go,' she said, climbing into the driver's seat.

I slid down into the passenger seat next to her, St William's Catholic School for Boys already a distant memory, as she drove down the long lane leading down towards the main road. I didn't even look back; I didn't have to – St William's and Brother James would be seared into my brain forever.

I waited a short while before striking up a conversation.

'So, where do I go now?'

I didn't care where she took me as long as it was far away from St William's. The relief I now felt was palpable.

She smiled as she shifted her gaze over towards me briefly.

'We've got you your own flat!'

'Flat?' I gasped.

'Well, yes, it's more of a bedsit, it's at the back of a pet shop.'

'A pet shop?' I repeated, trying not to laugh because I knew I sounded a bit like a parrot myself.

'Yes,' she smiled. 'The bedsit flat is owned by the people who run the pet shop. It's very nice, I think you're going to be very happy there.'

I scoffed and started to laugh.

'What? What's so funny?'

I rolled my eyes.

'Yeah, well, I've heard that before. The last social worker told me I'd like it at St William's and look at that place!'

Tell her. Tell her right now, the voice urged.

'Yes, but you were younger then and St William's was a place of safety.'

I gasped so hard that I began to choke, cough and then splutter.

She looked over at me.

'Are you okay?'

'Safety!' I croaked, in between lungfuls of air, 'St William's?'

'Yes.'

I coughed into my sleeve and then looked up at her.

'Well, if you call that safe, I'd hate to see what you called unsafe.'

She seemed baffled.

'What do you mean?'

'You lot, you don't half make me laugh. You lot knew what was going on there with Brother James and his mates interfering with us all, yet you did nothing. No one helped us. But it's still going on, right now,' I said, stabbing my finger in the air to drive home my point. 'It's happening right now under your noses, yet you lot and the police know all about it and won't get involved. You just don't want to know, do you?'

There, that was it. I'd finally said it, said my piece. I'd finally said the one thing I needed to say in order to be able to start my new life. I decided that if she did turn the car around and start driving back to St William's, I'd open the door and jump out. I'd escape and run somewhere they could never find me. But she didn't turn the car, indicate or even stop. Instead, she carried on driving.

'I hear what you're saying, Stephen, but the only way anyone can do anything about it is if they had absolute proof. Until then, no one's going to listen to a bunch of damaged children.'

And that was that – the end of the conversation. Afterwards, we drove in silence. I was disgusted but ultimately, I knew I'd be better off. I'd escaped the system and soon she would be out of my life for good. Secretly, I think she was relieved too – relieved that she wouldn't have to travel over to St William's to see me any more. A few hours later, we pulled up outside my new flat, in a place called Heanor in Derbyshire. The social worker hadn't been joking: it really was at the back of a pet shop, which was run by a lovely couple called Trevor and Sue. Even though it was hardly Buckingham Palace, it was all mine and I loved every square inch of it – apart from the noise, that is. I relished having my own space. Although it wasn't much, I could do what I wanted, leave when I wanted, and I didn't have to answer to anyone. But the best thing was I knew I was finally safe. For the first time ever, I had my own door key and I could just shut everyone else outside. I could make my own decisions and buy my own clothes without having to seek anyone else's permission and it felt bloody marvellous!

Having a pet shop as a neighbour had many benefits in that I always knew there would be someone on hand, should I need them. The downside was at night, when my neighbours became quite animated and noisy. The walls could only muffle so much noise, as parrots, budgies, cats and puppy dogs talked, chirped, meowed and barked for hours on end, trying to be heard above the din. I'd be there with my head buried deep beneath my pillow, attempting to block out the constant racket. Then, just when I thought it couldn't get any worse, Trevor and Sue bought a monkey! It set the proverbial cat amongst the pigeons as the whole place took on the smell and sounds of an all-night party at the zoo! Thankfully, I could escape it during the day because the social worker had managed to find me a job in a nearby flour mill. I was seventeen years old, tall and quite strong for my age, so it was my job to hump big, heavy bags of flour around the mill. It was exhausting work, but it paid handsomely – a whopping £25 per week, which was more money than I'd ever had in my life. For the first time ever, I felt rich!

★ ★ ★

I'd been living in my new flat for a year and I was just leaving work when I saw a familiar figure standing at a bus stop. It was a young lad who only looked about sixteen years old, but there was something about him that I recognised. I scoured my mind for clues.

Where do I know you from… Aston Hall? I shook my head. *No, not there. St William's?* I shook my head again. Nope, I'd only left there a year ago and I'd definitely know him from then. *No, it was someone I'd known ages before that. Someone I'd known…*

I ran across the street for a closer look and as I did so, the teenager turned and looked up at me.

'Are you Andrew?'

I watched as a small flicker of recognition flashed across his face.

'Yes.'

'I'm Stephen,' I said, pointing to myself. 'I'm your brother.'

He gasped as we both stood there, neither of us knowing quite what to say.

'Alright?' he nodded over at me coldly.

'I've been released,' I explained, as though I'd been a prisoner. 'I've been released from all those places. I'm working, I work around here…' I said, waving a hand over towards nowhere in particular.

Andrew nodded. 'Right.'

Another awkward silence followed.

'So, do you live around here?' I asked.

He shook his head.

'Nah, I'm waiting for a bus. I live in Loscoe Grange with Mary and the others….' he said, his voice trailing off.

And that's when I realised that I had absolutely nothing else to say to him. We had nothing in common. I couldn't help it – I blamed him and the others for keeping quiet for all those years. All those years that my father had kept me locked down in the cellar. Of course, I knew they'd been children, and so much younger than me, but they'd gone to school and they could have told a teacher, the milkman, the woman in the corner shop… Hell, they could have told anyone, but they hadn't.

'Right…' I said sharply. '…suppose I'll see you around.'

Andrew shrugged as though he didn't care either way.

'Yeah, suppose.'

And that was it – the last time I ever saw anyone from my family.

CHAPTER 27

JUSTICE AND MAYHEM

Soon, the sound of the monkey and his mates had driven me insane, so I left the pet shop bedsit, bade a fond farewell to Trevor and Sue, and moved to a better and much quieter place in Langley Mill, Derbyshire. I was out down the pub one night when I met a woman called Lucy. I'd become quite a regular in the bar – a bikers' bar – because it not only served ale, and lots of it, it also had a cracking jukebox full of heavy metal. I loved rock and metal music and I chose it because it suited my life and personality. I liked being part of a biker gang, and I loved wearing and doing things that I knew others would disapprove of. So I went out and got myself some leathers, grew my hair even longer, and had tattoos inked across my body.

In many ways, I felt I was reclaiming what others had taken from me. I refused to conform – I'd spent my life doing what other people had wanted or had forced me to do, but now it was my time and my choice, and I chose heavy rock. I was still only eighteen years old, but Lucy (who was the exact same age) and I hit it off straight away and within a couple of months, she said she had something to tell me.

'I'm pregnant, Steve.'

I was completely bowled over, though I suppose it wasn't unexpected because we'd not been using any contraception. I hadn't been taught about contraception at school but I knew the basics. However, we'd taken risks and now she fallen pregnant. I didn't want to be tied down with a baby, but I also didn't believe in abortion and so we agreed she would have the child. Of course, her dad soon followed. One day, he came around to pay me a visit.

'Well, well,' he said, looking me up and down with my long hair and biker clothes. 'You've been bloody stupid, haven't you?'

I nodded in agreement: he was right.

Although I was young, foolish and a bit of a selfish teenager, I'd been abandoned as a child so I had no intention of doing that to Lucy, even though we'd only known each other a short while. Instead, we got a house in nearby Heanor and tried to settle down into some sort of normal life, whatever that was. By this time, I'd left the flour mill and found a much better-paid job working in a meat factory as a butcher. I was nineteen years old when my first child, Debbie, was born. I'd love to say that I was a brilliant, hands-on dad, but I wasn't. I hadn't planned on having children and I'd been kept under lock and key all my life. Now I'd finally got out, I wanted to enjoy myself with my mates. I became known as the big bastard that everyone would come to see if they needed something sorting out.

In retrospect, I wasn't a very nice person back then. I'm not making excuses, because I drank and smoked far too much, but all the pent-up anger I'd kept buried for all those years rose to the surface. At that time, my motto was: I'll do anything I like and sod everyone else, a selfish mantra that I lived my life by. Lucy fell pregnant again and our second daughter – a beautiful little girl called Natalie – was born two years later.

I secured another even better-paid job making kitchen cabinets, then I moved again, this time to a position in a latex factory. The factory was the place where I suffered my first flashbacks. The company I worked for supplied rubber sheets for mattresses used in the NHS – the exact same type as in the treatment room at Aston Hall. At that time, I was in charge of the stores, but the sight and smell of those sheets made me feel nauseous. The rubber smell would drift up into my nostrils and, in a second, I'd be back there – a frightened little boy, his legs tied together with greying bandages as Doctor Milner moved in with the mask and needle.

One afternoon, a colleague of mine complained of having a cold and so nipped out to buy something to help unblock his nose. He popped a cough sweet in his mouth, but as soon as I smelled it in the air, I had to run straight to the toilet because I thought I would vomit. He was sucking Fisherman's Friends – a harmless mouth lozenge – but the smell was exactly the same as the chemical that Milner had dripped down onto the wire mask he'd covered my face with in the treatment room. I didn't appreciate it at the time, but certain smells would transport me straight back and I'd be trapped there – in the treatment room at Aston Hall or inside the headmaster's office at St William's. It wasn't until much later that I discovered the 'mask' chemical was called ether, something they once used in certain cough sweets. These smells, combined with the memories of what had happened, caused me to suffer from horrendous flashbacks and night terrors. Most nights I'd wake up screaming, unable to shake the horror visions of the past from my mind.

I loved my daughters but, like the selfish twat I was back then, I decided that I loved my new sense of freedom even more. Lucy grew tired of being stuck inside the house on her own with two kids, with me out all the time. Not long afterwards, I was working at the latex factory when I suffered a really bad work-related accident. I was just checking some boxes of stock when the chains on a nearby forklift truck carrying heavy goods snapped. The whole load shot up in the air and crashed down onto my leg, arm and shoulder, smashing them to smithereens. Somehow, the doctors managed to save my damaged leg and re-built it using metal pins.

I eventually woke up in intensive care, but Lucy was nowhere to be seen. Then I spent months on a set of crutches as I slowly began to recuperate. I remained in hospital for months, but Lucy never visited or came to see me. In many ways, I didn't blame her – I'd not been there for her and I realised that you reap what you sow in life. I also knew we were over. If she couldn't bring my kids to see me when my life was hanging by a thread, it meant we were over for good. Instead, on my release from the hospital, a mate of mine helped me find a new flat. Not long after that, I met my first wife, Lorraine. Lorraine was everything that I wasn't – she was kind and decent, and we fell in love. We met in 1985, when I was twenty-four years old, and were married two years later.

By this time, I was working as a steel erector and earning so much that we had cash to burn. I'd been given a chance by a big bear of a man called Dave Harding. I didn't realise it when I first met him in the pub, but Dave became the father I'd never had. He was, without a doubt, the biggest and roughest man I'd ever met. He was also the hardest man I knew, but he had a heart of solid gold. Everyone in the Langley Mill area knew that if you ever needed a job, then Dave would give you work. Not that he was a soft touch – anything but – however, he gave those people who others wouldn't touch with a bargepole a chance and I was one of them. I had spent my whole life fighting, but Dave taught me that I didn't have to fight any more. He knew more than most because he'd been just like me once. As soon as he heard I'd been in care, he offered me a chance to work for him.

'Tell me, why did you end up in care, Steve?' he asked one night as we chatted over a pint.

I flinched. I'd never told anyone about the cellar, the mental hospital or the sexual abuse I'd suffered, yet now here he was asking me a direct question.

'My dad used to beat me up, but I don't like to talk about it,' I replied, draining the last of my pint.

'No problem. Well, I've got a job for you, but it's on one condition…'

I put down my empty glass and signalled to the barmaid to bring us over two more.

'Yeah, what's that?'

'No more fighting.'

I thought for a moment and nodded.

'Okay, deal.'

And that was that, my job interview was over. In reality, I

was sick of the fighting and, if truth be told, the drinking. Over the past decade I'd done both to excess, yet there was still a part of me that wanted to self-destruct and I knew I needed to rein it in. The following week, I started working for Dave and soon me and Lorraine were cash-rich. I was bringing home £500 a week which, back then, was a small fortune. Meeting Dave turned out to be one of the best moves of my life and, after that day, he remained a constant father figure in my life.

Lorraine became pregnant and our son Simon was born in 1991. Simon's birth changed my life in more ways than one. I knew that I'd messed it up with Lucy and the girls and so this time I was determined to become the father I'd never had. With Dave's influence, I cut back on my drinking and spent time at home with Lorraine and my boy. We went on to have two more sons, Oliver, now twenty-six, and Jacob, twenty-three, and they became the centre of our world. I made a conscious decision that the abuse I'd suffered as a child stopped with me, and I'm proud to say that I never once raised my hand or my voice to any of my kids because I'd seen first-hand the damage that kind of 'parenting' does.

But outside home and work, I was still knocking around with a few nasty sorts. One night, and against my better judgement, I got involved in a fight and when the fists started to fly, I found myself in the thick of it. The following Monday, I was back at work when Dave came over to see me.

'Hi, Dave,' I said, my face lighting up as he approached.

SMACK!

His fist crushed my nose flat before it smashed hard into my chin. He'd hit me with such force that I found myself waking up on the floor. I dabbed a hand at some blood as it trickled down from my nose. Punch-drunk, I glanced up to see Dave's huge frame looming over me.

'What was that for?' I asked, looking down at my crimson bloodied fingers.

'That is what you get for fighting,' he said coolly. 'I told you, no more fighting. You do that again and you're out.'

Even though he'd punched me flat to the floor, I knew he was right and I was wrong.

'Sorry, Dave,' I said, and I meant it.

He was the last person I wanted to let down.

'I was like you once and I don't want you to follow the same route, understood?' he warned.

I nodded, my face throbbing as I did so.

'Yes, I won't. I mean, that's it. My fighting days are over, I promise.'

I knew that Dave had hit me to teach me a lesson and it had, even though I was by now thirty years old. He'd wanted to shock me, to set me back on the right path, and it worked. After that day, I changed my group of friends, gave up my driving licence so that I wouldn't be tempted to go out on my bike looking for trouble, and I decided to become a better man. Dave was right – my father had lived his life through violence and, in many ways, it was all I knew, how to survive and how to play the tough guy. The problem is, when you're the tough guy, there's always someone tougher than you, and for me that person was Dave. He encouraged me to become the best person I could and I decided that I would never ever let him down again. And I didn't. Sadly, my dear friend died of cancer many years later. Everyone who knew him was absolutely heartbroken and still is to this day. We all miss him deeply.

My work as a steel erector took me all over the country, and Lorraine and my wonderful in-laws supported me in every single way. We'd been married for around eight years and we'd never had a single row. I'd thought it had been a good thing, but then I realised that we didn't row because we were just friends, there was no passion left. It was around this time that I met Gail, the woman who was to become my second – and final – wife. Gail was a hairdresser, but me and Lorraine had got to know her because she worked a second job at night behind the local bar – the White Lion – to try and make ends meet.

As soon as I met Gail, I knew I'd found my soul mate, the person I'd been searching for all my life. It was 1996, and I was thirty-five years old but, in many ways, it felt as though my life had just begun. Not only was she absolutely gorgeous, she was my intellectual equal, my everything. I'm not proud of the fact that we embarked on an affair, but it turned out that Lorraine had also decided that our marriage had reached the end of the line. When I finally came clean and told her about me and Gail, she not only accepted it, the three of us remained good friends, which we still are to this day. Lorraine is still one of the most marvellous people I've ever met.

With an amicable split behind me, I decided that this was my final chance and I couldn't mess up again. Lorraine and I filed for a divorce and Gail and I set up home in a room above a pub. Nine months later, we moved into our first house. My boys would come and stay with us all the time, and Gail and I would pop around to Lorraine's to see them. I also made sure that my children were always well provided for. In time, Gail gave birth to our beautiful daughter, Jessica – the spitting image of her beautiful mother.

Gail made me the happiest man alive when she became my wife. We married at Ripley Registry Office when Jess was five years old.

* * *

I was still suffering with back problems, which I put down to the time I'd been almost sliced in half with the edge of the spade.

One day, I was in a hospital cubicle with Gail, waiting to see a specialist, when he popped in around the curtain and sat down.

'So, tell me, your knee has been giving you problems?'

I glanced at Gail, and we both shook our heads in confusion.

'No, I'm here to see you about my back,' I explained.

The doctor seemed a little flummoxed until a voice called out from a nearby cubicle.

'No, doctor. It's *my* knee, I'm over here!' a woman cried out.

Flushing red with embarrassment, the specialist jumped to his feet and dashed over to the correct patient, leaving my hospital notes sitting there in front of us on a table. Curiosity got the better of me and with nothing else to do, I began flicking through them. What I read blew me away. There, in my medical files, was proof that my father had physically abused me. I felt sick as I read how I'd been treated for a fractured skull when I was still a baby. I'd also spent time in hospital when I was a year old, suffering from Primary TB (tuberculosis). Homeless people and those in poverty are more prone to TB because they have little or no heating, and they live in dark, damp and filthy conditions, with no fresh air – just as I had done throughout my childhood. TB bacteria can live longer in the damp and dark because sunlight cannot reach it to kill it off.

The neglect I'd faced as a child was written right there in black and white for all to see. Strangely, there was no mention of any broken arms, or of me being locked in a cellar for thirteen years. I'd always thought my father had been a bastard, but finding out that I'd suffered a severe fracture to my skull when I was just nineteen months old left me sickened. I recalled the haircut he'd given me and the strange bumps I'd felt at the back of my skull – that had happened as a babe in arms. Deep down, I knew it was probably time to start searching for answers to how and why he'd been able to get away with doing that to me for so long when all the warning signs of abuse and neglect had been there. I had blocked it out for so long, but the constant flashbacks and night terrors convinced me that I had to tackle it once and for all. Up until that point, Gail had been the only person I'd confided in about St William's. She was also the one who would have to chase me and calm me down after I'd woken up screaming. Soon as I slept, I was instantly back there, trapped inside the headmaster's office or the treatment room at Aston Hall. I realised the only way I could free myself from the horror for good would be to face up to what had happened to me as a child.

I started by calling up Derbyshire Social Services to ask for my records. A short while later, I received a letter saying that my records had all been destroyed. Then, a few days after that, someone senior from Social Services phoned me to say it was 'unfortunate' but it sometimes happened. However, my solicitor told me such records should not be destroyed until after my death. I smelled a rat.

With a new sense of purpose, I set myself up with a Facebook account and stumbled upon a support group for boys who, like me, had survived their time at St William's. The group, which had been set up by other survivors, had been formed so legal action could be taken against the perpetrators. I knew there would be safety in numbers and I also knew that if nothing else, I wanted to bring those responsible to justice. I didn't hesitate, I decided to join.

In 2016, Brother James (real name James Carragher) and Anthony McCallen (who the boys had called the Black Spider) were convicted of a total of 35 sex offences against 11 boys between 1970 and 1991. McCallen, then sixty-nine, was jailed for 15 years, and Carragher for 9 years. It was the third time Brother James had been jailed for offences at the home, Leeds Crown Court heard. He'd first been tried in 1993, when he was jailed for 7 years, and again in 2004, when he'd been given a 14-year sentence. Judge Geoffrey Marson QC, sitting at Leeds Crown Court, told Carragher he must take into account the sentence that he would have passed had he heard the evidence from all three trials. Judge Marson said this would have led to a sentence of 30 years, but he had to deduct the 21 years Carragher had already served.

The pair had denied 87 sex offences against children at St William's, which finally closed its doors in 1992. Brother James (Carragher) of Cearns Road, Merseyside, was found guilty of 21 indecent assaults and 3 serious sexual assaults, but was cleared of a further 30 charges. Meanwhile, the Black Spider (McCallen) of Whernside Crescent, Ingleby Barwick, Stockton-on-Tees, was convicted of 11 charges, including a serious sexual offence, but acquitted of 8 others.

The jury was unable to reach verdicts on 13 charges and was discharged by the judge.

Judge Geoffrey Marson QC, sentencing the pair, said: 'Each of you targeted some of the most vulnerable boys. You groomed them and abused them for your own sexual gratification. The victims were effectively trapped and there was no escape from you. They were confused, frightened and in turmoil. It has blighted their lives and each of you has contributed significantly to their misery.'

The judge added: 'Each of you has a longstanding, deeply ingrained sexual interest in teenage boys. It's an interest, I have no doubt, that continues to persist.'

He warned that they would have to serve half their sentences before they could be considered for release on licence.

I took small comfort from the fact that Brother James had finally got his comeuppance, even if it was many years down the line, but I often wondered what had happened to his mates – the countless faces who had used and abused me. Had the long arm of the law or even death finally caught up with any of them? It's something I still wonder to this day.

CHAPTER 28

MUSIC, ART AND ASTON HALL

Before I learned of the fate of Brother James, I began drifting along another path and soon found myself drawn to it like a metal filing being pulled towards a magnet. That path was music. I'd always loved music since that fateful day when Mr Bradbury had brought the record player and his prized records to Aston Hall for me to listen to. Music has helped me through some of the darkest times of my life and given me a reason to go on when I just wanted to lie down and give up. Like Dave Harding, my old boss, they have been the two constants throughout my life.

Gail and I had been married a while when, one night, we were out having a drink in one of our old pubs in Langley Mill. The pub had a cracking jukebox with classic heavy metal and rock and even a whole section dedicated to Hawkwind, one of my favourite bands. Being the daft bugger I am, I'd often get drunk and sing along to songs, my voice booming across the pub as others joined in or covered their ears! It was after one of those barmy sessions that some fellas approached me and asked if I'd like to sing a few guest songs with their band.

'Me?' I said, laughing out loud. 'Are you sure?'

They were, and before I knew it, I was singing with them in pubs and bars. That's when Martyn Needham, from the band Dr Hasbeen, approached and asked me if I'd become his singer. Again, I couldn't quite believe my luck.

'Okay, why not?'

Martyn helped to organise festivals and soon I met other singers and musicians. Before I knew it, we were playing and attending them all, from early Glastonbury to Stonehenge and various bike festivals. The more people I met, the more I realised this was a world I loved and one which I belonged to. I played with more and more people until me and a mate of mine – a lad called Vince Cory – decided to set up our own band, Captain Starfighter and the Lockheeds – of which I'm still the lead singer today. Former members of Hawkwind, namely Dead Fred and guest musicians such as Nik Turner, Harvey Bainbridge and Alan Davey amongst others, have joined and played with us. Today, we play sonic rock at festivals all over the world.

★ ★ ★

In 2011, Gail and I were living in a house near Alfreton, Derby, when our neighbour knocked at the door. She was a lovely lady called Stephanie Smith so, bizarrely, our names were almost identical.

'Hi Steve, can I ask you a really odd question?' Steph asked, standing in our kitchen as I filled up the kettle with water.

'Yeah, of course, you can ask me anything, meduck.'

'Have you got a daughter called Natalie?'

I almost dropped the kettle in shock.

'Natalie?' I gasped.

Lucy had given birth to Debbie and Natalie, then she left me and I'd not seen them again since that day. Natalie would have only been about three years old then, so she would be twenty-one now. I'd often wondered where my girls were and if they were happy. I'd convinced myself they'd have a much better life without me because I'd been so messed up as a kid.

I nodded over towards Steph.

'Yes, I have. Why do you ask?'

'Because I've just had a conversation with a girl who was ringing all the S Smiths in the phonebook. She's looking for you, Steve, she says she's your daughter.'

My heart soared with joy.

'And what did she say? Do you know where I can find her?' I asked, desperate to know.

Steph smiled.

'Yep, I can do better than that, I've got her phone number.' She smiled again, handing me a piece of paper.

I could hardly believe it that after all these years, one of my girls had come looking for me. It felt like my second chance at being the dad I'd always wanted to be. I felt sick with nerves as I dialled the number and waited for someone to answer. Natalie was so delighted to hear from me that we arranged to meet in a local supermarket cafe. I was worried that I might not recognise her, but as soon as I saw her, I knew it was my Natalie because she was the spitting image of her mother. That day, we went out for a meal and I saw her every single week to make up for all the years we'd spent apart. I also became close friends with her boyfriend and we'd often all go down the pub together. Then, six months later, Natalie had some news for me.

'Dad, I'm pregnant!' she beamed.

'Oh, love!' I gasped, wrapping my arms around her. I was absolutely thrilled.

Months passed, until one Sunday morning when I was sitting in the house and there was a knock at the door. I opened it to find two police officers standing on my doorstep.

'Are you Stephen Smith?' one of them asked.

I nodded. He looked so serious that I was frightened to death what it was that he was about to tell me.

'It's about your daughter, Natalie…' he began as I felt my world fall from beneath me.

Natalie had been out with her friends to the cinema the night before. They'd been on their way back home, driving along a winding country road, when their car had collided with another. She and three of her friends had been killed instantly. The occupants of the other car had suffered serious injuries but survived. A blackness enveloped me as I looked for someone – anyone – to blame. But the police investigated and a resulting inquest found that it had been just that, a tragic accident. Natalie had been five months pregnant. Distraught and grief-stricken, I went along to the funeral, where I saw Lucy, but we didn't speak – the pain of losing our beautiful daughter was just too much to bear. It's hard to come to terms with losing a child, especially one that you haven't watched growing up. The only consolation is that I got to spend that wonderful year with my girl, one of the most precious years of my life.

Of course, the night terrors and flashbacks from my childhood abuse continued to haunt me. Poor Gail would often wake to find me screaming or running around. I'd have nightmares that I was trapped alone in the cellar; I'd dream of Doctor Milner coming for me with a needle and a mask, and finally, I'd have images of Brother James and what those other bastards had done to me at St William's. The flashbacks and night terrors became so bad that I had to go for counselling. It helped a little, but it couldn't take it away because all that horror was permanently imprinted on my brain. I was eventually diagnosed with Post Traumatic Stress Disorder (PTSD) and Dissociative Disorder, caused by a traumatic event in my earlier life, of which I'd had many. The disorder – there are three types – is the brain's way of coping with too much stress. It leaves you feeling disconnected from yourself, which explains why, when I was younger, I'd have a voice talking to me in the third person. Back then, I thought everyone had a voice that spoke to them in this way, but it had been my way of coping. I now know this is called Dissociative Identity Disorder, which is very unusual, but then the life I've led has been unusual, to say the least.

On 28 October 2013, I was interviewed by Elie Godsi, one of the UK's leading consultant clinical psychologists, so that he could prepare an independent psychological report for my lawyers. I told him all about the cellar, the abuse at both Aston Hall and St William's. His report concluded that I

would always have significant interpersonal problems including a general mistrust and suspicion of people, particularly anyone in a position of authority.

The report added:

The effects of PTSD on his identity, his self-esteem and his personality will be evident for the rest of his life.

His findings brought me comfort because at last someone – and not just anyone but one of the country's leading experts – had finally recognised what I'd been through and what I was still living with every single day of my life.

Four years ago, Gail and I decided that owning a house wasn't for us – it was far too tying and expensive. The night terrors continued and waking up surrounded by brick walls added to the anxiety, so we sold up, lived in a caravan and I spent six months building our own narrow boat. It turned out to be the best thing I ever did because after thirteen years of being locked in a cellar, then a mental hospital, and eventually being passed around the offices and rooms of paedophiles, I was finally free. I can now choose where I want to live or move to and no one can stop me. I find the freedom of living on a boat utterly liberating. Each morning, I have swans stick their heads in through my window, waiting to be fed. What could be better than being at one with nature and not hemmed in by bricks and mortar? But the very best part was being able to decorate my boat with the very same dragons and fantasy art that my father and the head teacher at Aston Hall had ripped up, time and time again. Now, no one can rip up my paintings because they've been decorated on solid wood, where they will always be with me.

A few people noticed them and commented kindly, asking if they could buy some of my artwork for themselves. So, whenever the mood takes me, I not only sing but I paint too. Today, my artwork sells all over the world, from Japan, Canada and America to Norway and even Russia. Some collectors have bought up to a dozen paintings that they display in their homes and that makes me very proud indeed. A few years ago, the band members from Iron Maiden asked if I would paint some fantasy backdrop artwork for a tour they were doing around Iceland and Norway. They wanted something Egyptian, so I painted these huge panels that took me forever. Not that I cared – I did them for free because it's what I love to do. They only thing I asked them to pay for was for the shipping because they weighed a tonne!

Since then, I've done album and book covers, cars, even a tank – you name it, if I can paint on it, then I will. I have also given hundreds of my paintings to charity so they can do some good. It doesn't matter how long a piece of artwork takes me, I sell them all at a reasonable price because I believe art should be accessible to everyone and not a chosen few. I love to paint and I don't wish to make any money out of it. I truly believe that money is just a means to an end and once you start putting a price on art and creativity, it stops being just that.

Not long ago, I received a phone call from a gallery. The owner had seen my work and wanted to display it in his art gallery.

'Can I ask you something?'

'Yes,' he replied.

'Do you put prices on the art that you hang on the walls?'

The man seemed momentarily baffled but replied, 'Yes, of course we do.'

'Well,' I told him, 'it's not an art gallery then, is it? It's a shop!'

I feel the same about music. If I could just perform at free festivals then I would, but sadly, there's not so many of them about these days, as festivals, like everything else in this world, have become a big business.

* * *

On 25 July 2018, I was sat on my barge boat, tucking into a sandwich, when the local news came on television. I heard a police officer read out a statement about Aston Hall, the mental hospital I'd been sent to as a young boy. I threw my butty down and I immediately rang Gail's mum, Marjorie.

'Have you got the telly on?'

'Yes, why?' she asked, a little taken back.

'That's one of the places they sent me. I was there, Marge – that's where they kept me after I got out of the cellar. Hang on,' I said, turning up the sound as a woman with red hair came on the screen. That woman was called Barbara O'Hare and she'd written a book called *The Hospital*. Now in her fifties, she had also been held at Aston Hall against her will and injected with something called sodium amytal, a truth serum. It turned out brave Barbara had blown the whistle not only on Doctor Milner, who had been carrying out drug experiments on children like us, but the whole system.

'If you were a child at Aston Hall, come forward now,' she urged. 'Come forward to the police and let them know.'

Astonishingly, Barbara, who'd survived cancer, had formed a help group on Facebook called The Survivors of Aston Hall. Thanks to this remarkable lady, hundreds of people had found the strength to come forward and stand together. I immediately searched for the group and contacted Barbara, who not only called me back but listened to my story.

'You need to read my book that I writ, Ste. And then you need to write one of your own,' she said in her distinctive and warm Liverpudlian accent, and I immediately knew I'd found a friend.

The news on the report carried out by Derbyshire Police, which I'd seen on TV, concluded assaults had been carried out by Doctor Milner on both boys and girls. He had sedated me and these other children with drugs, namely sodium amytal and who only knows what else in my case. Milner had died in 1976, so he could not be questioned or tried, and despite a huge investigation by Derbyshire Police – the biggest one the force had ever undertaken – allegations against other staff members were eliminated from the inquiry for various reasons because staff members could not be identified or had since died. In total, the police had interviewed 114 alleged victims, with 77 crimes having been reported, including ones of serious physical abuse, sexual abuse and 14 allegations of rape.

Milner had given truth serum to us before we had been sexually assaulted. The treatment, known as narco-analysis, involved interviewing us in a drug–induced state to try and make us recall and disclose our deepest thoughts, fears and feelings. Following the release of Barbara's book, the publicity surrounding it and the police report, another 43 people contacted Derbyshire Police, including me. As I write this, the survivors of Aston Hall have been told we will receive compensation from the Department of Health for what the doctor, Kenneth Milner, did to us. Not only that, but we have been told to expect a letter of apology from the Government.

A Department of Health and Social Care spokesperson told the press: 'This is an important milestone for everyone who was affected by these terrible events and we hope that all claims can be resolved as soon as possible.'

The police report also decided that had he still been alive today, Milner would be questioned over multiple allegations of rape and sexual assault. Not only that, he was illegally drugging children – some as young as twelve – against their will and without their parents' consent or knowledge. It was a scandal on an industrial scale.

I spoke to the police and gave a detailed statement of what had happened to me during my 16-month stay at Aston Hall. In the meantime, Barbara helped put me in touch with her solicitor, who later told me they believed I'd been one of 20 boys chosen by Milner to carry out extensive 'treatments' on. That is, while some of the children had been subjected to one or a few treatments, myself and 19 other lads had been given 'treatment' once, often twice, every single week. I now believe that in giving me multiple injections in both arms, Milner was trying to find the perfect concoction – the perfect truth serum – so that it could be used for potential interrogation work. All I know is that out of those 20 boys, only I, and possibly two more, have been traced. We will never know if there are others still out there. However, it's understood that the majority of them have already died, taking their secrets to the grave. This is why I've written this book. It's difficult for anyone, but especially a tough, hard man like me, to admit what has been done to him as a child, but if I can find the strength then I know others can too. I hope that by telling my long, brutal and, at times, deeply distressing story, it will give strength to others. If it helps just one other survivor, I will die a happy man.

I've had terrible things done to me, but it has made me stronger and also made me the person I have become today. My philosophy on life is this: you cannot allow your past to define what your future will be. Likewise, I do not see myself as a victim but as a survivor. Those who have been abused do not always go on to abuse others; we all decide who and what we become, and as I promised my dear friend, Dave Harding, I will try and become the best version of myself that I could possibly be, and I hope that I have. I actually consider myself a very lucky man because in spite of what has happened, I now have a great life – the best. I have a wife whom I adore, hundreds of great friends, and all my children, who are, and continue to be, my greatest achievement. I've done some stuff when I was younger that I'm not proud of, but I didn't know any better then.

Throughout my childhood I'd been locked up, hidden away, institutionalised and failed by a system and parents who should have been there to protect me. I'll never know for sure why I was kept locked down in a cellar. Over the years, I've seen lots of psychiatrists and psychologists, who have mooted various different theories, one being that my deeply religious parents, who were Catholic, had had me out of wedlock and so kept me hidden away. This could be true, but it doesn't explain my father's brutality towards me. Another explanation could be that he wasn't my actual father, but that he'd taken me on as his own. At the end of the day, I could send myself mad thinking of all the possibilities, but you cannot try and make sense out of something which makes no sense at all. I think he was just a sadistic bastard with a twisted mind that us ordinary folk could never hope to try and begin to understand.

Today, nothing makes me happier than spending time with my family, painting or performing. When I get up on that stage, I'm there to entertain and make people happy. In many ways, I feel like the luckiest man in the whole wide world. Other musicians might need chemical stimulants or alcohol to give them courage, but I don't. I never get stage fright and I never get nervous, not any more – I've spent a lifetime being frightened and I refuse to be frightened any more.

THE BOY IN THE CELLAR

Feedback rips through the black square amps stacked up on top of each other in tall, cubed towers. The screech pours from them like the howl of a wounded animal. A tangle of black spaghetti cables leads down like snakes as the crowd pushes against each other. Anticipation crackles through the air like electricity and there's a momentary dip in noise as the sound engineer walks on and taps his fingers against the lead mic.

One, two, one, two... he calls, his voice soaring high into the air.

Thousands of people become restless as a slow clap picks up from the back and moves towards the front – an audible Mexican wave. Legs ache as sharp elbows jostle each other for the best view.

Another stagehand walks on and thinking it's the band, a cheer rises quickly only for it to fall away almost as soon as it has begun. The sound of an electric guitar cuts the air like a scalpel as the instrument and others are tested on stage before fret boards are rested against waiting stands.

There's another pause as the audience begins to swell with excitement. Painted faces, old and young – but all smiling – stand shoulder to shoulder, waiting for the gig to begin. Someone shouts out from the back and the mosh pit – a swarm of black T-shirts – begins to stir. Digital lights rise and fall as the first stagehand rushes around, adjusting the height of the microphones. The slow hand clap starts up again. It travels through the crowd like a steam train as a crescendo of noise explodes. There are screams, shouts, and a girl with blue hair is hoisted up on her boyfriend's shoulders as he sways beneath her. Lager is spilt and the LED lights on the sound desk flash from green to traffic light red as a second roar erupts and the band walks out onto the stage.

The crowd surges forward and the volume burns like fire. A single ear-splitting strum of a guitar slices through and then the thick din of the drum reverberates through feet, travelling quickly up legs and into chests, causing hearts and ribcages to thud in unison.

Dry ice drifts and curls upwards; a sudden thrash of electric guitars slams into the audience like a solid brick wall. The spotlights dim as a single figure walks out onto the stage, his arms spread as the crowd screams for him, sending the lights off the scale. They rise and burn a blinding white and the mosh pit comes alive as he takes centre stage – arms, fists and feet all flying in a single spinning ball of energy. He looks up, his heart soaring, and then begins to sing. His voice leaves the fans punch-drunk with delirium and in that moment he realises just how far he has come and the journey he has taken to get here.

It is the boy in the cellar. He is no longer alone.

ACKNOWLEDGEMENTS

I'd like to start by thanking my lovely wife, Gail, for her strength, support and constant nagging! Also, my amazing children: Simon, Oliver, Jacob and Jessica.

To my band mates in Captain Starfighter and the Lockheeds, namely, Vince, Darren, Lee, Nige and Dead Fred.

Special thanks must go to Barbara O'Hare – the most tenacious woman I have ever met or known! Also, to the Bunny Hop Knights of the Round Table: Ant, Bones, Jon, Colin, Not Right John, Gary, Lee, Digger and Bimbo.

To my dear friend Dave Harding and his wife Sue, without whom I wouldn't be the man I am today. Also Tay, another great man.

To Veronica Clark, who was recommended by Barbara O'Hare, and who not only wrote, but helped me put this whole book together. Thanks for listening to my tale and for making sense of it.

Thank you to the brilliant Alan Sellars, my (and many other

people's) barrister at Bond Turner, for helping us not only to fight for justice but compensation for what has been done to us as children at Aston Hall.

To Pete Stanley – a fantastic photographer – who supplied all my professional 'stage' photos featured in this book.

Thanks to my literary agents, Eve White and Ludo Cinelli, for believing in me and my story, and to Kelly Ellis, Ciara Lloyd and the amazing team at John Blake Publishing for allowing me to tell it.

Finally, thank you for reading my story. I hope that in finally finding a voice to tell it, I can help others who have suffered for years in silence. If I can do it, so can you.

APPENDIX

Some of Stephen's medical notes from his childhood that he's only recently uncovered. They show a glimpse of the abuse he suffered at the hands of his father, and how many opportunities were missed to save him.

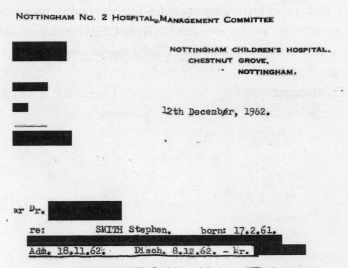

ar Dr.

re: SMITH Stephen.   born: 17.2.61.

Adm. 18.11.62.   Disch. 8.12.62. - Mr.

This child was admitted with a history of being rathe iet on the day prior to admission and a swelling being ticed on his head on the day of admission.   There was no own history of trauma but on examination there was an tensive soft swelling in the left parietal and occipital gion.   An X-ray of his skull showed a linear fracture on e left side in the posterior part of the parietal bone. e fracture extended in to the occipital bone.

He was observed in the ward for several days and after out a week he vomited twice, with a raised temperature and boccipital nodes ++.   His throat was slightly congested d there was blotchiness of his skin.   He was seen by the ediatric Registrar who suggested treatment with Syrup nicillin 1 tsp. t.d.s. for five days.   A white cell count this time was 10,000 per cmm. and E.S.R. 15 mm. in one hour. throat swab yielded a heavy growth of Alpha haemolytic reptococci and N. catarrhalis.

He settled down satisfactorily and was fit for discharge

317

home on the 8th December.

    We will see him again in the Orthopaedic Clinic in one week.

                Yours sincerely,

                Orthopaedic Registrar.

SHEFFIELD REGIONAL HOSPITAL BOARD

NOTTINGHAM No. 5 HOSPITAL MANAGEMENT COMMITTEE

NOTTINGHAM and DISTRICT CHEST CENTRE

"FOREST DENE," GREGORY BOULEVARD, NOTTINGHAM

Telephone : NOTTINGHAM 77884-5

Your Ref. :

Our Ref. :

8th June, 1962.

Dear Dr.

            Re: Stephen Smith.

    This child's primary tuberculous lesion in the left lung has regressed satisfactorily, and it would now be safe to discontinue the chemotherapy.

    We will keep him under regular observation.

                Yours sincerely,

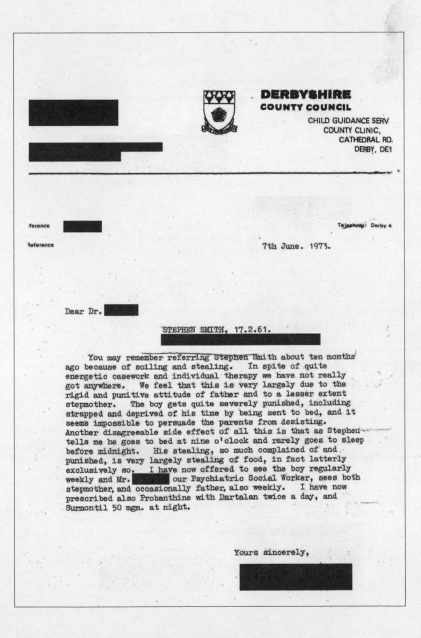

DERBYSHIRE
COUNTY COUNCIL

CHILD GUIDANCE SERV
COUNTY CLINIC,
CATHEDRAL RO.
DERBY, DE1

ference

Reference

Telephone: Derby 4

7th June. 1973.

Dear Dr.

STEPHEN SMITH, 17.2.61.

You may remember referring Stephen Smith about ten months
ago because of soiling and stealing. In spite of quite
energetic casework and individual therapy we have not really
got anywhere. We feel that this is very largely due to the
rigid and punitive attitude of father and to a lesser extent
stepmother. The boy gets quite severely punished, including
strapped and deprived of his time by being sent to bed, and it
seems impossible to persuade the parents from desisting.
Another disagreeable side effect of all this is that as Stephen
tells me he goes to bed at nine o'clock and rarely goes to sleep
before midnight. His stealing, so much complained of and
punished, is very largely stealing of food, in fact latterly
exclusively so. I have now offered to see the boy regularly
weekly and Mr.   our Psychiatric Social Worker, sees both
stepmother, and occasionally father, also weekly. I have now
prescribed also Probanthine with Dartalan twice a day, and
Surmontil 50 mgm. at night.

Yours sincerely,

319

MBERSIDE A.H.A. — BEVERLEY DISTRICT

EAST RIDING GENERAL HOSPITAL
BRIDLINGTON ROAD
DRIFFIELD
NORTH HUMBERSIDE
YO25 7JR

4th October, 1976.

Dr.

Stephen Smith, aged 15,
St. William's School,
<u>Market Weighton</u>

Thank you for your note about this lad, gives a history of falling backwards and injuring lumbar spine on a metal tent peg some two s ago.

On examination there was a scar from this ration which had healed well, but no obvious al signs. The big question, of course, was ther there was any foreign body in the scar, so -rayed the area and no F.B. was seen. I have not, refore, asked to see him again.

Yours sincerely,

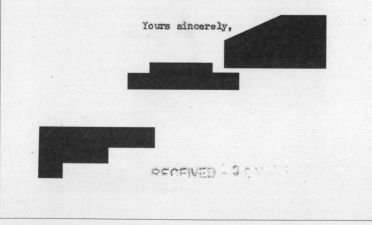

RECEIVED - 3 C V

Excerpts from the psychiatric report compiled by Dr. Godsi after recently assessing Stephen. The horrors of what he has suffered are plain to see, and shocking to read.

8.9	His highest score by some margin was for Dissociation, (which measures dissociative symptomatology such as depersonalisation, derealization, out of body experiences and psychic numbing). This was followed by a cluster of similar significant scores for Anger and Irritability, which measures self reported anger or irritable affect, as well as associated angry thoughts and behaviour; for Intrusive Experiences (those intrusive symptoms that are highly associated with post traumatic stress such as flashbacks, nightmares and intrusive thoughts) and for Defensive Avoidance (avoidance of stimuli reminiscent of a traumatic event). The remaining significant scores were for Tension Reducing Behaviours (those external activities engaged by an individual as a way to modulate, interrupt, avoid or soothe negative internal states); for Anxious Arousal (symptoms of anxiety, especially those associated with post traumatic hyperarousal e.g. jumpiness, tension) and finally for Dysfunctional Sexual Behaviour.

9   Opinion

9.1	The physical, sexual and emotional abuse that Mr Smith experienced at various points through his childhood would be classified as of sufficient magnitude to be traumatic and to have therefore had significant psychological consequences. As a young child he experienced serious physical and emotional abuse and neglect mainly from his father and this continued when he was at home▮▮▮▮▮▮▮▮▮▮▮▮▮▮▮▮. He was then seriously mistreated when he was at Aston Hall Mental Hospital for about a year between the ages of 12 and 13.
9.2	Mr Smith was placed as St William's on the 17th May 1976 aged 15. He recalled spending two Christmases there and estimated he remained there for a period of about two years until he was 17. If he left when he was 17 he would have been there for about 19 months. During his placement at St William's Mr Smith reported that he attended a local school because he was intellectually gifted and whilst there he was bullied by other pupils and then bullied at St William's by other residents for attending a different school. He also reported that he and other children were subjected to routine physical abuse and violence by different members of staff and that much if this was carried out openly. In particular he reported being seriously physically abused b▮▮▮r ▮▮▮▮▮▮n an▮▮▮▮▮▮d but also by Brother James when he refused to comply with his demands for sexual abuse. He also reported being routinely sexually abused by Brother James including repeated buggery, two or three time a month. Brother James also made threats to kill him which he took at face value. Mr Smith also witnessed Brother James sexually abusing another boy and was aware that this was happening to others. He also reported being raped by 'Sailor John' on more than one occasion and being sexually abused by a friend of Brother Jame▮▮▮▮▮▮▮▮▮▮▮▮▮▮▮'.
9.3	In my opinion the abuse at St William's has had an effect on his development as a person and on his ability to function in the world, caused him to have significant psychological and interpersonal problems and greatly exacerbated the problems he already had. There is no recorded history of any anti-social or violent behaviour or substance misuse prior to St William's. I have not seen his criminal records but he reported no convictions prior to St William's. The experiences of abuse at St William have therefore made a very significant contribution to the development of his subsequent violent and anti-social behaviour and problems with substance misuse.
9.4	Mr Smith has a limited history of criminal offending but a very extensive history of violence. He told me he had been involved in hundreds of fights, mostly as a younger man and up until his so▮▮▮▮n was born when he slowed down. He admitted that even though since then he had tried to avoid conflict, he had continued to be involved in the occasional fight and as recently as June 201▮▮▮▮▮▮▮▮▮▮k mentions that he told her he had been in a fight at a festival. Mr Smith told me he came out of St William's a very angry young man, anti-authority and with little or no respect for others. He also described being hypervigilant for threat and how he would attack people simply for

27

looking at him in ways he perceived to be threatening or if they made comments about his appearance. He also became involved with others who were routinely violent. He reported very limited violence in his personal relationships. In my view Mr Smith learned to use violence instrumentally (as a means to achieving an end, for example to gain a reputation as a hard man and thereby to protect himself from further harm) and for the 'excitement' of fighting, as a tension reducing behaviour. He has also used violence as a means of trying to deal with intense thoughts and feelings he cannot otherwise cope with.

9.5   Mr Smith reported an extensive history of problems with anger and violence. He reported little or no remorse for his behaviour, saw much his violence as justified and expressed little or no victim empathy ███████████████████████████████ ██████ Despite all these problems he has had consistent periods of legal employment and managed to sustain several long term and relatively healthy personal relationships. In my opinion Mr Smith's would not currently therefore satisfy the criteria for an Anti-Social Personality Disorder although his history of violence indicates he may have done when he was younger. His violence has been exacerbated through chronic abuse of alcohol and cannabis. If there is to be a process of calming down or maturation involved in such a disorder then this typically takes place when a person reaches their early to mid thirties: this seems to have been the case with Mr Smith who reported that he made a conscious decision to try to avoid conflict and violence when his first son ██████ was born (his eldest son was 23 when I met him which means this happened when he was in his late 20s).

9.6   The information gained from Mr Smith as well as the TSI test results support an assessment that he suffers from chronic and severe Post Traumatic Stress Disorder (PTSD). The main symptoms and behaviours associated with PTSD have been present since St William's but have all been exacerbated since he came forward and started to talk about the abuse for the first time in 2012: these include cognitive symptoms such as distressing intrusive recall and ruminations about revenge, waking terrors, post traumatic hypcrarousal and anxiety, and a wide range of avoidance behaviours.

9.7   Mr Smith clearly meets the criteria for a diagnosis of PTSD according to the recently released DSM V. He was directly exposed to sexual violence, actual serious injuries and threatened death (**DSM V criterion A: stressor:** one required, he reported 3). He has suffered persistent intrusive memories and traumatic nightmares, Dissociative reactions, reported intense or prolonged distress after exposure to traumatic reminders as well as marked physiologic reactivity after exposure to trauma-related stimuli, for example, media coverage about abuse in general and even more so when he found out about St William's on the internet (**DSM V criterion B: intrusion symptoms:** only one required, he reported 5). He also reported avoidance of distressing trauma-related stimuli after the event, for example, avoiding anything to do with religion which he associated with perverts (**DSM V criterion C: avoidance,** one required, he reported both). He reported an initial inability to recall key features of the traumatic event, persistent distorted blame of self or others for causing the traumatic event or for resulting consequences and persistent negative trauma-related emotions (e.g. fear, horror, anger, guilt, or shame) (**DSM V criterion D: negative alterations in cognitions and mood:** 2 required, he reported 5). Mr Smith reported trauma-related alterations in arousal and reactivity that began or worsened after the traumatic event: irritable or aggressive behaviour, self-destructive or reckless behaviour, hypervigilance and sleep disturbance (**DSM V criterion E: alterations in arousal and reactivity:** 2 required, he reported 4).

28

9.8   Mr Smith reported a history of distressing intrusive recall and ruminations about his past which, in the years immediately after St William's he tried to suppress through heavy alcohol and then drug abuse and through being involved in persistent violence. He has been reminded of the past, for example, through media coverage about abuse, or when he sees anything to do with priests or churches. In the 1980s he seriously assaulted a man who was charged with sexually abusing children. The memories and ruminations have continued throughout his adult life. He has employed other strategies to distract himself from them, for example working excessive hours, engaging in high risk activities at work or such as riding a motorbike at very high speeds or fighting. The recollections and the nightmares/waking terrors have been significantly worse since he reduced his drinking about 5 years before I met him and even more so since he came forward in 2012.

9.9   Mr Smith reported post-traumatic hyperarousal in a number of ways: he has always been guarded and found it very hard to trust anyone, even those closest to him. He has always been hypervigilant for threat and wary of others to the point that he adopted a violent 'strike first' attitude and a complete intolerance of men treating him in any way he perceived as disrespectful. He also reported an angry and at times violent reaction to seeing media coverage about child abuse. He does not tolerate having his personal space invaded.

9.10   His presentation and reported history also clearly indicated the other principal feature of PTSD which is avoidance: he has spent his entire adult life trying to avoid thinking about his past but has still experienced recall that, as stated already, has been internally generated or else been triggered by specific external triggers reminders. Importantly, the impact of his experiences as a child in St William's has been both traumatic and *developmental*, that is, as well as affecting him in terms of his mental health or symptoms, these experiences have had a significant impact on the nature of his personality and the way he relates to other people. Those experiences have contributed greatly to the development of all of his interpersonal problems including mistrust and aggression and also to his chronic problems with substance misuse.

9.11   Mr Smith reported limited symptoms of PTSD in terms of sexual traumatisation but did tell me he has ▓▓▓▓▓▓▓▓▓▓▓ a strong aversion to certain sexual acts associated with being sexually abused and he has also had extended periods when he had to wash straight after sex. It is of course significant that for much of his adult life he has been on drink or drugs and it is likely given his strong dissociative tendencies, that he has been on one way or another intoxicated during his active sex life.

9.12   It is significant that Mr Smith's highest score in the Trauma Symptom Inventory was for Dissociation, a form of psychological numbing, and that he has been told he has a Dissociative Disorder. One of the principal coping strategies adopted by victims of sexual abuse is to dissociate while the abuse is actually taking place and they often speak of this as 'not being there', an 'out of body' experience: imagining they were somewhere else or that it was as if the abuse was happening to someone else and they were looking on. This coping strategy then becomes established so that whenever the person recalls the abuse or is reminded then they dissociate again: this strategy can also then become a way the person deals with any painful or distressing events. In Mr Smith's case, dissociation has become embedded into his personality and the way he functions and this is likely to be one of the reasons why he has experienced his distress in the form of such disturbing nocturnal waking terrors.

29

9.13   Mr Smith has an extensive history of abuse of alcohol and cannabis which began only after he left St William's when he started to drink heavily. He continued to drink heavily for several years immediately after St William's and then started to smoke cannabis when he was 21. Alcohol and cannabis have continued to be a problem for him throughout his adult life. His records corroborate what he reported about his drinking which has been in the form of routine heavy use as well as periods of harmful binge drinking. Although he told me he had reduced the amount he drank and smoked in 2008, he continued to smoke cannabis and he continued to binge drink at harmful levels up until the point when I interviewed him late last year. In my opinion his long-standing abuse of drugs and alcohol should also be viewed as a process of avoidance that is an integral part of Post Traumatic Stress Disorder (PTSD): as a means of coping with both internal and external difficulties and as a means of detaching himself and thereby avoiding aversive thoughts and feelings associated with his past.

9.14   As well as substance misuse, Mr Smith has also employed other strategies to distract himself from his past. One of the ways he has done this is through working excessively and through risk taking adrenaline fuelled activities such as working in dangerous settings, hang gliding, riding motorbikes at high speed and also of course fighting. Mr Smith spoke about the enjoyment he derived from fighting and these activities which are also ways a person can manage or manipulate their feelings: a form of distraction as well as a tension reducing behaviour. In my opinion the processes of avoidance and dissociation that are an integral part of PTSD have become deeply embedded within his personality and are only likely to be amenable to change in limited ways.

9.15   Mr Smith's test results indicated continued problems with anxiety and his medical records also reveal a history of anxiety states and chronic sleep disturbance from at least as far back as his early 20s. He reported that his problems with anxiety began at Aston Hall and that he has suffered from this all of his adult life. Since coming forward in 2012 he has also experienced heightened depression although he did report he has had tendencies to depression all of his adult life. Mr Smith told me he had always used drugs and alcohol as a way of managing his anxiety: that anxiety in turn is directly linked to his PTSD.

9.16   In terms of attribution or causality for his continued psychological and psychiatric difficulties, as is so often the case, the picture is not straightforward. He reported being physically and emotionally abused by his father from an early age and records show he sustained serious injuries before the age of 2. Early medical records also show by the ages of 11 and 12 he was stealing (mainly food) at home in the context of the neglect and mistreatment he suffered there. He also had emotional problems which was manifest in the form of soiling at those ages. With such extensive abuse and violence at home from an early age, in my opinion Mr Smith will already have sustained a degree of long-term psychological injuries prior to being removed from home when he was about 12 or 13. He then reported being seriously mistreated at Aston Hall over a period of about a year: he told me there was objective evidence for the medical malpractice he told me about which I have not seen but which can presumably be verified. ▮▮▮▮▮▮▮▮▮▮▮▮▮▮▮▮▮▮▮▮▮▮▮▮▮▮

9.17   ▮▮▮

As described above, while at St William's he was subjected to routine physical and emotional abuse by different members of staff and also routinely witnessed others

30

being similarly mistreated as much of this was carried out openly. He was also repeatedly sexually abused and raped by Brother James and on fewer occasions by two other men. He witnessed others being sexually abused and was threatened with his life. In my opinion the experiences he reported at St William's have made a significant contribution to all of his long term difficulties. His experiences in this institution added substantially to whatever problems he already had, contributed greatly to the development of his violent personality and increased the likelihood of him developing subsequent substance misuse problems.

9.18 In conclusion therefore, some aspects of Mr Smith's long term injuries have been caused by his experiences at St William's whilst other problems have multiple causes. Some of those long term injuries may have arisen in the absence of any abuse at St William's, but those experiences at St William's will have greatly exacerbated any pre-existing injuries. Further, the physical, sexual and emotional abuse he described at St William's not only exacerbated the impact of previous traumas but created long term problems that would not otherwise have arisen, for example, the shame, stigma, guilt and self-blame he still experiences specifically in relation to sexual abuse.

9.19 In terms of his career and employment, in my opinion Mr Smith's education and academic/vocational prospects would have been adversely affected by his experiences at St William's. Despite the abuse and neglect he had already suffered by the time he was placed at St William's, he is the first former resident I have ever interviewed who was considered so academically bright that he was placed at a local school. This suggests his underlying academic potential must have been considerable. As an adult his employment history has been a reasonably consistent one: he was worked for several different employers with some of these periods of employment sustained over many years. He reported problems at work and being sacked from some jobs because of his anti-authority attitudes and more general interpersonal problems. Since his substance misuse, his interpersonal and mental health problems have all had a negative impact on his ability to seek or maintain employment as an adult, this indicates that without these problems his employment history is likely to have been much better. In 1985 he suffered a serious leg injury at work: since then he has worked but this injury caused him continued physical problems which in turn have severely limited his employment opportunities.

9.20 In terms of relative attribution it is extremely difficult to apportion degrees of causality in psychological or psychiatric sequelae, especially in cases where there is abuse or trauma across time, in different settings, by different perpetrators and particularly during or over the course of a person's childhood development. It is also very difficult to quantify any given abusive experience in terms of severity or impact and one has to consider such complex factors such as the nature of the abuse, the specific circumstance under which it took place, the length of time of each episode of abuse as well as the duration over time if the abuse was repeated. There is also a cumulative effect and each episode of abuse may make a child vulnerable to further abuse and create further more damaging psychological injuries, the sum total of injuries being greater than the parts. There will inevitably be an interaction of the effect of continued abuse over time and across settings.

9.21 In terms of relative causation I would *roughly* estimate the contribution of genetic endowment, his experiences prior to being removed from home, his experiences at Aston Hall and any other (post-care) experiences at around 30% of the total long-term

31

injuries. In my opinion therefore his experiences specifically at St William's would in my view account for the remaining 70%.

10   Recommendations

10.1   In my opinion Mr Smith will always continue to struggle with problems in terms of cognitive symptoms, nightmares/waking terrors, sleep disturbance and avoidance behaviours associated with Post Traumatic Stress Disorder (PTSD). Another integral aspect of PTSD is that he will remain hypervigilant for threat from others: the traumas he suffered as a child at home and at St William's have left him with significant difficulties relating to people and he will always have problems trusting people, even those closest to him. The processes of dissociation are deeply embedded within his psychological make up and are only likely to be altered in limited ways. Mr Smith will also continue to struggle with his identity and a sense of shame, stigma and self-blame about what happened to him specifically at St William's. Since coming forward he has experienced a deterioration in his mental health in the form of depression and heightened anxiety, as well as in symptoms more directly associated with PTSD. He may well require prescribed medication at various points in the future to help him manage these diverse mental health problems.

10.2   Mr Smith deserves credit for having tried to reduce his alcohol and cannabis consumption in the last few years, particularly given his heightened distress since coming forward in 2012. However, his abuse of both of these drugs has been a chronic problem and I have concerns about his continued use: he continues to smoke cannabis regularly and he continues to binge drink. Until he is able to develop alternative strategies for coping with aversive thoughts and feelings, which is unlikely in the short to medium term, his substance misuse is unlikely to alter.

10.3   Mr Smith's personality has developed in such a way as to avoid any feelings or situations of distress and vulnerability. He also has significant problems trusting people generally and those in positions of authority in particular. This is all likely to make engaging with any form of psychological treatment especially difficult for him. It should of course be recognised that any barriers to treatment such as his mistrust of authority have also been caused, at least in part, by the abuses he suffered at St William's. As reviewed above, his medical records show that he has engaged well with ▮▮▮▮ ▮▮▮▮ a mental health worker, over a consistent period of time. Although she is supposed to be helping him with trauma they have not discussed the abuse in any detail.

10.4   Mr Smith's continued support from ▮▮▮▮▮▮ is a positive influence and this seems to have helped him manage his panic and anxiety, at least during the day. However, this treatment has had little impact on his nocturnal waking terrors and I am not convinced EMDR is ultimately the most appropriate treatment given his complex needs. I would therefore recommend at least 3 years of highly specialised and weekly psychological treatment specifically with a Clinical Psychologist or other mental health professional that has extensive experience of working with adults who were sexually abused as children, preferably with experience of adults who were in institutional care. It is unlikely such extensive and specialised therapy will be available from the NHS since psychological treatment there is often severely limited by time constraints and limited expertise. He will probably need to seek this on a private basis. ▮▮▮▮▮▮

32